DEATH IN CENTRAL PARK!

A four-inch-long blade—luminescent and dazzling in the light of the moon—ripped into Michael's forehead, slicing a five-inch-long horizontal trail from one side to the other. The knife then slashed both his left and right upper eyelids, leaving a long bloody laceration. A third strike ripped into the midportion of his face, partially detaching his nose from the skin and soft tissue, and fracturing his nasal bone. A fourth pierce sliced his left cheek to the midportion of his face, just above his lip. Perhaps endorphins took over and he didn't know he was stabbed. Body fluid oozed from both his nose openings. Blood ran down his face. He was alive. He was still standing. The stabbings continued.

The knife struck the right side of his face, next to the corner of his mouth. Then it struck again. It pierced through the depth of the cartilage of his right ear.

BABY-FACED BUTCHERS

STELLA SANDS

PINNACLE BOOKS
Kensington Publishing Corp.
http://www.kensingtonbooks.com

For Jess and Sass, of course

Some names have been changed to protect the privacy of individuals connected to this story.

PINNACLE BOOKS are published by

Kensington Publishing Corp.
850 Third Avenue
New York, NY 10022

All Kensington Titles, Imprints, and Distributed Lines are available at special quantity discounts for bulk purchases for sales promotions, premiums, fund-raising, and educational or institutional use. Special book excerpts or customized printings can also be created to fit specific needs. For details, write or phone the office of the Kensington special sales manager: Kensington Publishing Corp., 850 Third Avenue, New York, NY 10022, attn: Special Sales Department, Phone: 1-800-221-2647.

Pinnacle and the P logo Reg. U.S. Pat. & TM Off.

ISBN-13: 978-0-7860-1803-1
ISBN-10: 0-7860-1803-8

First Printing: May 2007

10 9 8 7 6 5 4 3 2 1

Printed in the United States of America

CHAPTER 1

New York City's Central Park covers 843 lush acres of the most valuable land in the world. Stretching north from Fifty-ninth Street to 110th Street, and east from Central Park West (CPW) to Fifth Avenue, it sits serene and resplendent, the center jewel in the dazzling crown of Manhattan.

The park celebrates the seasons in a brilliant kaleidoscope of colors and aromas. In summer, Frisbee players energetically toss plastic comets above the emerald carpet of Sheep Meadow, an expansive, manicured quiet area that serves as a communal picnic blanket and sunbathing haven. Guitar players, perched on benches in Strawberry Fields surrounding the "Imagine Mosaic" in honor of the late John Lennon, strum Beatles tunes as the crowd sings along.

In the fall, red leaves from European beech mingle with yellow and orange from pin oaks, while the acrid pungency of ginkgo permeates the crisp air. After the leaves have fallen and the temperature plummets to single digits, some 26,000 trees, 29 sculptures, and

36 bridges and arches take center stage—stark subjects in a muted and still background.

In spring, cherry blossoms cheer the winter weary. Lining the slopes below the track surrounding the Reservoir, they offer a downy pink protective canopy for joggers. Thousands visit the Children's Zoo to see some of the fourteen hundred animals. Others head to the Carousel for a ride on some of the largest hand-made horses in the world.

In every season, during the daytime, dogs, finally freed from their apartment confines, retrieve balls and look for their barking buddies. Bikers, Rollerbladers, joggers, and power walkers share the lanes abutting the roadways, jockeying for position as they try to get the most out of their sandwiched exercise time.

Never as dark or as silent as the country, Central Park at night is as close to mysterious as the urban landscape gets. Officially closed from 1:00 to 6:00 A.M., the park, however, is never totally empty. Late at night and into the early hours of the morning, certain areas stay alive with people high on booze, drugs, and even life. High-school kids out beyond their curfews mingle with dropouts, as runaways from upstate make fast friends with slick hipsters. Old people who've been down on their luck for years mix with energetic, anxious teenagers.

Some of the night parkers are longtime regulars, people who live in the park by choice—mostly the homeless, variously labeled as "weirdos," "losers," "boozers," "druggies," and "vagrants" by the media. The most articulate and lucid of the nighttime parkers insist that they are independent-minded citizens who have chosen an alternative lifestyle, while those with the least tenuous hold on reality are unable to explain or even comprehend who they are.

Most night parkers know each other by face, if not by name, and often congregate in the same area night after night—in Strawberry Fields, at the Bandshell, on the perimeter of Sheep Meadow, on the Great Lawn, at the playground near the southern end of the park, or in the Ramble. Each location has a distinct personality and an unwritten set of rules.

Police cars from the Central Park Precinct, located along the Eighty-sixth Street transverse, patrol the roadways and even ride on some of the fifty-eight miles of footpaths and 4.25 miles of bridle paths. Most of the time, the officers simply tell late-night drinkers and assorted NYC nightlifers to move along.

Frederick Law Olmsted, who, along with Calvert Vaux, designed Central Park in 1858, remarked that the park "exercises a distinctly harmonizing and refining influence upon the most lawless classes of the city— an influence favorable to courtesy, self-control, and temperance."

However, in the early hours of Friday, May 23, 1997, courtesy, self-control, and temperance were not in existence as a blast of violence engulfed Central Park in a murder that horrified a city, where, all too often, crime is a distinct fact of life.

CHAPTER 2

Thursday, May 22, 1997, was a perfect spring day. The breeze was gentle and comforting.

For Daphne Abdela, it was a perfect day to hang out, Rollerblade in Central Park, and get high with friends. She had more than enough time on her hands. Just two weeks before, she'd been asked to leave Loyola School, the exclusive Jesuit-run private school she'd attended as a freshman since the fall. The administration cited disciplinary reasons. Her attitude was unacceptable, way off the chart of the school's norms for tolerable behavior. She picked fights, disrupted classes, and acted in a loud, hostile, and aggressive way. Often she arrived at school already wasted, and during lunch and sometimes between classes, she could be seen smoking up or gulping down liquid in a brown paper bag. Drinking early in the day had become relatively routine for this B student. In one particularly bravura performance, she celebrated her school's basketball win by parading through the halls in her bra, after having yanked her T-shirt over her head.

But now, free at last, her days were no longer confined to sitting in sterile classrooms and attempting to pay attention to boring teachers droning on about topics of little interest to her. Instead, she was pretty much on her own with only a few tasks that she really needed to do: study for finals, which the school said she could take at home at the end of the term, and read pamphlets for out-of-state boarding schools, which her parents had sent away for in the hope that she would find a place of interest for next fall.

That Thursday morning, with the temperature a mild 65 degrees and the sky already a slate blue-gray from car exhaust, smoke, and chemical fumes, Daphne left the apartment she shared with her parents, on the corner of Seventy-second Street and Central Park West in a building known as the Majestic, crossed the street, and entered Central Park through Women's Gate—not an actual gate, but bookends of stone between which the Seventy-second Street park transverse road begins. Once inside, it took her no time to hook up with a group of guys to share a six-pack. That was the great thing about the park. You could always find someone willing to join you in the vice of your choice, no matter how bizarre. If you wanted to take acid, for example, there was always someone around to trip with you; if you wanted to get laid in the grass, you could count on a willing sex partner. If you just wanted to find someone to chat with about the Yankees, the Grateful Dead, or even politics, you could always find someone willing to comply.

After drinking and chilling for a while, Daphne decided to head east toward Carl Schurz Park. At around 3:00 P.M., as she was walking along Madison Avenue at Eighty-second Street, she recognized two older boys she'd met somewhere before. After engaging in small

talk, she asked them if they'd get her Phillies—cigars
she used for rolling fat joints called blunts—and a
"forty"—forty ounces of beer. They told her she was a
loser for drinking forties in the middle of the day. By
now, she'd already downed two wine coolers and three
pints of Guinness and wasn't the least bit bothered by
their comments. It was just around then that she
began boasting to anyone who would listen that she
couldn't wait to get totally wasted.

Armed with her goods, she continued on to East
End Avenue and Eighty-fourth Street, the southern
entrance to Carl Schurz Park, also called "East Side's
best-kept secret." There, visitors are treated to spectac-
ular views of the East River, the Triborough Bridge,
the Queensboro Bridge, Randall's Island, and Roosevelt Island. At its northernmost end sits pristine and
elegant Gracie Mansion, home to many of the mayors
of New York. Arriving at around 4:00 P.M., Daphne immediately made her presence known. With her stan-
dard fare—a six-pack of Coors, a forty, some Phillies,
and a wad of $20 bills—it was obvious that she was al-
ready buzzed. Animated, provocative, and defiant, her
bravado was oozing like an ulcerous, festering sore.
Hangdog behind her was a newcomer, a nerdy-look-
ing guy with rimless glasses, a fade haircut—short and
tapered on the sides, longer on top—and a vacant
look on his face. All the regulars knew Daphne, but
no one recalled having seen the kid before. Truth is,
they were surprised Daphne had shown up at all,
since she hadn't been around for the past couple of
weeks.

Wearing her signature loose-fitting grunge clothes,
she wasted no time laying claim to her domain and
staking out her parameters. The chess tables. The Cat-
bird Playground. The benches by the basketball courts.

Within minutes of putting on her Rollerblades, she approached hunky sixteen-year-old José Gonzales and started slap boxing with him, a customary way of saying hello and bonding all in one. Swinging at each other with open hands, she did her best to make a go of it, but after only a few seconds, it was clear that she was no match. In fact, she was pathetic, unable to land even a good one close to his face. José didn't want to take advantage of her. It wasn't his style, so he called it quits. Daphne cursed at him. She wanted action, but José wasn't taking the bait. He walked away and then rode off toward home on his bike.

Meanwhile, the regulars were engaged in their usual MO. A newcomer? Test his mettle. On their bikes, they began darting at him—again, and again, and again—missing his feet by inches. Would he flinch? Fight? They needed to find out. It was part of the initiation.

But the kid did nothing. He didn't move. He didn't yell. He didn't challenge. He stood stock-still and stone-faced— unfazed. Just as well, cause if he dared challenge them, they'd icc him. With no reaction from the robot, they soon became bored and left him alone.

Restless and on the prowl, Daphne looked for another slap-boxing partner. Carlos Magriz was hanging out nearby, so Daphne skated up to him. Magriz, however, wasn't interested, but Daphne kept taunting him, hitting his face again and again. Finally, he slapped back, knocking Daphne to the ground. Seemingly unfazed, she picked herself up and moved on.

Daphne then Rollerbladed up to a girl she'd seen before, trying to engage someone—anyone—in anything at all, and asked her what school she went to. The girl shot her a chilly stare, turned her head, and went back to talking with her group. Daphne cursed her out and skated off to the chess tables. Seeing the girl's father there playing chess, she bolted over to him. Moving in too close, she hung over the man, breathing on him. Annoyed, he barked, "You looking for trouble?"

"We are trouble," she shouted; then she skated off, back to some of the regulars to persuade them to kick the crap out of the man. Always up for an adventure, the gang returned with her, ready for action. But when they saw that the target was just some old dude playing a game of chess, they backed off and told her to do the same. After some convincing, she finally relented and reluctantly left the man alone.

Still pulsating with aggressive energy, she approached Brian Miller, a fifteen-year-old who many thought was her boyfriend, at least until she arrived today with this weird new guy, whose name they learned was Christopher. Daphne tried to kiss Brian. Rebuffed, she went up to an old flame, Nick. They had had an on-again, off-again, relationship—by most accounts, mostly off-again—with Nick breaking up with her time and time again. She asked him if he liked her, if he had a problem with her. He pushed her away and rode off on his mountain bike.

Meanwhile, Christopher, sitting on a park bench alone, was drinking beer and munching Pringles, a solitary bird on its perch, watching.

Increasingly more desperate—no romance and no one to fight with—Daphne began bragging, tossing off hyperboles like some mini Muhammad Ali. She told one group, which included friend Francisco Lopez, she was going to slice someone. To another, including Michael Thomas, she screamed that before the day was over, she would kill someone. She implied that she had a knife and was looking forward to using it. By that time, she was really feeling it, riding the bullet. But no one who heard her took her seriously. Anyone that wasted would say anything.

As Daphne's bluster grew more belligerent, the new kid began to show signs of life. At first, Christopher talked to Daphne quietly, trying to calm her down. But when her threats continued and she became even more combative, he began feeling nervous. Soon his agitation turned to panic. Trying to deflect attention from Daphne, he began challenging people to take *him* on, boasting he could kick their butts from one side of town to the other. In spite of all the bravado, it was a piss-poor performance. Nobody paid him any mind. Nobody, it seemed, was the least bit interested in either of them.

At around 7:00 P.M., bored and restless, the pair left Carl Schurz and skated over to the West Side. Along the way, they picked up two other bladers. Now they were a pack on the move. As they entered Central Park, at Seventy-second Street and Fifth Avenue, they saw a group of homeless dudes sitting on the benches. Daphne dashed over. Scanning the group, she singled out one man, an enormous guy who weighed around four hundred pounds. Looking straight at him, with unflinching eyes, and speaking in a loud voice so everyone could hear, she screamed, "That fatty there, that's the one I'm gonna gut like a pig." And then off she zoomed, a speeding train heeding no signals, hell-bent on a bloody wreck.

The intended target, Frank, was stunned. For a split second, he wasn't sure he had heard right. "Did she say what I think she said?" he asked Billy, who was sitting next to him reading the newspaper.

"Sounded like she just threatened to kill you," Billy said.

"She's gotta be kidding, right?"

"Didn't sound that way to me."

"Me neither."

For the first time since he began living in the park, several months before, Frank felt fear. In fact, for the first time in his life, he felt afraid. "I could barely breathe," he recalled later. "My stomach was churning. I knew something crazy had just taken place, but for some reason that's not easy to explain, I didn't doubt that she meant what she said. It was something about the look in her eye. She was capable of it. I knew it was real."

As a kid growing up in College Point, Queens, as a trucker in Texas and cross-country, and as a mover in California, Frank had always been able to take care of himself. Nobody messed with "Big Frank." Homeless by circumstance—all his belongings were stolen from the storage compartment in a Greyhound bus on his way from California to New York—he wasn't what many people consider a "typical" homeless person. Frank never drank, smoked, or asked for a handout. A tournament-winning bowler, he was among the smartest people in his high school in Queens, New York. With sympathetic clear blue eyes, a bushy white beard, and long white hair, Frank was a friendly figure on the park benches, always ready to chat it up or lend a hand. "But you gotta understand," he said softly, "when I was sleeping in the park, once my eyes were shut, anything could happen. Even a ten-year-old could do damage—with a switchblade." Recently he'd read a story in the newspaper about a homeless woman who was doused with gasoline and set on fire. And then there was the article about a man sleeping on a park bench who was kicked and punched until he died on the spot. "Hey, look at me," he said, "don't you think I can handle anything while I'm awake? But when I'm asleep, I'm as vulnerable as a baby."

Leaving the guys on the park bench to figure out just what the hell had happened, the teens continued on their way. Eventually Daphne and Christopher broke off from the others and skated over to Blockbuster, on Sixty-eighth Street and Amsterdam Avenue. It was only a five-minute trip, but it gave them a sense of power and invincibility. People had to move out of the way as they took over the sidewalks. Each long glide or quick, deliberate crossover, each swing of the arm, each dart in and out, assured them that they owned their ground. They were somebodies.

Arriving at Blockbuster, the two skated up and down the aisles. At one point, Daphne sprawled out on the floor between the rows, a snow angel on wooden ground. Christopher stood over her, awed by her bravado. After racing up and down the rows, they finally picked out *Reservoir Dogs*, a violent, tension-filled, and gut-wrenching movie that included the torturing of a cop by cutting off his ear. When Daphne's turn came to check out the video, she was rambunctious and loud. Looking at her with concern, the counterman asked, "Have you been drinking?"

"Have you?" she snapped back angrily before grabbing her video and racing out with Christopher shadowing behind.

The two skated the seven blocks to Daphne's apartment and went directly to Daphne's room. As they milled around, they considered watching the video, but soon decided that live action of their own was more enticing. Simmering with anticipation, the two skated off to the nighttime park, its powerful pull luring them like the sweet songs of the Sirens.

On that same Thursday, May 22, 1997, Michael Mc-Morrow awoke in the apartment he shared with his eighty-one-year-old mother, on Ninety-second Street and Second Avenue, eager for a new day at work. He loved his job at Sir Realty, where he'd been employed for the past three months. The people were friendly and welcoming. His boss, Glenn Golub, appreciated the great job he was doing renting apartments at 252 West Seventy-sixth Street. Plus, Michael loved talking about the Yankees with Angel Colon, the building's handyman. That day, Boston was playing at Yankee Stadium, in the "House that Ruth Built." With David Wells against Tom Gordon, he knew there'd be a lot to argue about. No doubt, it was going to be a great matchup.

Waking up at around 11:00 A.M.—his workday began at 1:00 P.M.—he got dressed in black pants and a gray shirt, had a quick cup of coffee, kissed his mother good-bye, and reminded her to eat the leftover lamb for lunch. Then he headed west and into the park, making use of his usual mode of transportation, his legs, to get to work.

When he got to Broadway, he made a quick stop at the corner deli, Broadway Express, at Seventy-seventh Street, and bought the usual, cigarettes and beer. He stopped at the deli every day before work and exchanged a few words with the deli owners, nice guys who always had a positive take on the day. The beer he bought he would put in the refrigerator at work and take out when he headed to Strawberry Fields for his usual nighttime activity of hanging out with his buddies. Sharaf Al-Gotaini and Amin Alhalmei, the deli men, liked and trusted him. He was one of only two customers they allowed to keep a tab. That day, they put $9.75 on his bill for three bottles of Guinness and a pack of Kools.

"See you tomorrow. Maybe I'll be the lucky one then," Michael said as he walked out of the store, referring to the Queens woman Niki Barkoutsis, a twenty-three-year-old counterwoman at Chirping Chicken, who a month before had bought the winning $22.5 million lottery ticket from the Broadway Express clerk.

"Inshallah," replied Amin. God willing.

But it seemed that God—or fate or Karma or simple bad luck—had something altogether different in store for Michael.

CHAPTER 3

Covering 2.5 rolling green acres of Central Park, Strawberry Fields is a teardrop parcel of land dedicated to the memory of John Lennon. Named for the 1967 Beatles classic "Strawberry Fields Forever," the area is located just across the street from the Dakota—the apartment building where Lennon lived with his wife, Yoko Ono, and their son, Sean. The area is the destination of over a million visitors a year, who pay respect to their fallen hero by placing flowers, candles, and other memorabilia on the black-and-white-tile mosaic on which the single word "IMAGINE" implores visitors to be dreamers.

Meticulously maintained by a $1 million donation from John's widow to the Central Park Conservancy, the pristine patch of land boasts over 161 plant species donated by various countries in the United Nations when it was dedicated in the singer's honor in 1985. But no matter how hard you look throughout the undulating sea of green, you won't find any strawberry plants. Strawberry Fields is the name of the orphanage in Liverpool that John frequented with his friends as a young boy.

Each park bench that borders the mosaic offers a tribute in the form of a small plaque to a loved one:

"For Gianfranco Mantegna, Have you seen a horizon lately? Y.O. 2001."

"For our grandchildren's peaceful thoughts, Amy and Oppy."

"Frances Alexander Miller, 1913–2000, Go placidly amid the noise and the haste and remember what peace there may be in silence."

"In Memory of Michael 'Irish' McMorrow, 'Oh for the touch of a vanished hand, And the sound of a voice that is still.'"

CHAPTER 4

Arriving in Strawberry Fields at around 10:00 P.M. on Thursday, Christopher and Daphne immediately recognized the sight as one they'd seen most nights of the week. Two distinct groups were hanging out on opposite sides of the center path. One, stationed on the patch of grass to the north of the walkway, was listening to a radio station that played '70s tunes. Hard-core rock 'n' rollers, they considered themselves a peaceful group who watched each other's backs. Most were high on reefer and booze and had been hanging out together, on and off, for maybe ten or twelve years, with different guys coming and going. Every night they gathered and listened to music—the Grateful Dead, the Beatles, Led Zeppelin, James Brown, the Allman Brothers, and even Fats Domino and Little Richard—almost anyone who strummed a guitar and had something to sing or wail about. Whenever they could, they'd go to concerts, often getting in free by hanging out at the stage door. Much of their conversation centered around the performances they'd seen, hoped to see, and even those they thought they'd seen. Basically, the guys just loved rock 'n' roll almost as much as they loved getting high, but taken together, there weren't a whole lot of things in this world any better. The core group consisted of Gary, known as "the Mayor of Central Park," Laird, Robert, two Erics, Billy, Cliff, Marcos, Maynard, Patrick, Shorty, and Michael. Park culture meant that no one knew anyone else's last name. "It's irrelevant," said Gary. "We all go for first names and nicknames and slang. That's the way it is. Mostly, we talk about music and sports. About what concerts are taking place. About the weather. About who we saw that day—Lauren Bacall, Yoko Ono, Mitch Miller, others. During the day, we like to help the tourists find the places they're looking for. They look at the flower petals I lay out in a peace symbol on the mosaic and ask me about it. Sometimes they give me tips for my artwork. At night, when they're all tucked in tight in their hotel rooms, that's our time to chill. Our living room. Our extended home."

That night, with honeysuckle blooming only feet away from their lounge area, the air oozed perfume. "Dazed and Confused," Led Zeppelin's elegy to crazy love, blared from Gary's Emerson boom box.

Another group, just to the south, was a younger crowd, mostly Bladers, maybe eight or ten of them, edgy kids, always looking for action. Some wanted to start fights. They'd hang out every night starting at around eleven or twelve, chatting it up, smoking, and drinking, and then in the early hours of the morning, they'd head back home, usually to the comfort of a warm bed in a safe house. Many were private-school kids who liked to get twisted and act like hoodlums. They were tense, overly sensitive, and stressed-out— thoroughbreds with no race to run. Parkers could always tell where they came from by the sneakers they wore. According to regular Eric Horvitz, "They all had the name brands."

That night, Daphne walked up on her skates to the people in each group and introduced herself. She said her name was Daphne and her friend was Chris and she wondered if anyone had any pot or acid. The laid-back regulars—that night, the core crew consisted of Gary, Maynard, Marcos, and Mike—felt she was loud and pushy, but, most of all, spooky, and they didn't even bother to answer her. Gary knew her generous side because she'd often share her beers with him and the other regulars, but he didn't really like her. "That crazy broad was a flirt," he said. Besides, now they were chillin' to James Brown.

When no one answered her, Daphne said to the air, as much as to any one person, that she was going to get some beer. At around 11:30 P.M., she skated off, leaving Christopher to fend for himself. He lay down on the grass and stared up at the twinkling stars, which, if he read them correctly, could point him in the direction of home. But he had no interest. His focus was less celestial and more corporeal, single-mindedly fixed on Daphne. After she'd been gone for a few minutes, he became agitated. He skated over to one guy and asked if he knew where Daphne was. Getting a negative response, he tried another and another and another. No one seemed to know or even care. Then he skated up to Gary and asked him if he knew where the hell Daphne was and what was taking the bitch so long. Deep into his own increasingly private and hazy world, Gary simply looked at him, shrugged his shoulders, and settled back into a dreamy and delightful daze.

Unable to wait any longer, he skated off in the direction Daphne had taken. He figured she'd be at the deli, buying beer. And she was. When he got there, Daphne was mouthing off to some guy who had just paid for a pack of cigarettes, telling him he was an alcoholic and daring him to take her on. He had no interest, and quickly left the store. Around twenty minutes later, the two teens reappeared in the park carrying 4 six-packs of Heineken. With Christopher following behind her, Daphne began distributing bottles of beer, a modern-day Dionysus tending to the Central Park flock. The rock 'n' rollers gratefully accepted the offering, high-fiving their thanks without skipping a beat of the music that blared from the radio.

Handing a bottle to one guy who looked familiar, Daphne asked him if he remembered her. She said she was Daphne, from rehab. She sat down next to him and casually put her arm around his shoulder. The man looked closely at her and nodded yes, he remembered her. Daphne from rehab. He introduced himself as Michael and thanked her for the beer. She gave him two pecks on the cheek, then skated off to be with Christopher.

It was now closing in on midnight and everyone was mellow, as usual. No one was acting loud or crazy. No one was up in anyone's face. It was another run-of-the-mill spring night in Strawberry Fields.

Then, as if the lawn had magically morphed into a Broadway stage with a spotlight shining directly on the main characters, the searchlight of Officer Fernando Losada, in a three-wheeled police vehicle, illuminated the group. "Move along!" he demanded. "Park's closed."

They'd heard it before and knew that the cop meant business, but they also knew—damn well—that they still had an hour before the park *officially* closed. However, no one had any interest in pointing out this discrepancy to the officer and risking the possibility of getting arrested. Spending the night in the slammer was about as bad as it got, way worse than sleeping in the park, under a tree, near a perimeter fence, or even out in the open. At least there, most of the time, nobody harassed you.

The night parkers began gathering their belongings. Some of the regulars reclaimed their carts, which were piled high with clothing and special items, such as radios and toiletries. Others gathered their shopping bags, which were filled with a few essentials. The young transients headed out of the park with what was on their backs, strategizing how to sneak into their apartments long past their curfews. As happened most nights, some of the regulars walked away alone to their usual nighttime spots, while others meandered away with a friend or in a group, maybe to find a new, more secluded spot in the park to chill or to sleep.

Daphne headed off with Christopher toward a deserted path that led east out of Strawberry Fields, two brown bags filled with Guinness and Zima clutched tightly in her arms. Gary and Michael, Heinekens in hand, walked a short way north together and then parted. "Peace, brother. See you tomorrow," said Gary, his customary sign-off to Michael for the past ten years. "Say hello to your moms."

"Will do. See you tomorrow," replied Michael.

"Peace out," said Gary.

The two friends then parted, Gary walking west on his way out of the park at Seventy-second Street, and Michael heading north, then east through witch hazel and rosebushes, toward West Drive, on his way home. As Daphne and Christopher were ambling out of Strawberry Fields, their paths crossed with Michael's and together they decided that it was too early to end the evening. They still had plenty of beer and nobody was the least bit tired. The three walked down a path, crossed West Drive, and headed for the gazebo at the southwest perimeter of the park's lake, just east and slightly north of Strawberry Fields. It was a perfect spot—always deserted and out of the watchful gaze of the cops. Plus, it offered free front-row seats to the shimmering light show that glistened off the lake, where patches of light and shadow played tag as the full moon played peekaboo from behind gauzy clouds and through filigreed leaf canopies. Eerily quiet, richly aromatic, sensuous, and mysterious, that's the way it was.

Who could ask for anything more?

CHAPTER 5

The Lake at Central Park is a twenty-two-acre, amoeba-shaped body of water that is home to mallard ducks, Canada geese, mute swans, and innumerable treasures resting on its muddy bottom. Originally created from a swamp, Central Park Lake was intended to provide boating in the summer and ice-skating in the winter.

Today, ice-skaters head to Wollman Rink in the southern part of the park, and Lasker Rink in the north. Boaters can still row the waters of the Lake at Central Park and stop off at any of the four landings that dot its perimeter. During the daytime, each roofed, open-sided gazebo is used as a rest stop for strollers, a shelter from the rain, or a launchpad for tossing bread to the waterfowl. In the dark of night, however, the gazebos serve a totally different purpose. They become rustic, romantic hideaways—isolated dens for making passes, making love, and getting wasted.

CHAPTER 6

Settling in at the wooden retreat, the three continued their evening—drinking Zima, Heineken, and
Guinness and smoking joints. They were twisted, loud,
and having a good time. No beef had ever passed
among them. Daphne and Michael had met once or
twice, maybe at AA meetings, but they'd never exchanged more than a simple greeting. They brought
no baggage to the gazebo that night. Christopher had
never met Michael before that evening, so he didn't
harbor any negative feelings toward the man. And
Christopher and Daphne had been friends for about
a month, maybe even lovers—no one could say for
sure—so no obvious antagonism existed between
them. It seemed like a perfectly congenial group, and,
by the standards of the park at night, a perfectly logical one. Park camaraderie had nothing to do with age,
class, race, education, values, or religion—the more
classical predictors for pairings. Instead, groups were
serendipitous and random, based on who was hanging
out at a certain spot at a certain time, who was game
for whatever was being offered, or who was on the

same wavelength or feeling the same degree of intoxication at the same time.

After they chatted for a while about the Yankees' pathetic 8–2 loss to the Red Sox, the weather, the beer, or the Beatles, the night that had been so pleasant and peaceful suddenly turned violent.

Perhaps Michael put his arm around Daphne, or Daphne kissed Michael, enraging Christopher. Perhaps Michael kissed Daphne, enraging Daphne. Maybe Christopher and Daphne started kissing, enraging Michael. Maybe Michael made a disparaging remark about Christopher, enraging Daphne. Perhaps Daphne tried to get Christopher jealous. Maybe Christopher wanted to prove himself worthy of Daphne. Maybe Michael didn't like the arrogance—or youth—of the teenagers. Perhaps all three got into a pissing match about whatever—enraging all three of them. Whatever it was that took place, it ignited a spark that, within no time at all, set off an explosion with tragic—and fatal—consequences.

A four-inch-long blade—luminescent and dazzling in the light of the moon—ripped into Michael's forehead, slicing a five-inch-long horizontal trail from one side to the other. The knife then slashed both his left and right upper eyelids, leaving a long bloody laceration. A third strike ripped into the midportion of his face, partially detaching his nose from the skin and soft tissue, and fracturing his nasal bone. A fourth pierce sliced his left cheek to the midportion of his face, just above his lip. Perhaps endorphins took over and he didn't know he was stabbed. Body fluid oozed from both his nose openings. Blood ran down his face. He was alive. He was still standing. The stabbings continued.

The knife struck the right side of his face, next to the corner of his mouth. Then it struck again. It pierced through the depth of the cartilage of his right ear. Again

and again and again. It sliced into his head. Michael was
still standing, but he was staggering. Soft tissue began
hemorrhaging under his scalp. Blood gushed all
around his head. He let out an agonized wail. And another. He was still alive. And the stabbings continued.

A half-inch-long slice opened his chin. Below it, the
blade slashed a four-inch-long horizontal path with
jagged edges. To the right, another horizontal slice
with sharp edges stretched two inches long. Fading in
and out of consciousness, he was still upright. He
could barely see or hear. And the stabbings continued.

A 1¼-inch stab, with sharp edges, penetrated
through skin and soft tissue, fracturing his left clavicle. A sharp pierce perforated his left jugular vein. Soft
tissue hemorrhaged. With her Rollerblades, Daphne
kicked Michael's leg, causing three circular contusions
on his right mid-thigh, each one inch in diameter. As-
toundingly, Michael was still standing. Daphne struck
his ankles with her Rollerblades, knocking his feet out
from under him. Michael was now on the ground, lying
on his back, still alive. And the stabbings continued.

The blade sliced into Michael's chest. One time.
Two times. Three times. Four times. Five times. Six
times. Seven times. The wounds were horizontal, all
with sharp edges. Of the seven, six entered the chest
cavity. Three hit bone. The uppermost wound superfi-
cially perforated his spleen. Another fractured his
fourth rib, entering the midportion of his heart and
extending through the entire length of the septum.
The track went backward, leftward, and downward, to
a depth of four inches. Of the remaining five stab
wounds, four intersected each other. One pierced the
upper lobe of his left lung, which collapsed. The direction of these wounds was backward and slightly downward, to a depth between one and three inches. The

seventh wound, which went back and left to a depth of three inches, fractured his second rib along its attachment to his sternum. It perforated his anterior pericardium—the double-walled sac that surrounds the heart and contains the roots of the great blood vessel—and his right ventricle and extended into his aorta. It perforated the wall along the right aortic coronary sinus. It severed the aorta. Michael was now dead. But the stabbings continued.

A two-inch-wide, three-inch-deep obliquely oriented strike slammed into the right midportion of his abdomen. A five-inch-long, three-inch-deep horizontal slice with sharp edges cut into the lower quadrant of his abdomen, perforating it and leaving it partly gaping, with extrusions of loops of intestines and membranes that line the abdominal cavity. Ten more stabs, each one from one-half to three-quarters of an inch long, and up to three inches deep, penetrated his abdomen, close to the incised wounds in the left lower quadrant. A long slash nearly severed his right wrist, slicing the underlying tendons and portions of muscle. Multiple incisions, half an inch in length, cut into his thumb. A blow caused a blunt impact to his head.

Michael's wallet was wrenched from his pocket and his ID was removed. A match was lit and several of the cards were burned. His money was confiscated and put in Daphne's pocket. "Gut him," Daphne ordered. "He's a fatty. He'll sink." And with that, Michael's intestines were pulled out of his body.

With his right wrist nearly cut off, his nose dangling, and his intestines hanging out, Michael was dragged to the edge of the water. From there, he was rolled and then pushed into a shallow and accepting temporary watery grave.

By now it was early Friday, around 12:30 A.M., and

the start of the much-anticipated three-day Memorial Day weekend.

A little after midnight, Officer Lawrence Moran was in his patrol car, parked at the corner of Seventy-second and Central Park West. Occasionally a car screeched to a halt, fearing a ticket for running a red light. Occasionally a group of revelers passed by, arms slung around one another's shoulders, lock-step in bawdy badinage.

As the uneventful evening wore on, from some-where deep within the park, two agonizing screams drifted west, like plaintive blues notes held painfully too long.

Occasionally a thing like that happened. In the early-morning hours, when the park was supposed to be empty of people, drunk friends, enraged lovers, and even frantic loners sometimes raged against real or imagined injustices and personal pain. Especially on nights with a full moon, every variety of weirdo emerged from his den, eager to rail at the madness of it all by howling at the distant lit-up orb.

Although screams often drift up, out of the park, Moran decided to investigate. He turned his car around and started cruising the park roads, searching for anything that looked the least bit suspicious. After taking several loops, he found nothing out of the or-dinary. The park was quiet and serene. No one was hanging out near the roadway. Nothing looked out of place. He soon returned to his lookout spot.

About half an hour later, he noticed two teenagers coming out of the park. Occasionally things like that happened, too. Kids who have stayed out too late walked, raced, Rollerbladed, lumbered, or staggered out of the park on their way home to salvage the little sleep they could get. As the pair rounded the corner and noticed the cruiser, first one, then the other, sank to the ground. Most likely, they were getting in one last smooch before saying their final, precious farewell. Possibly, they were making plans for another outing the next night. Whatever, the two sat on the grass for about five minutes, then slowly got up and calmly skated out of the park, passing directly by the patrol car on their way.

To Moran, nothing about them was the least bit noteworthy.

Another uneventful Central Park Precinct night watch.

Thank goodness.

CHAPTER 7

While Moran was sitting in his patrol car around midnight, Angelo Abdela was becoming more and more agitated in his apartment, which was located just across the street from Moran's lookout. It was past Abdela's daughter's curfew, and although this was not the first time Daphne had ignored his demands—far from it—he didn't want her getting into any more trouble. He didn't want her hanging out in the park drinking, smoking, and doing who-knows-what-else. As recently as March, she had spent several weeks at Arms Acres, a substance-abuse program in Westchester, with the expectation that she would get her drinking under control. He had to give her credit. She had agreed to continue the program by attending Alcoholics Anonymous (AA) sessions at the YMCA on Sixty-third Street and Central Park West, and by all accounts, she was doing just that. Angelo certainly did not want her arrested—again. She already had a juvenile record, and only six months before, he had filed a harassment complaint charging that she had slapped him. Six months before that, he and his wife had filed a report claiming she was a runaway. Moreover, only two weeks ago, she had been asked to leave Loyola School, where she had gone since the fall as a freshman, and before that, a similar situation had occurred at Columbia Grammar and Preparatory School, the Upper West Side private school she had attended earlier. Then, too, the Abdelas had been asked to find a more appropriate school for their daughter. Enough was enough.

At 12:49 A.M., Angelo reached the end of his rope. Weary and fed up, he placed a 911 call and reported Daphne missing. As he waited for the officers to arrive, he paced his living room, occasionally looking out onto the lamplit park, which now stretched before him like an eerie bastion of evil. It was surprising how *splendid* could turn into *sordid* in just a matter of hours. Disheartened and anxious, he went downstairs to the lobby to await the officers' arrival.

At 12:49 A.M., Officer Lee Furman, from the Twentieth Precinct, located on Eighty-second Street between Columbus and Amsterdam Avenues, was riding in a patrol car with Officer Phil Anchick and rookie cop Rachel Nichols. They had been assigned "David Eddie" that night, the sector that extends from Seventieth to Seventy-sixth Streets, and from Central Park West to the river. Compared to other precincts, like the "3-0" up on West 151st Street, which covered only about one square mile and had seventy-three homicides in a single year, the "2-0" was among the lowest-crime areas in the city. Furman liked being a part of the "2-0." Having been there for four years, he felt comfortable and even proud to call it his "home away from home." Riding through the streets that he knew better than his own neighborhood, he felt energetic and alive. He loved his work, but he also loved his time off and this was the last day of his 5-2, 5-3 rotation: on five days, off two; on five days, off three. The Memorial Day weekend would be all his—spending time with his family, barbecuing, playing touch football, and watching TV.

Just as the three officers had settled in for the long night ahead, the radio crackled. "Missing person. One-fifteen Central Park West. Abdela residence." Furman radioed back that it was his. With no need to turn on their sirens—even in the city that never sleeps, traffic thins out to a trickle on most streets after midnight— Furman raced to the address. Within minutes, the three arrived at 115, the Majestic apartment building. Doorman Angelo Goetze, manning the main entrance on Central Park West, greeted them.

"Evening, Officers," he said. "What's up? We got a problem here?"

"Missing person," replied the officers as the three headed toward the elevator.

As always, the police didn't give out any more details. If bystanders overhear what has been said, they can alert others before the cops get a chance to do their job, and the investigation can be compromised.

A man pacing in the lobby, seemingly waiting for a guest to arrive, stopped the officers. He stated that he had made the call. That it was his daughter who was missing.

A surprised Goetze turned to him and told him that his daughter wasn't missing. In fact, she had gotten in a short time ago with a friend and they were in the utility room.

As soon as he heard this, Abdela raced through the lobby, past the elevators, down a hallway, and finally to a doorway on the left. All the while, Furman, Anchick, and Nichols sprinted to keep up. Abdela pushed open the door and barged in. When he saw his daughter, he yelled at her, asking what she was doing, where had she been, and why she was here.

An angry Daphne told him to get the hell out.

An awkward moment passed. Then, seemingly cowed, Angelo Abdela started to back out of the room. Furman put his foot in the door to keep it open and, at the same time, to prevent Mr. Abdela from leaving.

Able now to get a good look at what was going on, Furman saw two teenagers—a female with short brown hair facing him directly and a male facing the other way—sitting in a huge slop sink. The two were nude, and they were washing and rubbing each other's bodies.

Caught in the act! Teenagers fooling around, having sex, and snagged! No wonder the girl's pissed.

But as Furman walked closer to the tub, he noticed a pinkish red color to the water. Then he looked at the heap of clothes strewn on the floor and the two pairs of Rollerblades nearby. Bloodstains dotted them all.

"Mind telling me what this blood's from?" Furman asked.

"Why are you bothering us?" snarled Daphne. "We didn't do anything."

Surprised by her attitude—usually kids from privileged backgrounds are respectful, even meek, when confronted by police officers—Furman demanded they get out of the tub and get dressed.

Reluctantly the teens did as they were told. While they were putting on their clothes—Daphne in homeboy jeans and baggy T-shirt, and the boy in the same, only neater, less ghetto-looking—Furman asked the boy his name. He didn't answer. He looked to Daphne, who stared him down, silently telling him not to say a word.

"Chris. Chris Vasquez," Daphne replied for him.

"And the blood. What's it from?"

An annoyed Daphne retorted, "We fell—Rollerblading. Look."

Daphne showed Furman a deep gash on the back of her head. She pointed out Christopher's bruises, small cuts to his face and hand.

That could explain it. Not much blood on the clothes. Easily could've come from cuts like those.

Having been an emergency medical services (EMS) worker for 2½ years, Furman had seen his share of blood—blood from car-crash victims, blood from shooting victims, blood from attempted suicides—and the amount of blood on their clothes and blades barely made it onto the radar screen.

Satisfied that nothing unlawful was going on—the "missing person" was safely home, the minimal amount of blood didn't raise any red flag, and no calls had come over the radio to raise suspicion—Furman and Anchick agreed it was best to let the father handle things from here. The group left the utility room, and Angelo told the officers that he would be calling Chris's parents to come and pick the boy up. In the hallway, Angelo spoke softly to his daughter, telling her that he had been looking for her.

Daphne screamed back that she didn't care.

"Leave her the hell alone," Chris yelled. "She didn't do anything."

Hearing those words, Officer Furman stopped the boy and put his back up against the wall. "You're a real wiseass, aren't you? You give her father a little respect, ya hear."

"I'm not afraid of you," Christopher yelled. But then, as if the air had all of a sudden been sucked out of him, he looked nervous. His eyes, staring from behind rimless glasses, darted back and forth between Daphne and Furman. Furman immediately realized that the boy was just trying to look big, to be way cool, in front of his girl—but he didn't have the stuff to back it up.

At the elevator, Angelo Abdela thanked the officers for their help and apologized for any inconvenience he may have caused them. Within seconds, he disappeared into the elevator with the teens, an elevator operator taking them up to the Abdela apartment.

The officers got into their cruiser and headed back to the precinct. Another case of hormone-raging, rebellious teens breaking their curfew on a warm spring night. Typical adolescents. Typical early morning at the "2-0." As they drove along, they managed to find some humor in the situation—as always. With a job so overwhelmingly filled with tragedy and heartache—as, for example, when they had to tell the parents of a fourteen-year-old that their only son has been knifed to death or the fiancé of a college student that his bride-to-be had been sexually assaulted and strangled—if they didn't find a way to lighten up situations, they just might end up on the wrong side of the dark world they inhabited.

As they pulled up in front of the "2-0," Nichols hopped out. Her shift was over at 1:00 A.M. "Hey, stay outta tubs, you hear!" she yelled.

At the precinct, Furman and Anchick filled up the car with gas. What the "vampires" liked best about their midnight-to-eight shift was that the calls they got were mostly for real. There wasn't a lot of bullshit, as sometimes happened during the day, with crank calls and false alarms. Time passed quickly at night as they cruised the 'hood, investigating burglaries and car break-ins.

Meanwhile, back at the apartment, Angelo Abdela called Christopher's mother, who said she would grab a cab and pick up her son in just a few minutes. Abdela went downstairs with Christopher and waited with him until his mother arrived. It was around 1:35 A.M.

Satisfied that the boy would soon be safe at home, he returned upstairs to his apartment, still annoyed and agitated, but relieved that Daphne was finally back home, safe and sound.

At 1:42 A.M., an anonymous call was placed to a 911 operator. With a radio blasting in the background, a calm caller said, "My friend jumped into the lake and didn't come out. Go have your boys check out Central Park and drain the river. You'll find a body." The caller continued, "You can't miss it. You can't miss it. You can't miss it." The operator asked for more details. The voice continued, "I didn't know what it was at first. Then I saw it was a body, and I freaked out and left." After a few seconds, the voice continued, "It's a man, I think. I don't know. I saw that shit floating, and I was like, *what*?" Then the operator asked the caller, "Are you a male or female?"

"I'm female!" screamed the caller in a loud and angry voice, obviously offended by the question.

"Can I have your phone number?" asked the operator.

"I'm sure you have it on caller ID right now," the voice quipped, and hung up.

Just as the gas tank was filled and Furman and An-chick were ready to continue their patrol, the radio crackled again: "Dead body in the lake. Anonymous female caller." The officers immediately radioed back asking for details.

The dispatcher elaborated. "The caller stated: 'My friend jumped into the lake and didn't come out.'"

The officers asked where the call came from. With new technology called "enhanced 911" or "E-911," which had been in effect for the past sixteen months, the operator was able to trace the call. The telephone subscriber's name and address lit up on the emergency operator's screen. "An Angelo Abdela," the dispatcher stated. "One-fifteen Central Park West."

Furman and Anchick looked at each other. "You gotta be kidding," said Furman.

"What the hell's that all about?" queried Anchick.

"Payback time," said Furman. "We saw her in the tub. Now she's in trouble, so she's gonna bust our balls."

Furman radioed back: "We were just there on a missing person. We'll take it."

Like all cities, New York City has certain procedures that immediately go into effect whenever there's a report of a dead body or a possible homicide. Night watch is notified right away. They are a group of detectives that work from midnight to 8:00 A.M. and cover a borough, as opposed to a precinct. Manhattan Nightwatch is located in the Thirteenth Precinct, on East Twenty-first Street. A detective from night watch assigns the case to either Manhattan North or South, depending on the location, and also makes other calls to crime scene detectives, for example. Immediately, Emergency Service Unit (ESU) is notified. Located far west, on 126th Street, next to the Twenty-sixth Precinct, the ESU provides specialized equipment and expertise to support the New York Police Department (NYPD). Also notified is the duty captain, the person in charge of all the police officers in the borough, as well as the police precinct where the possible crime took place—in this case, the Central Park Precinct.

As Furman and Anchick pulled up in front of 115 Central Park West, a car from the Central Park Precinct with two police officers—Lawrence Moran and Sam Brenner—screeched to a halt. Furman quickly filled them in on what had occurred within the last hour, suggesting that the girl was probably screwing with them this time.

As they walked past the doorman, a perplexed Goetze greeted them—again. He couldn't remember a single night when the cops had shown up two times. Except for an occasional burglary, the building was free from police activity.

The four officers went directly to the twentieth floor and rang the bell. Angelo Abdela opened the door. He was clearly upset—Daphne was in some kind of trouble, again.

The officers asked to see Daphne, and the men were taken to the kitchen, passing first through a spacious foyer that looked onto a sunken living room, which stretched before them like a grand ballroom. It was filled with antiques; the parquet floors were covered with expensive Persian rugs. Framed grand paintings hung on the walls. The immediate impression was one of elegance and grandeur. Two huge chairs faced directly onto the park—a perfect place to relax and take a long view of life.

In the kitchen, on the subzero refrigerator door, were dozens of pictures of Daphne, dating from when she was a little girl, up until recently. Everything was sparkling clean and appeared to be new. It was the kind of place where a family could feel comfortable sitting down to enjoy a meal, chatting about the day's events, and even chuckling about the ironies of life.

Daphne stood calmly at the counter, wearing a pair of pajamas, eating a plate of macaroni and cheese. Seeing her so composed, Furman was even more convinced that she was putting the screws on him and his partners. Nevertheless, he began to question her. "We have a trace to this apartment. Know anything about it?"

Before answering, she coldly told her father, who was standing off to one side, to leave the room. The look on his face suggested that Daphne was going to give the cops a hard time and they'd better be prepared. He took a step toward the door.

After taking a few more bites, she put down her fork. "I just witnessed a murder, man," she told the officers.

Right, thought Furman. *A fifteen-year-old girl from a posh address—not from the projects, where murders are not uncommon events—just witnessed a murder and she's calmly eating mac and cheese. Give me a goddamn break!*

Angelo cautioned his daughter to be careful about saying anything that might incriminate her.

"I don't care," she replied. "I know they are writing it down."

Daphne resumed eating. "My friend Chris. He did it."

"The guy in the tub?" asked Furman.

"Yup. That's him."

Then, seeing her father still standing in the doorway, Daphne demanded he get the hell out. This time, he left.

"You want to tell me what happened?" asked Furman, his mind now racing, rethinking and reinterpreting the chain of events that got him to the apartment in the first place.

"He cut him up and gutted the body."

"Where's the knife?" Furman asked.

"Chris has it. He went home."

"Who'd he kill?" Furman asked, almost expecting her to give it up now and come clean.

"Michael McMorrow," Daphne responded calmly, taking another bite.

"You know him?"

"Yup. Met him in rehab. A friend."

Where's the emotion here? Furman thought. *No uneasiness. No nervousness. No sadness. She's totally nonchalant. Like she's giving a goddamn weather report.*

Furman looked at her skeptically. "Hey, look at my watch," she snapped. "There's blood on it. I ain't messin' with you, man. Chris freaked out!"

After hearing that, Furman decided to call Sergeant Carolyn Fanale. Officer Moran called the Central Park lieutenant. If things turned out to be as Daphne was saying—as unbelievable as that was—this was drop-dead serious. A murder in Central Park? About as big as it gets. Daphne would have to be read her rights. All the details would have to be checked out. Someone would have to go to Christopher's house and hear his side of the story and locate the knife. Someone would have to go to the park and locate the body.

Turning back to Daphne, Furman asked, "Why didn't you tell me this before?"

"I was scared of Chris," she replied. "He was crazed. I was terrified by the look in his eyes. I was afraid he was going to kill me."

Within five minutes, the sergeant and lieutenant arrived at the apartment, as well as Duty Captain Davin. The officers filled them in. Fanale started talking to Daphne, trying to spark a conversation. The two hit it off immediately, with the conversation flowing easily. Daphne mentioned that her parents gave her a hard time. That she hated them. Fanale said she understood. Daphne went on to say that she was adopted, and Fanale responded that she, too, was adopted. What a coincidence! They talked about how adoption can affect a person, make you wonder where you really came from. But then as quickly and smoothly as Daphne glided into the conversation, she abruptly stopped and said she wasn't talking anymore, telling the detective that she got what she needed. Other detectives began questioning Daphne and soon realized that for much of the time she was talking, she was faking hysteria.

Having questioned enough people to know when to push and when to back off, Fanale eased up. After a while, trying to change the subject, Fanale asked Daphne if she could see her bedroom. Feeling calmer now, Daphne willingly took her there. The officers followed. In the bedroom were an extensive CD collection, fancy audio equipment, a TV, a computer, and scads of books. Obviously, it was the room of a privileged New Yorker.

Fanale complimented Daphne on the nice digs and then noticed bloodstained Rollerblades on the floor and blood on Daphne's watch and asked where it came from. Daphne responded it came from when Chris cut up McMorrow. Fanale asked to see the clothes that Daphne had worn that night.

"They're in the washer-dryer. Come on upstairs. They're probably still warm."

On the way upstairs to the second floor of the duplex apartment, Fanale asked where Chris "cut him up."

"In the park. At the lake."

"Where at the lake?"

"Hey, I'll take you there. Come on!"

Now, for the first time, Daphne was animated. In fact, she seemed downright energized by the prospect of taking the officers to the lake. She quickly changed into baggy jeans and a sweatshirt and urged Fanale to come on, to hurry up. And with that, she raced out the door. Immediately behind her was Sergeant Fanale, followed by Duty Captain Davin, Officers Brenner and Moran, and her father. Furman and Anchick stayed behind to secure the scene.

After they left, the apartment was eerily quiet. With no distractions, the officers began to go over the events that had gotten them to where they were. They started to rewrite the scenario that had begun a few hours before.

There's been a homicide in the park. A man is dead in the lake. Two teenagers are somehow involved. The blood-stained clothes and Blades are possible evidence. Daphne is eager to show her trophy. If this isn't bull—and it's looking more and more like it isn't—this is huge.

Meanwhile, Christopher Vasquez was at home in his bedroom making a telephone call to his friend Diana, who attended Marymount School, a prestigious private school on the East Side. Diana's mother picked up the phone and Christopher demanded to speak with Diana, but her mother wouldn't let him. Christopher yelled and cursed her out, but she wouldn't budge.

Christopher then changed into pajamas and went into the living room to be with his mother. He knew he was in big trouble and that he was about to be scolded. After all, he had stayed out way past his curfew.

CHAPTER 8

Cops like to say that anything more serious than a broken cuticle in Central Park is big news. That's because Central Park is not *merely* a wonderland that serves as New Yorkers' personal patch of paradise, as well as the destination for innumerable tourists, but it is also a highly politicized arena in which the city's pulse, its emotional and physical well-being, is monitored on a daily basis.

A murder in the "2-0" or the "7-5" is news, but a murder in Central Park is a metaphor. Magnified a hundredfold, a park homicide equals more than one dead person. It is a symbol of urban decay, of the financial and cultural capital of the world gone to the dogs.

Some of the most vicious murders that ever took place in Central Park happened in the decades before the new millennium.

In July 1986, Officer Steven McDonald stopped a group of teens on the East Drive and was shot and paralyzed.

On August 26, 1986, Jennifer Levin, eighteen, was

murdered by Robert Chambers, nineteen, in what became labeled the "Preppy Murder" case. Six-foot four-inch Chambers's defense was that he was merely protecting himself during rough sex with five-foot four-inch Levin.

On September 6, 1988, David George, thirty-two, was fatally shot as he walked through the park with a friend.

In April 1989, in an incident labeled the "Central Park Jogger" case, a twenty-eight-year-old investment banker was beaten with a brick, raped, sodomized, and left for dead in the northern part of the park near 102nd Street.

In July 1994, two homeless women were raped and a third was stabbed to death in a pup tent they had set up near the Boathouse, at Seventy-second Street.

On September 17, 1995, Maria Isabel Monteiro Alves, forty-four years old and a native of Brazil, was jogging when she was raped and beaten to death near Lasker Rink, midpark at around 108th Street.

The murder of Michael McMorrow on May 23, 1997, was the first in Central Park since Alves was killed.

CHAPTER 9

With Daphne in the lead, followed by Sergeant Fanale, Duty Captain Davin, Officers Brenner and Moran, and Angelo Abdela, the group crossed Central Park West and entered the park at Seventy-second Street. After walking about one hundred yards, they came to a deserted and pitch-black Strawberry Fields. Passing the mosaic, they headed down the path leading out of Strawberry Fields and crossed West Drive. After walking about a block north, they dipped right, down an overgrown path, to a secluded wooden shelter, invisible from the walkway. About five feet to the left of the landing, a body was floating faceup in lake water that sparkled with shards of light from the full moon.

Breaking the stillness, Daphne screamed, "I tried to help you. I tried to give you CPR."

Within seconds, word went out over the police radio that there was a corpse floating near the gazebo at the southwest section of the lake.

After securing the site at 115 Central Park West, Furman and Anchick looked out the window, stunned. Four helicopters were already flying low, circling the park.

Patrol cars with their sirens blaring were racing to the West Drive. As the two officers talked about the strange set of circumstances that had gotten them to the ritzy duplex on CPW, where they now found themselves, a woman in a nightgown appeared in the living room. Groggily she asked what was going on and where her husband was.

Furman replied that her husband was with their daughter, probably still at the lake, but maybe at the precinct, the "2-0."

Immediately her face dropped. Noticeably upset, Catherine Abdela asked what had happened. The officers hesitated. They knew they couldn't say much, so they simply urged her to get in touch with her husband immediately.

Mrs. Abdela glanced out the window. After a few seconds, she turned away and abruptly left the room. She walked down the hall and into a room, shutting the door behind her.

Down at the lake, the officers were questioning Daphne. They asked her where Christopher lived. She told them: 65 East Ninety-seventh Street. Two detectives then drove to the five-story walk-up building. Because they didn't have an apartment number, the officers had to call Christopher's telephone number over and over again while they canvassed the halls listening to hear a telephone ring. Finally they heard the phone ringing on the fifth floor and knocked on the door. Christopher was in the living room with his mother, wearing only a pair of pajama bottoms. The officers asked him to get dressed. They were taking him into custody.

Meanwhile, Daphne and her father had been driven to the "2-0," where she was taken to the Youth Office on the first floor, just off the lobby.

There, a full investigation was about to begin.

* * *

When officers from the Central Park Precinct arrived at the lake, they immediately cordoned off the area with yellow police tape. That done, they stepped back and looked over the crime scene: the gazebo, the surrounding rocky and grassy area, and the nearby lake.

They were shocked and shaken. "It was a gruesome sight," reported one cop. "A dead guy's floating in the water, faceup. His intestines are hanging out, some of them are drifting nearby. His neck is slit. One hand is dangling, almost completely cut off at the wrist. I never saw anything like it, and I'm no rookie."

"He was gutted," said another cop. "You could see his nose was almost cut off."

"It was an extremely vicious crime," stated a veteran officer, "with a lot of gratuitous injuries. One of the worst I've ever seen."

One detective, describing the body, said, "They basically cut him up like a deer."

Even veteran cops who were on the scene were horrified—and revolted.

Prosecutors rushed to the "2-0," hoping for an interview with Daphne before the family invoked counsel. As they came into the room where she was being held, they found her sleeping, with her father sitting in a nearby chair. They asked Mr. Abdela if they could have a word with his daughter. Daphne awoke and yelled, "Jesus Christ!" and promptly went back to sleep. It was as if she were saying, "This is what you woke me up for?!"

Immediately both families hired lawyers. By all accounts, the less well-off family, the Vasquezes, hired the more seasoned and pricier attorney. Robert Fogel-nest, fifty-two, was a top trial lawyer and considered by some a courtroom brawler. He was the immediate past-president of the National Association of Criminal Lawyers. The Abdelas hired George Weinbaum, fifty-two, a former special assistant to the state attorney general and a lawyer who specialized in white-collar crimes from his office in White Plains, New York.

Fogelnest had been in the spotlight most recently the previous year defending the so-called firebomber, Edward Leary. Leary had been charged with two counts of attempted murder after igniting firebombs in New York City subways, which injured fifty people, sixteen of them critically. In that case, Fogelnest argued that Leary was psychotic after having taken Prozac, along with other prescription drugs, and therefore didn't know what he was doing. It didn't fly with the jury. Fogelnest was said to have had a mesmerizing effect on the jury in the case of Scott Jackson, a Tiffany employee who was accused of masterminding a $1.9 million heist of the store and plotting the armed robbery of a store courier. To the surprise of court watchers and even the judge, Jackson was sentenced to fifteen years for the courier robbery and acquitted of the store heist.

In 1992, Weinbaum successfully argued a case involving Dr. Ronald Tauber. He asked that the doctor be granted a New York medical license, even though he had been released from prison just two years before after serving time for molesting a six-year-old girl and had had both his Michigan and Florida medical licenses revoked. Before that, in 1986, Weinbaum represented Romual Piecyk, who had accused Mob boss John Gotti of assault. Piecyk subsequently withdrew his charges.

CHAPTER 10

A little after 2:00 A.M., about the same time that Furman and Anchick were speaking with Mrs. Abdela, Detective Hal Sherman was sitting at his desk on the fifth floor of 1 Fordham Plaza in the Bronx, a ten-story building where crime scene detectives from the Crime Scene Unit of the police department have their offices. It was a typical night. Ten detectives and one sergeant were hard at work, performing administrative duties, preparing diagrams and reports from past homicides, and reviewing notes and reports for upcoming court cases. A TV was on low, and the citywide radio was being carefully monitored. The telephone rang. It was a detective from Nightwatch. "A male's been discovered in Central Park, in the lake. He's been eviscerated and there's a blood trail leading away from the scene." The case was given to Sherman. He was up next.

Sherman became a crime scene detective after spending five years in law enforcement. He began as a uniform cop in the Forty-second Precinct, in the Morrisania section of the Bronx, and worked that job for four years. In 1986, he was transferred to

Bronx narcotics. In 1987, a year which saw some two thousand murders in the city, many of them drug-related, ten guys from narcotics were transferred into crime scene investigation because narcotics expertise was needed to solve the crimes. Sherman was one of the ten. (In 2001, he would be promoted to first-grade detective—the highest rank attainable by a detective, with fewer than 2 percent of all detectives in the city reaching this level—after he was able to lift fingerprints from newspapers inside the getaway van within twelve hours after two cops had been ambushed.)

As soon as he received the assignment about the body in the lake, Sherman, along with Detective Tommy Shaw, shot to the park in the mobile crime scene lab van. It took them around twenty minutes. When they arrived, eight or ten people were already there: detectives, uniform cops, and several bosses, all standing outside the taped-off crime scene.

Although many TV shows portray crime scene investigations as taking place in five minutes flat, most investigations take far longer—many hours or even several days. For one thing, the crime scene is often vast, including not only the specific area where a body is found, but also the vicinity around it, where an access or escape route might be, or where footprints, clothing, or other items might have been left behind. Plus, crime scene investigators must meticulously document everything they see—in photographs and in detailed, accurate diagrams—then collect and label all the evidence in such a way that the investigation won't be compromised. "It's time-consuming, exacting, and often difficult work. Good police work takes time," said Sherman.

Some evidence is fragile and must be collected immediately or it will be of no use. Footprints, for example, can easily be stepped on and wiped out or destroyed in a sudden rain. Other evidence is hard to find—fibers or hairs in grass, blood droplets, soil samples, pollen—and all must be collected and evaluated.

Investigators' minds must be alert and nimble. Crime scene detectives have to consider not only evidence that has been left behind but also evidence that is not at the scene, but should have been, such as a wallet or a vehicle. Investigators are constantly thinking, rethinking, and revising theories as new information comes to light. The best of the lot are like chess players, coolly evaluating what is in front of them, while keeping their eye on the endgame. Memory, experience, analysis, and inspiration are all brought to work when solving a crime. Sherman, like all top crime scene investigators, had to rely on his keen observation skills, deep knowledge of crime scenes, and intuition to lead him to the truth.

When Sherman arrived at the lake, he nodded to the officers, but did not speak to any of them. That was his usual MO. Not only did he not like to talk while doing his work—so focused was he on the task—but he also didn't want to hear anyone else's point of view about what might have taken place. "It compromises my work and taints my view of the scene. Maybe somebody's remarks will lead me along a path I wouldn't have followed, and the path ultimately turns out wrong. Let me do my work. If I'm able to do my job without interruption, I'll end up telling everyone else what's happened—even an eyewitness."

After Sherman made sure the crime scene was secure and protected, he did a preliminary survey to determine the boundaries where he would be working. Once satisfied that things were in order, he proceeded to photograph the entire area—overall, medium, and close-up views of the victim in the lake, the gazebo and surrounding areas, and the Central Park Lake itself—with his Nikon F3. He then did a quick walk-through, photographing each object he saw, in its place. In all, he took about seventy-five color pictures, which would later be developed in the police's own photo unit. Then he began making a diagram of the immediate area. It recorded the exact measurements of where every piece of evidence was in relation to every other piece and to the layout of the scene. On it, he numbered where each blood droplet and every other item was, to establish the distance and size relationships. Diagrams supplemented the photographs. Among other things, they could include the date, the specific location, the time, the name of the preparer, the weather, the lighting, the scale, the compass orientation, and the measurements, as well as the major items of evidence. Diagrams would be invaluable later, when detectives were piecing together all the pieces of the puzzle.

Once all the evidence had been photographed and placed in the appropriate spot on the sketch, Sherman, wearing his Tyvek suit and using latex gloves, began to collect, lift, and package items. In between each sample, he changed gloves to prevent any chance of cross-contamination.

At the scene, Sherman immediately saw many blood droplets. "You can put a time frame on blood," said Sherman, "but not on fingerprints." Examining the droplets closely, he discovered two things. First, they were fresh. They were still red, so they had not been there long enough to have oxidized into a deeper brownish color. And they had not caked or flaked, which also would have meant they were old. Sherman noted their directionality—up the pathway and away from the crime scene, not down toward the lake. From that, he knew that the assailant or assailants must have been injured.

Sherman also saw three bottle caps: Guinness, Heineken, and Zima. From the variety, he surmised that there were probably three different people drinking at the spot. His past work and his intuition told him that the Zima drinker was most probably a female, the Guinness meant a hard-core drinker—maybe even an alcoholic—and the Heineken, a more social drinker—certainly not an alcoholic.

Sherman then began to swab every other bloodstain. He carefully placed each sample individually inside a manila envelope, called a coin envelope. He signed and dated each one, then fully described the kind of evidence it was and its exact location. All in all, he took around thirty-five blood samples. Then he instructed ESU to take out sections of asphalt that had blood droplets on them. Using a jackhammer, the workers removed well over a dozen. Right outside the gazebo, Sherman saw diluted blood and a bloody handprint on some asphalt. Someone had washed his or her hands in the lake water. Sherman asked ESU to remove that piece of asphalt as well.

Carefully looking over the gazebo, Sherman saw several overhead blood droplets. The overhead blood droplets revealed that the source of the blood was standing still—the droplets were traveling straight down and there was no directionality, which would have shown the most likely path that the assailant was traveling toward. After seeing a blood trail leading away from the gazebo, Sherman theorized that the gazebo was the most logical place for the assault to have taken place.

Looking around the grassy area on three sides of the gazebo, Sherman saw other items of interest: a set of keys and a business card, which had been set on fire. It said "Sir Realty" on it. Looking further, he saw a sneaker near a tree.

It took Sherman around an hour to do his initial look-over of the crime scene—the grass, dirt, bushes, flowers, trees, paths, and gazebo—and another twelve hours to take photographs, make diagrams, and hand over all the labeled and packaged items to a uniformed cop at the "2-0," whose job it would be to voucher everything and send it on to the appropriate department. "There is a strong chain of custody," said Sherman. "Some stuff goes to the medical examiner's office. Other stuff goes to the property clerk, until the item is required for additional analysis or in court." Among the items Sherman collected were blood, grass, pollen, weeds, rock, bottle caps, and floating human tissue from the Lake at Central Park. He had to prepare special protective packages for one-foot-square pieces of concrete so they wouldn't fall out of their bags.

While Sherman was collecting all the physical evidence, police officers in scuba gear from the NYPD Harbor Unit waded into the lake to look for weapons and any other evidence that might be submerged, and, most important, to bring the body onto the shore. After searching the waters for half an hour, the divers recovered only a gun, which turned out later not to be a part of this crime. They dragged the faceup body out of the water and placed it on a green waterproof sheet. Immediately Sherman looked it over. The corpse would tell a truthful tale. After he examined, photographed, and documented the body, along with the medical examiner Barbara Butcher, the corpse was placed inside an ambulance and removed to the medical examiner's office, where the coroner would then begin the autopsy.

By the time Sherman finished his work at the site, it was around 3:00 P.M.—a full fourteen hours after he had begun. By now, some forty people in various official capacities, along with reporters and crowds of curious onlookers, were there—all being kept outside the taped-off area.

Later, when asked about the scene, he said, "This was one of the most gruesome murders I ever saw. And I've seen over fifteen hundred, all pretty awful, but this one was particularly horrific."

(Sherman is retired from the NYPD today but hardly inactive. After working at the World Trade Center site in 2001, searching for victims, he started working in bioterrorism and has been teaching classes in bioterrorism all over the country for the past five years. He is in great demand as an expert witness in trials throughout the United States and even as far away as Israel. He testifies about the validity of physical evidence, particularly fingerprints, hairs, fibers, and blood spatter patterns.)

"I have always found the work fascinating," Sherman said. "Those who examine crime scenes and victims have the obligation to speak for the deceased. Dead men do speak. They can speak volumes when the scene is documented properly and the evidence is collected properly, always being mindful that the items that you recover can assist in proving someone guilty or innocent of what they have been accused." His 2005 book, *The Illustrated Guide to Crime Scene Investigation,* is a testament to his skills, written to educate investigators on how to process a crime scene properly.

* * *

At 8:00 A.M., Friday, May 23, Detective Rob Mooney arrived at Manhattan North Homicide, at 3280 Broadway, at 132nd Street, his "home away from home" for the past three years. At six feet four inches, and weighing some 330 pounds, Mooney commanded attention not simply by the measure of space he occupied, but by the aura surrounding him. Impeccably dressed and immaculately groomed, with a voice as smooth as fine bourbon and a kind, avuncular face, he could easily be labeled a gentle giant—unless, of course, you happened to be the object of his shrewd and relentless interrogations. Then *gentle* might change to *merciless*. Playing roles as diverse as unyielding interviewer, harsh inquisitor, psychologist, friend, father figure, and moral standard-bearer, he can intuit the best method for getting the information he needs—and usually gets what he wants. With kind eyes that look right at you and then right through you, he was an expert at knowing who was telling the truth now, who might tell it later, and who will never fess up, no matter what.

Mooney was on chart change that morning, working the 8 to 4, instead of 4 to 1, because he had to be in court that afternoon. He liked the variety of the four-and-two chart—4:00 P.M. till 1:00 A.M., two days in a row, 8:00 A.M. to 4:00 P.M., the next two days, followed by two RDO's (Rostered Days Off). To him, nothing was as boring as doing the same thing over and over, evidenced by the way he lived his life—learning Spanish in his thirties, taking up the mandolin in his forties, and finally signing up for formal music lessons after playing the guitar by ear for some thirty years. Mooney was looking forward to testifying in court later that day, and he was good at it, too. Some defense attorneys, having witnessed his measured restraint followed by his precise and damaging testimony, refused to even call him to the stand, knowing he would make mincemeat out of them.

The minute he stepped into the familiar squad room, he knew something was up. The nine or so detectives were all in motion, some getting ready to leave, others signing out, and others making telephone calls, when usually they would be sitting calmly at their desks, sipping coffee, eating a bagel, reading the newspaper, and getting ready for the day ahead.

Sergeant Tommy Dolan immediately told him there was a fresh one in the park and that Bill Alee, the chief of detectives, wanted everyone to go. Mooney knew at once he had to get out of his afternoon court date. He got on the phone and called the district attorney (DA) on the case. He told him he couldn't make it that afternoon and would call back later to reschedule. Then he went to the book to sign out. On the left-hand page, he had just signed in: name, rank, time. Now, on the right side, he signed out: to Central Park. It was 8:15 A.M.

Billy Johnson and Timmy Hartnett, both second-grade detectives, were already in the squad car. Mooney was a third grader. He got in the backseat of the black Ford Crown Victoria, and the three set off for the crime scene. On the way, the men didn't talk about the little they knew so far about the crime. They were aware that getting the facts ahead of time about a case was worse than playing telephone, so they waited to figure things out for themselves.

Johnson dropped Mooney off on the West Drive and returned to the precinct. The area had already been secured. Two ESU cops stood in wet suits by the body that had been pulled out of the water. Barbara Butcher, from the medical examiner's office, was inspecting the area. It was her job to offer opinions about what might have taken place.

As he looked around, Mooney felt a sense of calm. Detective Hal Sherman was there. To Mooney's mind, Sherman was one of the best at crime scenes. He was already directing his men to cut out pieces of bloody asphalt. Two morgue employees, known as ghouls or drones, wearing coveralls, were about to put the body into a body bag and take it to the medical examiner's office, where an autopsy would be done and a coroner's report filed. When Mooney saw the body, he was stunned. The number of facial cuts and slices was the first thing that startled him. Then he saw dozens of incisions in the torso and other parts of the body. Looking more closely, he noticed that the nose was nearly detached. He saw a hand dangling. But what really startled him was the huge cavity where the intestines should have been, and about forty feet of intestines were lying nearby.

Mooney, unlike Sherman, spoke to everyone on the scene. He learned that two teenagers were in custody at the "2-0" and that they had already invoked counsel. He would not be able to talk to them. He knew he had to start his investigation somewhere and decided to in-terview the cops who had first learned about what happened—separately, to make sure he got the best information.

Investigators like Mooney approach a case this way: This is what I know. This is what I think. This is what I want to find out. Mooney was poised to proceed. Although this was a ground ball—the perps were already presumably known—there was still a great deal of work to do.

* * *

At around 8:00 A.M., the same time as Mooney got the call to go to the Lake at Central Park, Furman was replaced by another officer at the Majestic and returned to the "2-0." He now had the tedious task of preparing the paperwork—meticulously detailing exactly what had taken place.

At 9:00 a.m., Maria Luz Alandy, M.D., acting deputy chief medical examiner, was in the medical examiner's office about to begin an autopsy on the body of Michael McMorrow, in the presence of doctors Tennant, Milewski, and Smiddy. The corpse was wrapped in a green fitted bedsheet. After they took it off, they began writing their report.

It stated that the body was that of a well-nourished, slightly heavyset, light-skinned white male, with curly grayish brown hair, approximately one inch long. He looked to be somewhere in his late forties or early fifties, weighing 210 pounds, measuring six feet one inch.

The report noted that the following was observed: White jockey shorts underwear, soaked. Dark-colored pants, soaked. In one pocket, a soaked letter. Brown belt inserted through the loops of the pants. Long-sleeved dark gray shirt with multiple slitlike defects on left chest area, lower lateral and right frontal abdominal areas, corresponding to stab wounds on body. Soaked shirt stained with blood. Short-sleeved white T-shirt, soaked with water and blood, with multiple slitlike defects, corresponding to stab wounds on chest. The back of the torso without injuries. Both hands bagged.

* * *

At the "2-0," Furman walked past the Youth Office, where juveniles in custody were taken. He saw Daphne sitting inside.

"That's him! He's the one!" screamed an angry Daphne, her words echoing throughout the hallways.

Furman flinched. *That's the topper: she is blaming me for the fact that she's here!*

At around 3:30 P.M., Friday afternoon, Detective Kenneth Gannon, of Nightwatch, filled out four affidavits for search warrants. One was "to take scrapings from, on, and under the fingernails of Chris Vasquez, where there is reasonable cause to believe that the following property may be found: blood and soil." In the affidavit, Gannon wrote, "On May 23, 1997, at approximately 2:45 A.M., I observed the dead body of a male floating in the lake at Central Park in the vicinity of West 72nd Street." He wrote that Officer Lawrence Moran, of the Central Park Police Precinct, told him that Daphne Abdela had led Moran and others to the body and stated that she observed Chris stab and cut the throat of the deceased. Further, the affidavit stated that Detective Neal Parchen, of the Crime Scene Unit, observed Christopher at St. Luke's/ Roosevelt Hospital and saw a laceration and a bruise on the teen's left pointer finger, bruises on his right hand, a bruise and abrasion on the right side of his head, and an abrasion on his back. He reported that the injuries appeared to be recent. Parchen also said that "there appeared to be blood and dirt under several of Chris Vasquez' fingernails and in several of his cuticles."

Another affidavit was filled out to look for specific property at 65 East Ninety-seventh Street, including

U.S. currency, a baseball cap, a jacket, a license or identification of a Hispanic male, a brightly colored shirt, and other clothing possibly containing blood-stains or soil. These items were of interest because, according to the report, Officer Moran had observed the two teens Rollerblading away from the scene a short time after he heard screams, and that one of the teens, Christopher, was wearing a brightly colored shirt, jacket, and a baseball cap. The affidavit included the information that Daphne informed Moran that she and Chris tried to destroy the deceased's wallet and his ID, and that they removed and kept U.S. currency from the wallet. The affidavit also stated that an uncle of Christopher's, Michael Tantillo, had allowed officers to enter the Vasquez apartment earlier in the day, after it was sealed off, and once inside, "I recovered blood-stained socks, a bloodstained white shirt, bloodstained rollerblades, bloodstained jeans, and a knife in the pocket in said jeans." Gannon reported that there was no visible blood on the blade of the knife, but it was submitted for forensic testing.

A third affidavit was issued to search the premises at 115 Central Park West, to look for bloodstained Roller-blades, a bloodstained watch, a green fleece vest, U.S. currency, and clothing with soil or blood inside a washing machine and/or dryer, a license or ID of a Hispanic male, towels, or other evidence. In requesting the search warrant, Detective Gannon stated that he had reasonable cause to believe that the items were there because Officer Moran, in the early-morning hours of May 23, was present and observed them.

A fourth affidavit was submitted in support of a search warrant to obtain a blood sample from Christopher Vasquez and to submit such sample for serological testing. Barbara Butcher, the investigator from the medical examiner's office, said that the blood sample—one 10 ml Vacutainer tube—would be taken at the Twenty-fourth Precinct, on West 100th Street. The warrant was issued for this to be done between 6:00 A.M. and 9:00 P.M.

In the course of executing the search warrant at Daphne's apartment, Detective Robert Mooney, of Manhattan North Homicide, observed a pager and a wallet on a table and identification inside the wallet belonging to Christopher Vasquez. He also observed another pager on top of the pajamas that Daphne was wearing when Officer Moran first arrived at Daphne's home in the early morning of May 23. Rollerblades, which were on the floor, along with a bloodstained watch, had been placed in a bag. Crime Scene Unit officers began packing up several large cardboard boxes with potential evidence and loaded them into their Crime Scene Unit truck.

After the search warrant was issued for Christopher's apartment, officers seized a variety of items, including U.S. currency, a baseball cap, a jacket, and a brightly colored shirt.

CHAPTER 11

As Friday morning dawned, runners and bicyclists, fueled by obsession, caffeine, sheer will, or sheer force of habit, were already out in full force, zipping through the park like a determined band of human roadrunners. Passing by the cordoned-off site on West Drive, they barely gave the spot a second glance, and those who did, raised their eyebrows, shrugged their shoulders, and continued on their way, contented that whatever had taken place had little relevance to them and their already active and productive day.

However, a different reality altogether greeted those who had awakened and turned on the radio or TV: "A horrific and particularly brutal murder took place in Central Park in the early hours of the morning. Two teenagers have been taken into custody."

The shocking details were recounted over and over again, in ever increasing decibels of hysteria, and the ignoble yet magnetic intrigue of the sordid took hold, swelled, and eventually enveloped the good people of New York.

Scrambling to assuage the fears of New Yorkers that

their prized Central Park was unsafe, Mayor Rudolph Giuliani, Police Commissioner Howard Safir, and Parks Commissioner Henry Stern held a news conference urging New Yorkers not to panic.

Commissioner Safir summarized the most pertinent details. Giuliani then tried to calm the fears of New Yorkers: "The fact is that Central Park is a place of very little crime. It is a safe place. It is a place people can use without being worried. This particular crime was not a crime between and among strangers." He went on to say that it was a "particularly gruesome and horrible crime, but it was not a random act of violence. I think this is an incident that really has no bearing on the park." Giuliani reminded New Yorkers that this was the first murder in the park in over a year, and that during the entire year of 1996, only 219 crimes were reported. Because Central Park is so treasured, he went on to say, when something happens there, it gets more attention.

Parks Commissioner Stern reinforced the mayor's main points: "This crime is totally unrelated to recreational use of the park. It was close to midnight and they were drinking beer, drinking Zima. It's deviant behavior." He continued: "There have been past crimes in the park where people involved in legitimate park use have been victims of vicious crimes. This is not one of them. Only one thing will keep people away from the park this holiday weekend. Rain."

Regardless of what spin the politicians tried to put on it, New Yorkers were nevertheless stunned. It was certainly not a loss of innocence that they experienced. They had lost that a long time ago, almost as a rite of residency: living in the urban jungle included such a high concentration of humanity that New Yorkers had seen and heard it all. No, the murder was a

reminder of something far greater than the existence
of decadence, wickedness, or even degeneracy. It was a
reminder of the existence of evil, and that even young
people—those with baby faces from fine, upstanding
places—were capable of doing the unthinkable.

Even the most hardened city dwellers were shaken
and upset, wondering not only what role might they
have unwittingly played—as friends, teachers, and
fellow citizens—in this deadly drama, but also what responsibility their prized city played—with its atmo-
sphere of freedom and anomie—in the actualization
of the horrifying drama.

As the day wore on, and those less hurried took the
time to stop near the crime scene and inquire what had
happened, reactions varied. Several onlookers were
nonplussed. If you use common sense, they remarked,
nothing bad is going to happen to you, and they wondered why anyone would go into the bowels of the park
in the middle of the night. One passerby said that Central Park was the best place for sunbathing and people
watching, and that this wouldn't deter her from enjoying the park. She added, however, that she never went
there at night. Another person echoed the feeling,
saying that the park was safe and comfortable, but the
rule was not to ever go there after the sun set. One bystander admitted that being a New Yorker had made
her almost numb to killings and that she felt sad about
that, but she quickly added that that was just how it was.

However, most New Yorkers at the site were visibly
upset. They said it was a stark reminder that danger
lurked within their cherished magical garden and
that, sadly, there was little that could be done to rid it.

By late morning, the names of the two teenagers
were released. The name of the deceased came after a
call had been made to the home of Michael's brother,

Charlie. His wife, Kathi, answered the phone. Later, remarking about the conversation, she said, "You simply can't believe it is true. You wonder if you heard correctly. How could you have? How could Michael have been killed? I was told that because of the location of the murder and the age of the alleged perpetrators, the incident would be receiving an extraordinary amount of media attention. It was the worst day of my life."

Kathi immediately called Michael's younger sister, Joan. She was at work on the far west side of Manhattan, ready to go to the gym for a lunchtime workout. Joan later recalled that as she was walking out the door, the phone rang, and she said to herself that she really should take this one last call. When she heard Kathi's voice, she thought they would be discussing the holiday weekend plans. Instead, Kathi said that Michael was dead.

"The following hours are a blur," Joan recalled. "My boss drove me to my mother's apartment, but I don't remember much of the ride. In fact, I don't even remember walking out of the office. I was in shock. My brother—my sweet, caring, loving brother—was dead. It was beyond comprehension."

When Michael hadn't come home Thursday night, his mother, Margaret, didn't give it much thought. Sometimes he stayed at a friend's house overnight. She knew she'd see him Friday, and maybe he would even call her during the day. Michael never stayed out two nights in a row without calling.

By the next afternoon, however, the only call she had received was from Joan, who said she was on her way to her apartment and would be there in about an hour. Joan wanted to talk with her. Margaret immediately sensed that Joan was upset, but something held her back from asking what was wrong. She would see her daughter soon and would find out then. Maybe Joan had gotten fired. Maybe her love life had veered off track. Whatever it was, they would talk about it and, no doubt, everything would fall into place.

The second Joan walked in the door, Margaret knew something terrible had happened. Her daughter's hands were shaking; in fact, her whole body was trembling, and she could barely speak.

Margaret and Joan embraced and, through tears, Joan told her mother what had happened. "I was the one who had to tell her. Can you imagine what that is like? We both just cried and cried and cried. My mother was hysterical. I was hysterical. We couldn't believe what had hit us."

Once the word got out, the McMorrows' phone didn't stop ringing. Joan recalled, "Family and friends came to the apartment to offer support and keep us company. It was a comfort, but nothing could change the reality. Michael was dead, killed by two teenagers, and nothing could bring him back."

Nobody in the McMorrow family slept that night. Between tears and half sentences, through anger and disbelief, they somehow made it until the morning, drifting though the apartment like disembodied souls in a world they barely recognized.

"The next day was a lovely spring day," Joan later recalled. "We almost believed it didn't happen, that somehow we had gotten it wrong. But we didn't. Every time we looked at each other, we broke down. We simply couldn't stop crying. But we had to make funeral arrangements. We had to bury Michael. It was unbelievable. You wake up one day, and it's the start of the Memorial Day weekend and you feel so happy and hopeful. Then this happens. It was the saddest day of my life."

CHAPTER 12

Three New York newspapers vie for the attention of New Yorkers, and each succeeds, with its loyal following swearing that that the other two aren't worth the paper they're printed on.

The average weekday circulation for the *New York Times* during 1996 and into 1997 was approximately 1,100,000, while the *Daily News*'s was 725,000, and the *New York Post*'s around 440,000. The *Post,* owned by Rupert Murdoch, has a penchant for being outrageous, but is valued for having the buzz and for dishing out the latest dirt on all the celebs, with sass and fizz. Some consider it a decadent dessert to dip into after dining on the more wholesome meal of the *Times,* the no-nonsense paper that appeals to those who consider themselves intellectuals or, at the very least, serious students of the news. The *News,* which calls itself "New York's Hometown Newspaper," prides itself on being the newspaper for the working class, the paper that calls it as it sees it and speaks in strident tones to the ordinary folk.

BABY-FACE BUTCHERS, screamed the headline in thick

letters that splashed across half the front page of the *Post* on Saturday, May 24, 1997. It was followed by: "Altar boy and his rich-kid girlfriend charged with brutal Central Park murder." Below those chilling words were side-by-side photographs of two teenagers. On the left was a shot of a sulky, pouting girl; on the right, a solemn-looking boy, with eyes cast downward, his face partly obscured by a baseball cap. Below the pictures was this caption: "Police say lovebirds Daphne Abdela and Christopher Vasquez, both 15, robbed and killed a 44-year-old man during a booze-filled night in the park." The identity of the dead man was given. Michael McMorrow.

The *Daily News* headline, sprawled in huge type across the bottom of the front page, was also sensational. DEADLY ENCOUNTER, it read. Next to it were these words: "Cops: Teen and preppie girlfriend slashed man in jealous frenzy." Above the pictures of the two teens, this time with Daphne's face almost totally obscured by strands of hair, were the words "Vicious Murder in Central Park." The story continued on pages 2 and 3. The paper also identified the dead man by name.

From the Metropolitan Desk of the *New York Times*, on page 21, was this column: "2 Teen-Agers Held in Stabbing Death of Man Found in Park." The paper identified the teens by name, but not the "44-year-old man [whose] body was slashed open by as many as 50 stab wounds."

On Sunday, the chilling front-page headline of the *Post* read, in huge bold letters: HE LAUGHED—UNTIL HE DIED. Below it were these words: "Before two troubled teens allegedly murdered him in Central Park on Friday, Michael McMorrow happily spent his nights doing what he liked to do—hanging out." Inside, the report stated that "an autopsy revealed his jugular vein, heart, aorta and lung were perforated during the attack, and his intestines had been pulled out of his body."

The front page of the *News* again on Sunday was devoted to the murder: TERROR TEENS, it said. Above it was "Central Park Butchery," and below it read: "She was a rebel. He was a loner. Together, cops say, they killed in cold blood." On the side were these sentences below a picture of Daphne: "A sullen Daphne Abdela is arraigned on murder charges yesterday. She and friend Christopher Vasquez are accused of brutally killing a man in Central Park." Next to an inset showing a happier Daphne are these words: "Last year, Daphne smiled for the camera."

On Sunday, May 25, on page 1 of the *Times,* an article began, "Body in Park Was Mutilated To Hide Identity, Officials Say." Another article in the paper had this headline: A SON, A COLLEAGUE, A MAN WITH PROBLEMS.

On May 26, running across the entire spread of pages 2 and 3 of the *News,* were these words: PARK TEEN PINS GUY PAL IN SLAY. Other observations on the pages read: "Troubled girl in long spiral. Tells police she feared for her life." "Shock over altar boy turned suspect." "Kin, pals mourn victim."

Throughout the weeks that followed, headlines continued to bombard—and intrigue—New Yorkers:

PUZZLEMENT OVER TEEN-AGERS' SUSPECTED INVOLVE-
    MENT IN GRISLY CRIME
THE MURDERS THAT STRIKE AT US ALL
SUSPECT'S EX-TEAMMATES RECALL COLDNESS
SHRINE FOR PARK VICTIM: HIS FAMILY GATHERS IN
    FAREWELL
MORE QUESTIONS THAN ANSWERS IN LURID CASE

LOVE CAN'T KEEP KIDS OUT OF THE ABYSS
AT VICTIM'S FUNERAL, LOSS OF GOOD NAME IS FEARED,
   TOO
VICTIM GAVE HIS KILLER A FIERCE FIGHT
A TEARFUL FAREWELL TO VICTIM
CENTRAL PK. TEENS MAY BLAME EACH OTHER
A SMALL BOY AND BIG EVIL
I WAS JUST A WITNESS WHEN MY FRIEND DID THE
   KILLING

Reports in the papers offered various accounts of the precipitating events. The *Post* reported that the two were lovebirds and that Vasquez flew into a "psycho rage" and a "booze-fueled jealous rage" after an older man, identified as Michael McMorrow, put his arm around Abdela. It stated that Vasquez then slashed and stabbed the man about thirty times and dumped him into the Central Park Lake. It went on to say that in butchering the man, McMorrow's neck was slit and a hand was severed at the wrist. He was gutted, and stab marks were found all over his body. His body was mutilated. The *Post* also reported that Vasquez "allegedly exploded after McMorrow asked Abdela to perform a sex act in exchange for the beer he'd bought them." The paper reported that on Thursday night, the pair were guzzling beer with the victim before Vasquez stabbed Michael dozens of times. A cop reported to the *Post* that the body was dumped and found floating just left of the gazebo. The report stated that Daphne watched while her boyfriend stabbed him in the stomach, face, hand, back, and throat. She watched as he "viciously sliced up" the victim, before telling him to enlarge the wound in his stomach so that he would sink.

The *News* reported that a "slash frenzy" took place in

the park after a night of boozing. It stated that the boy slashed the man from ear to ear after he put his arm around Abdela. Then, upon receiving an "order" from the girl, he "eviscerated" the victim, after taking cash from his wallet and burning his identification. The report noted that there were thirty stab wounds to the face, neck, chest, and stomach, as well as multiple cuts and stab wounds to the abdomen, after the man was dead. The teens disemboweled the man, the report stated, and almost completely severed his hand in an effort to conceal his identity before they dumped him into water.

The *Times* stated that there were as many as fifty stab wounds and that Abdela observed Vasquez stab and slash the victim. She admitted to police that she told Vasquez to gut the body so it would sink, before the two of them threw the body into the Lake at Central Park. The only information coming from police officials, reported the *Times*, was that the teens and the victim had had an argument before the stabbing.

Depending on the newspaper report and the columnist's slant on what took place, McMorrow was mutilated, slit, gutted, gruesomely slashed, slashed open, disemboweled, gutted like a pig, or eviscerated. McMorrow was dragged, pushed, thrown, dumped, or heaved into the Central Park Lake.

Commenting on the media frenzy that was taking place, Jerry Nachman (deceased, as of 2004), a former editor of the *Post*, and a former news director at WCBS-TV, said: "Is there a test of what qualifies as news that this story fails?" It seemed not.

The story included, among other things: youth, wealth, race, gender, drugs (both illegal and prescription), alcohol, adoption, divorce, agoraphobia, motive, a weapon, viciousness, the park, and, yes, even love.

* * *

Youth: The accused were teenagers. One had turned fifteen only days before the murder. The other was almost 15½.

Wealth: one of the accused was from a multimillion-dollar household.

Race: One of the accused was white; the other was Latino. Neither race was on the top of the list of typical juvenile offenders.

Gender: one of the accused was female, which was on the bottom rung of typical juvenile offenders.

Drugs: Both teens were drinking heavily that day and both may have smoked pot. One may have taken LSD. One teen had a serious enough alcohol-abuse problem that she had been in treatment for years. The other teen had been on Zoloft since he was nine and was also on Lorazepam.

Adoption: one of the accused was adopted at three days old.

Divorce: one of the accused's parents divorced two years before the murder.

Agoraphobia: one of the accused had been diagnosed with agoraphobia, particularly a fear of school, in the third grade.

Location: Central Park, a sanctuary that for many New Yorkers was as holy as the church or temple they attended, was the scene of the murder.

Motive: it seemed to have been a spur-of-the-moment kill—a thrill kill or one prompted by jealousy rage.

Weapon: A knife was used, not the more popular form of murder weapon, a gun. Killing with a knife was up close and personal—where the attacker saw a face, heard the moans, felt the blade as it sliced through skin and touched bone, watched as the victim fell to the ground, saw blood and other fluids coming from the victim's body, and possibly observed the moment of death as well.

Viciousness: The murder was an overkill of great cruelty and brutality. The body was disemboweled and tossed into a lake.

Love: the accused may have been in a "relationship."

Most papers focused on the question of what could have gone wrong with this rich white girl, while showing little surprise that a Latino would be involved. That, in spite of the fact that Daphne had been in trouble before and Christopher hadn't. Nevertheless, they wrote Christopher off. He fit the stereotype.

Perhaps it was because most of the reporters were white and middle-class, and in Daphne, they saw someone who could be their own daughter: a rebellious adolescent flexing her muscles and trying to assert her independence—just like their kids, who enjoyed Roller-blading, watching violent movies, hanging out with friends, and acting tough.

The newspapers raised many questions regarding the teens and the murdered man, and each person's motives. Among the most often repeated were these: Why were the teens in the park that late? What was a forty-four-year-old man doing drinking with teenagers? Who did the actual stabbing? What role did each play? Why was the murder so brutal, and why did it last so long? What was the motive for the murder? What role did drugs, alcohol, and sex play?

Only hours after the murder, people began weighing in about it on the Internet.

One person wondered if the Abdelas knew that

their daughter was doing drugs and hanging out at night drinking booze with a forty-four-year-old. She wondered why the parents weren't more involved with their kid's life. Another writer wondered why the two were permitted out of the house after dark, much less in Central Park among the alcoholics.

One writer questioned how a child became a thrill killer—through a steady diet of horror, mayhem, and cruelty brought home through TV, movies, music, and video games? But, citing Jack Levin, director of Northeastern University's Program for the Study of Violence, she went on to point out that there is a lot more violence on Japanese TV than here, and almost no murder takes place on the streets in Japan.

One writer expressed sympathy for Daphne and Christopher in his note, and a responder questioned why anyone's heart would go out to the teens and their families—unless that person is suffering from "sympathy-for-the-devil" syndrome.

Another person stated that people can sympathize with whomever they wish, but certainly no one deserved the butchery that Michael suffered.

One person commented that Michael McMorrow may not have been a hero, but he was certainly a victim of a barbaric murder. The writer went on to say that anyone who sympathizes with the teens is misguided and has a sad and frightening point of view.

A city school teacher wrote that she was outraged that people were casting blame only on the teens when Michael was committing several crimes himself—including spending the evening providing alcohol to—and drinking with—a couple of 15-year-olds.

When Daphne's Sunday-school classmates learned about the murder, they struggled to keep their negative feelings in check. They felt betrayed and devastated not only because she was "one of them" and had done something unthinkable, but also because of the viciousness of the crime. Many of the kids were so upset that they required counseling. Seminars were held to help them try to understand the unfathomable. They—as well as the teachers—were forced to do a lot of soul-searching: Why hadn't they seen that something was horribly wrong? What could they have done to have prevented this from happening?

At thirteen, fourteen, and fifteen years old, Daphne's Sunday-school classmates were confused, shocked—and livid.

But they weren't the only ones. When park regulars heard about the attack, they, too, were stunned. "Parkers," who also call themselves "parkees," "hippies," "rockers," and "gypsies," emphasized they were a peaceful lot, who were not dirty and who cleaned up after themselves. They looked out for each other and never sought trouble. The problem that night was that the cops came around and harassed them. In fact, several of the night parkers blamed the NYPD for the murder. They said that if the cops hadn't come along and chased them, Michael would still be alive today. They would have chilled until the wee hours of the morning, then gone their separate ways, without a hint of violence—just like every other night of the year.

In interviews, they claimed that the park was basically safe at night. In fact, they said, they felt safer in the park at night than on the streets of the urban jungle. Some did admit, however, that for those who were not used to it, the park could have a hint of danger. But for them, the park was pure bliss. They had the freedom to strum their guitars into the wee hours of the morning. They could lead the life of an

artist and meet "real" people, or they could simply
be whoever they wanted to be and do whatever they
wanted to do in the most luxurious and serene setting
in all of New York. One park dweller, Youm, twenty-
one, stated that he preferred spending nights in the
park to staying in his parents' home because he enjoyed hanging out with friends and playing his
acoustic guitar without restrictions. Another park
dweller, Damon, a wealthy business consultant's son,
stated that he didn't like "to hang out with robots. I
want to hang out with real people."

Parker Gary recalled Michael's cheerful "Peace"
greeting and his park nickname, "Madness," which
was Michael's definition of the world outside the park.
Gary said he'd miss Michael forever and feared he'd
never come to an understanding of what could drive
teen-agers to do such a thing.

Madness, indeed, he surmised.

CHAPTER 13

Christopher Vasquez was born on New Year's Day, 1982, a precious little bundle who was certain to be a harbinger of even greater happiness for the growing Vasquez family, which already included a baby girl, Jennifer, as well as Christopher's parents, Patricia Reidy and Gerardo Vasquez. The two had been high-school sweethearts, growing up within a block of each other on East Ninety-seventh and Ninety-eighth Streets. Theirs was a mixed neighborhood, with a large entrenched Irish-American population, followed in the 1960s by a wave of Hispanics. Reidy and Vasquez were representatives of each. After they married, the couple rented an apartment on the block they knew so well, Ninety-seventh Street, between Madison and Park. It was a modest five-story walk-up building, and their apartment was on the top floor. Across the hall lived Patricia's parents, Marie and Daniel. Close-knit and deeply religious, the families were parishioners at St. Francis de Sales Church, on East Ninety-sixth Street, where Daniel was an usher. He also worked as a doorman on Park Avenue.

Like many neighborhood kids, Christopher attended St. Ignatius Loyola Grammar School, on East Eighty-fourth Street, where Catholic moral values were stressed and morning and afternoon prayer were an integral part of school. One day, while he was in the third grade, Christopher became increasingly anxious and claustrophobic. When it became impossible for him to sit still a second longer, he bolted out of his seat and raced out of class. Soon after, he was diagnosed with a form of agoraphobia—a condition in which a person becomes highly anxious in a place or situation from which escape or help might not be available. Christopher's particular form of agoraphobia was manifest in public spaces, especially in school. Doctors treating him prescribed Zoloft, an antidepressant drug, which at the time had not been approved by the FDA for children. Later he was also put on Lorazepam, an antianxiety drug.

Even with the drugs, however, Christopher was unable to return to school, so instead he was home-schooled. Although his mother worked as a secretary at Regis High School, not far from home, and his father held various jobs, including working as a store manager, they both pitched in and helped him with his studies. All the while, they looked forward to the day he could return to school.

By all accounts, Christopher was a neat, quiet, and polite boy who listened to his parents and rarely got into trouble. He was known to take home sick and stray animals and take good care of them. As a Boy Scout, he attended meetings and outings with Troop 241. He loved to Rollerblade and play roller hockey, and was considered skilled at both. Like other kids in the neighborhood, he was an altar boy at St. Francis de Sales Church, and, like most of them, he showed up infrequently. Most Sundays, he would walk his

mother and grandparents the three blocks to the
church, on Ninety-sixth Street, for 10:30 A.M. Mass,
and then go back home or to the park to Rollerblade.
During the week, he would accompany his grandmother to the supermarket, usually wearing a tie and
khaki pants. Rarely, if ever, did he hang out on the
streets of his 'hood, unlike most of the other neighborhood kids.

Although Christopher was bright, his parents
couldn't find a suitable high school for him. Patricia
had written to the Board of Education in November
1996, asking for a recommendation. On January 3,
the committee suggested Benjamin Cardozo High
School in Bayside, Queens, a school known for its special program for students who had school phobias.
However, Patricia decided against the school in favor
of the closer Beekman School, which was geared
specifically to students with special emotional, physical, and learning needs. She enrolled Christopher
there and he attended school for half a day, from
12:30 to 3:00 P.M., taking three courses: English, history, and science.

It was at Beekman that he met up with the East
Coast Vandals (ECV), a loose gang of kids who hung
out together and garnered some clout at school. (The
East Coast Vandals, also known as "Encouraging Child
Violence," as some of the crew liked to brag, were a
bunch of high-school kids—rich punks, according to
some—from the city's better private schools. Most of
the gang wore North Face and Hilfiger. The group
started with about a half-dozen kids hanging out and
scrawling graffiti. By the time of the murder, their
numbers had burgeoned to around sixty kids, from all
over the city and from all different races. Most members said they mainly just chilled; they didn't rob or

hurt anyone. Others said they moved in a pack, picking on young kids, even beating up other private-school kids. By some accounts, they liked to video themselves beating up people and then have it shown on a cable-access show that highlighted crew life, called *Temple of the Intoxication.*) Christopher was intrigued by the members and liked to proclaim that the crew were his boys. Although he still avoided fighting, he hoped to impress them in other ways. Some say that was when he started carrying a knife—a four-inch-long folding one. According to the ECV members, they never considered Christopher to be a part of the crew, even though he constantly tried to hang out with them and followed them wherever they went.

Like many high-school kids, Christopher sometimes took drugs, but he was not a druggie. He wasn't a big drinker, either, although when he did drink, his personality could change and he could become antagonistic. But most of the time, he was a quiet kid who kept to himself. "He didn't talk much and he didn't get in anyone's way," commented George Rudovic, fifteen, a friend of Christopher's who attended St. Ignatius Loyola Grammar School with him. According to some friends, he was even too quiet. One acquaintance remarked that it was difficult to have a real conversation with him, because he'd say only a sentence or two, and that was all. Another acquaintance reported that Christopher told him he was depressed and had a low image of himself in the lower grades, which "screwed him up in the head." Some acquaintances spoke of the blank expression on his face. Others said that if someone looked at him a certain way, he'd get a real crazy look in his eyes. His peers, accustomed to labeling kids, called him a "Herb," a person who could easily be swayed and dominated.

Even when it wasn't cool to say so, Christopher proclaimed how much he loved his parents. He was particularly close with his mother, who kept a tight rein on him. Usually, Christopher observed his curfew and came home on time. Sometimes, however, he did not, and his mother would beep him ten or more times a night.

The Vasquezes were a close-knit, warm, and loving family, so when his parents separated in 1995 after twenty years of marriage, Christopher was devastated. Some friends reported that that was when his look became empty—not rough or tough—just a spaced-out, crazy look. One neighbor reported that Christopher's mother told her that "he was taking medication to help him after his parents separated."

Something must have changed dramatically for Christopher in the early part of 1997, because it was then that, on at least two occasions, his grandfather Daniel sought counseling and prayer at church. He was deeply concerned about his grandson's behavior. It seemed that Christopher was now staying out until all hours of the morning.

It was not that Christopher had become a bad kid. He had simply become a different one.

CHAPTER 14

Daphne was born on May 18, 1982, and adopted when she was three days old by the Abdelas—Catherine, a former Paris model, and Angelo, an Israeli and vice president of CPC International, Inc., a large food-service company that owned brands such as Hellmann's and Skippy peanut butter.

Daphne's immensely successful father worked long hours, so it was usually her mother who took her to and picked her up from after-school activities. Catherine spoke with a pronounced French accent, which was difficult for some people to understand. At home, all three spoke French fluently. In fact, French was the language Catherine used if she needed to say stern words to Daphne in front of her classmates, so as not to embarrass her daughter. It was also the language Daphne used to teach her friends some choice words, not necessarily ones her parents would approve of. Catherine was considered gentle and gracious, although some said she suffered severe bouts of depression. With no family in this country, she was thought to be lonely.

Daphne and her parents lived at 115 Central Park

West, known as the Majestic. It is located just south, across Seventy-second Street, from the Dakota. Both the famous and the infamous have lived there, or at least rubbed elbows with its residents, including Bruno Richard Hauptmann, the convicted murderer of Charles and Anne Morrow Lindbergh's baby, who worked as a carpenter there when he committed the crime; gangster Charles "Lucky" Luciano; Mafia boss Frank Costello, who in 1957, while crossing the lobby to go up to his seventeen-room penthouse, was shot in the head, and survived; and Walter Winchell, gossip columnist and radio and television broadcast journalist.

The Majestic is a co-op, with approximately 250 apartments—some selling for more than $8 million. At the time of the murder, Daphne lived in a twentieth-floor duplex facing the park.

Most everyone who knew Daphne while she attended Columbia Grammar and Preparatory School considered her spunky and independent. Headmaster Richard Soghoian recalled that she had a great smile and was an active kid, very sports-minded. He remembered seeing her zipping around on Rollerblades. Her parents, he noted, were wonderful people.

As was the case at many private schools, each child's parents are called in for a yearly conference. At one of these, a counselor pointed out to the Adbelas that because of Daphne's looks—her solid physical build, her short-cropped blond hair, and her boyish way of dressing in pants and shirts—older kids in the yard and visitors to the school would mistakenly call her "he." The counselor suggested that to avoid these uncomfortable situations, they might consider giving their daughter a more feminine look. The parents heeded the advice. Daphne came to school wearing a pair of gold earrings. The counselor also reported that Daphne was definitely not a part of the group that enjoyed playing with dolls, and that although she was smart, she often had to be put on social probation for unruly behavior. At various times, she was required to attend meetings to deal with social issues. Remarking on Daphne's parents, the counselor recalled that they were stunning, in a regal way. The mother, the counselor recalled, could have been a duchess.

One parent who traveled as a chaperone on a bus that the children took for a fall outing commented that Daphne's mother looked very proper and controlled, exhibiting almost "Germanic control." With her fine features and elegant dress, Catherine looked more like an Upper East Side woman than one from the more "casual" West Side. The chaperone observed that Catherine did not chat with the other mothers, but stayed to herself, looking very much like a loner. Daphne, the parent observed, had her hair cut straight across the front, and she looked as if she had been sitting around a lot. With a solid, square body, she looked like a "tight blob within herself." The parent noted that Daphne showed no animation during the bus ride— she was stolid and unresponsive—and her demeanor suggested that she had a difficult life going on inside. Looking at the mother and daughter, the chaperone felt that "it looked like the worst match."

When Daphne was nine, she was enrolled in an after-school swim program at the YMCA on Sixty-third Street and Central Park West, where she competed on the West Side Marlins swim team. People on the team remarked that there was something strange about her. She was cold and haughty. One swimmer, Heather Morelli, said that Daphne never really talked to anyone on the team. She labeled her "hard" and "difficult," reporting that she never seemed to fit in. "She didn't have her own groove. I don't know how to say it. She was very independent. She didn't mold to anything." Gail Slatter, the mother of a girl who was on the Marlins with Daphne for two years, noted that unlike the other girls, Daphne seemed unhappy despite all her privilege. While most of the kids would run and jump around with unbridled energy, Daphne was removed—never laughing and rarely smiling. It was important for all the team members to work together toward the same goal. Daphne, however, would simply stop swimming whenever she felt like it and didn't seem to care. Even at that age, Slatter remarked, Daphne seemed to look down on her parents with "frosty disdain." She would walk ahead of her mother and seemed to bully the older woman. When Daphne came out of the pool, Catherine couldn't get close to her. When her mother asked her questions, Daphne wouldn't deign to answer, but would simply ignore her. Her mother seemed both ashamed of and intimidated by her, unable to control her strong independent streak, which many labeled, less positively, "brash and temperamental." At one meet, a parent told Catherine that Daphne had used a racial slur against a swimmer. Catherine tried to get Daphne to apologize, but to no avail. This mother recalled that Catherine seemed to find it hard to control Daphne.

Around the age of twelve, Daphne played in the Safe Haven Basketball League, which met on most Saturdays, indoors or outdoors, depending on the weather. The year Daphne was on the Suns, she was considered an excellent player. One teammate remarked that she was quiet and not as social as the other girls in the league, but she was a nice person who was never mean or nasty to her or to any of the other girls. She also noted that Daphne had a boyish

physique and would wear baggy or oversize clothes
most of the time. In fact, she recalled, it was often
hard for people who had just met her to tell if she was
a boy or a girl.

Like many preadolescents and adolescents, Daphne
focused on her weight and seemed upset that she was
not as svelte as the other kids—or as her mother. Self-
conscious about being heavy, even though her mother
reassured her she looked good, she attended Camp
Shane, a weight-loss camp, on several different occasions. Each time she attended the nine-week $4,650
camp in the Catskills, she lost some weight, but soon
gained back all the pounds. Although people praised
her looks after she slimmed down, she didn't seem
to relish the positive reinforcement. One person close
to her surmised that perhaps she didn't like being fit
into a mold, or maybe even looking too girlish. To
some, her voice and body language said "boy."

By around sixth grade, she began dressing tough,
wearing street jeans, uptown style. She was a "homeboy" to the point where you had to take notice. When
she was younger, she seemed to dress to cover up;
when older, she seemed to dress to be noticed.

Over the years, the Abdelas attended West End Collegiate Church, where a diverse group of people from
the neighborhood worshipped. The church had many
interfaith, multiethnic, and international members.
Daphne attended Sunday school there with some reg-
ularity from the time she was around eight years old.
Inquisitive and attentive at times, she would become
engaged in discussions and ask thought-provoking
questions, but often she would use her time on the
floor to bring in her own side stories from the street—
about herself, her friends, and the kinds of aberrant
behavior they engaged in. She was also known to

curse, saying things like, "Look, what the 'f—' is this Genesis?" Most people felt she did it for shock value.

Throughout the years that Daphne attended the church, no one could recall her ever making any close friends, and teachers reported that, overall, she was extremely difficult. She liked nothing more than a good argument and had the capacity to get very angry. At the least provocation, she would fly off the handle, slam her hand down on the table, and march out of the room. There was a disturbing element about her that the teachers worked hard to understand. They felt there was something dark deep inside her. When she entered a room, they reported, it changed and the energy was disruptive. One teacher lamented that he simply couldn't get through to her, no matter what tack he took. He recalled that she disregarded her parents and treated them like nonentities. Although rebelliousness was classic teenager conduct, her behavior was an outlier, far distant from even the most deviant conduct. In spite of all this, the kids in her Sunday school were supportive and kind and tried their best to keep an open mind and a Christian attitude.

During the summers of 1994 and 1995, Daphne attended Campus Kids, a weekday sleepaway camp. When interviewed later about Daphne, counselors recalled they had predicted a troubled future for her. They said that she swore all the time and always insisted on doing things her way, even when her way defied the rules. She desperately yearned for attention—or perhaps love, the counselor said, even though "her dad gave her everything."

That same point of view was echoed by friends later, in 1996. They said that by then, Daphne no longer spent much time at home, preferring to hang out on the streets. Many believed that she had begun drinking at around thirteen or fourteen years old. Her tough, bad-girl attitude had become a provocative, pugnacious, up close, and in-your-face stance. She'd smoke outside stores and restaurants on the streets close to her home. She'd start an argument with a person who was simply walking by—for no reason at all. A friend at that time reported that he never saw her without "beer on her breath or a bottle in her hand." If there wasn't one in her hand, she'd be walking down the street to buy one. George Rudovic, Christopher's pal who also hung out with Daphne, remarked that she had more freedom than any of the other kids, but that didn't stop her from complaining that she wanted more. He went on to say that Daphne's father was a kind and loving man, but Daphne always complained that they couldn't get along. Another friend, Larry Cappelli, called her a rebel, but insisted that she was "more a misfit than a murderer."

When she was around fourteen, a deli owner on the block where she lived reported her hanging around outside his store, drinking and smoking almost daily. He said she hung out with anyone who came by, even the most unsavory characters. And she didn't do those things quietly; rather, he said, she flaunted her badass behavior, yelling at passersby and making a loud and ugly nuisance of herself.

At a time when most kids used pay phones to answer a page, Daphne had both a pager and a cell phone. At a time when many of the kids she hung out with had a curfew and stuck to it, Daphne had a curfew and ignored it, staying out into the early hours of the morning, often Rollerblading throughout the park.

At the end of the eighth grade, Daphne was asked to leave Columbia Grammar and Preparatory School and find a school that would better meet her needs.

In the fall of 1996, Daphne enrolled in Loyola School to start her freshman year. The learning institution had been founded in 1900 by Jesuits, and Loyola students were accepted based on results of an extremely competitive exam. Approximately two hundred students attended the school. In the beginning, many classmates praised Daphne as being concerned, friendly, and big-hearted. She was part of a group who helped feed the homeless. She would give friends money to take cabs home if they needed it, and she would buy beer for just about anyone. One time, she treated a bunch of classmates to fake IDs in Times Square—practically a private-school ritual. She was known to hook up friends with whatever they needed—drugs included. One friend recalled that Daphne stopped her from experimenting with pot, after admitting to the girl that it had messed up her life and she didn't want the same to happen to her. She also told the friend she was going to seek help.

By all accounts, Daphne was treated respectfully, almost reverentially, by her classmates in her first few weeks at Loyola. She was among the most sought-after of the freshmen girls. She had spunk, bravado, and audacity in a place where those qualities were in short supply. Here was someone who wasn't afraid to be bad, to defy authority, to have attitude. Here was someone who could act out her classmates' fantasies.

However, within a short time, the qualities that initially brought her props (respect) now brought her scorn. She was too audacious. Too edgy. Too unpredictable. She was a confrontational and belligerent tomboy. She would walk into class and boast that she was so high. Sometimes she would scream in class. Curse out loud. She was often rude to teachers. Friends reported her being boisterous, seemingly with an impulse-control problem. On many days, she'd forget to wear the school's mandatory uniform blazer and would have to "rent" one. She seemed out to break any rule that existed, however unimportant, just for the hell of it. To most observers, Daphne was out of control, doing whatever she felt like doing, whenever she felt like doing it. After one particular incident, when she punched a girl in the face for no reason anyone could ascertain, her glow began to fade. Classmates started looking at her differently. Many began avoiding her.

Described by friends as a wild spirit, she often drank too much, even drinking hard liquor during school hours. One friend said that although she loved her, she had to admit that Daphne could become violent when drunk. Some classmates reported that she had rum in her locker. Friends reported that she'd been drinking for years before her parents knew. When they did find out, they sent her to a rehab program in Westchester for two weeks, and when she returned, she was supposed to attend AA meetings. She did, but reportedly used them as a way to find other like-minded people to drink with. She proudly declared that she was an alcoholic. Big deal. Some friends said she also used drugs. Others, however, said that they never saw her taking drugs. She was reportedly on a waiting list at Daytop Village, an organization that helped people with drug addiction, and was in counseling.

One senior at Loyola noted that Daphne didn't get along with her parents and surmised that Daphne didn't feel loved. The friend said that her parents did, in fact, love her, but that Daphne messed up. Some friends remarked that her parents seemed almost afraid of her. They didn't seem to be able to understand or control her.

Daphne liked to brag. She bragged that she dated a guy who was the leader of a small gang called "357," from the .357 Magnum gun. She bragged about beating up kids and about her expert fighting skills. She bragged about doing drugs. She bragged about spending time with older men and drug dealers. She bragged about being an alcoholic. She bragged about not getting along with her parents, and she bragged about how she bad-mouthed them to their face every chance she got.

In early May 1997, Daphne went on a one-day religious retreat in Manhasset, New York, with her freshman class. Many remarked that it seemed to have a positive effect on her and heard her vow that she was going to get herself together. However, only weeks later, Daphne was asked to leave Loyola for both substance abuse and disciplinary reasons. When informed of the school's decision, classmates reported she was indifferent. "So?" was her attitude.

After she was no longer attending Loyola, she popped in at school one day, purportedly to pick up a book. Final arrangements for a party and auction were taking place. It was the school's yearly awards evening, honoring long-serving staff members. Called "Knights in the Garden," it was a semiformal evening, so most girls wore fancy dresses, and most boys wore bow ties. Daphne strolled in, wearing a pair of loose-fitting brown jeans and a rust-colored T-shirt with a boy's oversize jacket on top. Those who observed her said that for the time she was there, she adopted a different pose. She seemed to be sincere and truly care about her high-school days: "Do you think there will be any awards for me?"

Daphne wandered between two worlds. At home, on vacations snowboarding in Vermont or sunbathing in the south of France, and at expensive private schools, she lived the sought-after world of privilege; at night in the park, on weekends in Times Square, and even in the recesses of her mind, she lived the sometimes glorified, often horrifying, world of the alienated.

It wasn't that Daphne was a bad kid, exactly, but she was definitely a different kid.

CHAPTER 15

Several months before the murder, while Christopher was in the park watching two guys fighting, he met fourteen-year-old Daphne, who was among the crowd. They soon started hanging out together. Most of their park posse felt that they weren't romantically involved, although some thought they could have been. Christopher told acquaintances that he liked Daphne; he liked how free she was and how she did whatever she wanted to do.

To some, they were an odd couple. Brash, hostile, and rich, Daphne could have been a poster child for certifiable badasses. Introverted, timid, and working-class, Christopher could have passed for an archetypal Boy Scout. Perhaps what drew them to each other was their differences, with one teen's shortcomings complemented by the other's strengths. Maybe Christopher found in Daphne the leader he desperately needed to follow, the voice he couldn't find within, the aggressiveness he longed to have, the casualness—or guts—not to give a damn what anybody thought of him, and, if he dared even dream it, a girlfriend he could call his own. And maybe in Christopher, Daphne found someone who would accept her unequivocally, someone who would look up to her, respect and admire her, someone who would stick by her no matter what, and someone who would do whatever she asked, without question or judgment.

Whatever the attraction, they soon started chilling in the park, drinking, smoking, and Rollerblading.

On the Saturday before the murder, Christopher and Daphne were in the park drinking Zima and wine coolers. A friend of Daphne's, a senior at Loyola, reported that after drinking became old that night, the three headed out in a cab to another friend's house, where they spent the night smoking pot. The friend recalled that Christopher was "on the weird side," although she thought he seemed nice.

A week or so before the murder, a major event took place in each teen's life that may have been a turning point, a watershed, which impelled each one forward— from outcast to outlaw.

For Christopher, the moment came one afternoon as he was riding the number 6 train. As usual, he was minding his own business when all of a sudden from out of nowhere, a half-dozen kids jumped him. After stealing his money, the gang beat him up. It was a scary, crushing, and humiliating experience.

Later in the day, he went to Sheep Meadow in Central Park, where some kids from Beekman and other schools hung out. He figured he'd recount his ordeal and get some support. Maybe the guys would even be willing to revenge what took place. Go after the thugs. Give them what they deserved. When he got to the park, he immediately found some members of the ECV gang and recounted what had taken place. He asked the crew to find the assholes who did it and return the "favor." They told him that he wasn't down with them and that he shouldn't expect them to watch his back. In fact, they said, they'd been telling him for months that they wanted nothing to do with him. Didn't he get it yet?

Shamed, he left the park alone, tears barely held back. The walk was sobering. He had plenty of time to think. Finally, finally, he got it. "His" boys weren't going to get his back, now or ever.

After this incident, some friends reported, Christopher started carrying a knife for protection. It was a hunting knife and reportedly a gift from his father. It was also after this incident, friends reported, that he started drinking heavily. Some say he was drinking so heavily and so often that they feared he was on his way to becoming an alcoholic.

While Christopher was dealing with the mugging and the subsequent humiliating and heartbreaking rejection, Daphne was dealing with her own crisis.

By February, her behavior at Loyola had become so alarming that her parents decided to send an increasingly out-of-control Daphne to Arms Acres, a rehab center in Westchester. She was to stay there for several weeks, with the goal of getting her life under control and kicking what looked to be an addiction to alcohol. She spent a few weeks there, and when she returned, she began attending AA meetings at the YMCA on Sixty-third Street and Central Park West. However, when she went back to school, her behavior didn't seem all that different, and after some more inappropriate incidents in early May, she was asked to leave. She would, however, be allowed to take her finals at home.

Being asked to leave a private school in Manhattan is not an everyday occurrence. Most kids are able to create something that works for them in whatever school they find themselves and even play the system to their advantage. There is always someone to hang out with, someone with similar interests, subjects to get involved in, teachers who want to listen and counsel. And even if a student acts out once in a while—skips classes, smokes, disrespects another student—the school gives a warning, talks to the child, maybe even calls in the parents, and within a short time, everything returns to normal. For the most part, students conform to the rules and regulations, as asinine as they might appear to be, and manage to ignore or embrace the homogeneity, the boredom, and even the physical constriction of sitting still in an uncomfortable chair in a small room for hours on end.

Daphne was asked to leave two private schools. That was an anomaly. And no matter how nonchalant she tried to appear or how she tried to spin it, being expelled was a major rejection, which, like other repudiations, tunneled deep within and bubbled to the surface one day—in a new and unrecognizable form.

Realizing that their daughter's days at Loyola were numbered, the Abdelas had sent away for pamphlets from boarding schools in the Northeast. This was their latest—and maybe last—best hope for their daughter.

Friends of Christopher's who didn't believe it was the subway incident that catapulted him over the edge, and friends of Daphne's who didn't believe that her expulsion from Loyola tipped the scales, came up with their own conclusions as to what snapped and made them either a participant or a bystander in a murder. For Christopher, they cited the breakup of his parents' marriage of twenty years. Friends of Daphne's said that moment came the day she reached puberty.

Christopher was devastated when his father moved out of the house. The family that had been the backbone of his existence was no more, and he felt untethered, as if he were floating away alone. After the separation, friends recalled, he started drinking heavily and defying his mother, staying out late and getting roaring drunk. And, said many, he was not a happy, carefree drunk.

Puberty hit Daphne like a tornado, twisting her around so ferociously that when she emerged, she was barely recognizable. She put on weight and, instead of dressing neatly, only wore baggy boys' clothing. She became uncontrollably quarrelsome with her parents, defying them at every turn, and testing her limits as she teetered dangerously close to the edge.

But some had an even different take on Daphne. As soon as they learned that she was adopted, they cited that as the cause of her delinquency. They latched onto the stereotype of adoptees—they don't know where they came from; they have been "rejected" by the one person who theoretically should love them more than anyone else in the world; they are forever lost and unsettled. They cited research showing that during adolescence, adopted children face an even more difficult time of trying to sort out who they are. Maybe, they suggested, Daphne looked at her parents—suave, svelte, savvy, and successful—and wondered how in the world she could ever "belong" to them, and thus began acting out in defiance so as to distance herself and become as different from them as she could.

But others viewed adoption differently. When Ronny Diamond, a counselor who dealt with families of adopted children at the Spence-Chapin adoption agency, heard about the murder, his first reaction was "Please don't let her be adopted." He knew the news would rekindle the stereotype of adopted kids being problem kids. Diamond noted that many studies showed that adopted children do not have greater developmental problems than kids reared by their biological parents. He admitted, however, that some adoptees have certain issues that other kids don't have, such as "Who were my real parents and why did they give me up?" But all kids have certain issues that others don't have. He believed that adoptive parents provide love, discipline, special schools, and counselors, just like biological parents, and that adopted children should not be unfairly stigmatized.

CHAPTER 16

Michael McMorrow was born on May 30, 1952, to Margaret and Charles McMorrow. Charles had immigrated to the United States in the 1930s, but returned briefly to Ireland in 1948, after serving in World War II, to marry his childhood friend and sweetheart, Maggie. Both had grown up in the small village of Drumkeeran in County Leitrim. Neither had received much education in Ireland. One of four children, Maggie was taken out of school in the eighth grade to help around the house after her mother had hurt her foot. Charles was taken out of school in the sixth grade to work on his family's farm.

By the time Michael was born, two older siblings— Anne and Charlie—were already romping around their floor-through apartment in an old brownstone at 133 West Ninetieth Street, between Columbus and Amsterdam Avenues, only a block from Central Park. Two years later, Joan was born. The park served as all the kids' limitless playground.

For grammar school, Michael attended St. Gregory's. Every afternoon, Michael and his friends would race out of school, quickly change out of their uni-forms, and meet up in the park. There, they'd play softball, football, and basketball in the endless acres of green and return home only when one of the mothers yelled it was time to come in for supper.

Down the street from their brownstone was the fancy El Dorado apartment building, home, at various times, to Marilyn Monroe, Faye Dunaway, and Groucho Marx. When Michael was around eight years old, he often visited a friend there, whose mother made wigs for Bozo the Clown. Michael was invited to go on the show, and he went several times, each time feeling like he was the luckiest kid in the world. On weekends, he would go to the park with his mother, who sat on a bench while her son zoomed around on his bike. One day, Shelley Winters strolled by. She remarked to Maggie that Michael was a handsome young boy and encouraged her to take him for acting lessons. Reluctantly Michael went, but he soon quit. It wasn't really something he enjoyed.

Life for the McMorrows was idyllic until Michael was in the fifth grade and a renovation project on the Upper West Side targeted their brownstone for demolition. The family was faced with the difficult task of finding a new place to call home. Although they were assured of an apartment in the new buildings, that brought them little solace. They loved where they lived, and even if they took up the offer, they still would have to find somewhere to live for the next two or three years—and in the meantime, their beloved home would be gone.

One day, not long after the order to vacate was given, Charles came home from his job at Metro North and told the family that he thought he might have found a good place to move. A friend at the office knew of a great neighborhood in the Bronx and urged them to check it out. The family took the number 4 train to Fordham Road in the University Heights section of the Bronx and immediately fell in love with the neighborhood. The St. Nicholas of Tolentine Parish was a densely populated and tightly knit community of Irish immigrants and their descendants, affectionately known as "Bronx Irish-Catholics." Margaret and Charles, with their thick Irish brogues, fit right in and felt very much at home. A soon-to-be neighbor recalled, "We all had similar values: God, country, and family," and they all had a strong work ethic. "Everybody back then was poor," said McMorrow childhood friend Jim McShane. "We were children of immigrants, and we were all in it together. We paid sixty-five dollars a month for our apartments—and some of us had six rooms."

The McMorrows rented an apartment on the fifth floor of a prewar walk-up building, and Michael was enrolled at St. Nicholas of Tolentine Elementary School. Catholic schools were the choice for most Irish immigrant children. After school, the choice of all the kids in the neighborhood was Devoe Park, where they played basketball, football, and other sports.

Like most of the other mothers, Margaret stayed home, taking care of the children and the household. Her four children would often bring their friends home, and she would always cook a meal for them. If she had made something one of the children didn't like, she would make something else. A special treat back then was roast beef, with the blood running out of it. It was Michael's favorite.

Within two years, the McMorrows "moved up" to another classic six, only this time in an elevator building. Charles's steady job afforded them this luxury.

When Michael was twelve, in 1964, he played on a Little League team. A friend from those days, Colin Meagher, recalled that although they played on the same team, "Michael was a much better athlete than I." Basketball was Michael's favorite sport. He was considered tenacious and talented. In high school, he played on junior varsity, "which was a big deal back then," said Frank Ferrante, another childhood friend. "Since there were a lot of kids at the school on scholarship from outside the parish and Michael was a local kid who made the team, we looked up to him."

"He had a really sweet jump shot," remarked Gus Simpson. "His right hand would be on top, his left hand on the back of the ball, and he'd finish with two hands in the air. He'd kinda pose there for a second or two. It was a sight to see."

"We'd play basketball from morning till night," recalled McShane. "Michael was a forward. Back then, it was beer and basketball. Life was good."

Every kid in the neighborhood had a nickname. With both of his parents from Ireland, Michael was given the nickname of Irish, even though everyone else, it seemed, also had parents from Ireland. Michael was known as Irish for the next thirty years.

At All Hallows High School and at Bronx Community College, which he attended for two years, Michael, like all the other kids, tried to project a "hippie" image. "We had long hair and wore tie-dyed clothes," said one friend. Michael was a hard-core music fan—he followed the Kinks, the Beatles, the Stones, the Doors, the Steve Miller Band, Jethro Tull, Hot Tuna, Crimson, Procol Harum, Canned Heat, the J. Giles Band, and Santana. But his all-time favorite was Captain Beefheart and the Magic Band. Michael loved going to concerts, and a group of neighborhood kids would invariably go to concerts practically every weekend. "Basically, we never wanted to grow up," said McShane, "and managed not to, for much longer than we should have."

Michael's childhood friends recalled that Michael was friendly, smart, and never hesitated to speak his mind. "He knew more than any of us about sports, politics, music, and celebrities," said one friend. "He was funny, even irreverent, and had this biting wit. Not the type to be labeled 'Big Man on Campus,' instead he was down-to-earth and always championed the little guy. I remember that Michael was comfortable with everyone and everyone was comfortable with Michael," said Jack Baxter, another friend from the Bronx. Simpson recalled that Michael had a strong personality. "We all had our opinions. It was the late '60s and early '70s. There was a lot of turmoil, and we shared similar political views, particularly against the Vietnam War. We went to protests. We even went to Washington, to the huge protest in '72. We were part of the lottery and had high enough numbers. But since Michael was in college, he couldn't be drafted anyway."

"We all drank back then," recalled Baxter. "The Irish kids called it 'going down the Deegan,'" referring to the empty lot overlooking the Hudson River where every Friday maybe a hundred kids or so would gather to drink beer and hang out. "It was a more innocent time. No one had a knife or a gun. There were some fistfights, but that was about all. If you said something another person didn't like, you got a fat lip. Nobody'd even think of taking out a knife and cutting you up."

"Although Michael was successful meeting girls," Meagher remarked, "he never settled down. He fit the mold of the classic Irish bachelor. As a comparison, I was the same way and only got married at age forty-four." Another friend recalled that sometimes Michael lacked some social graces. He could be "too forward with women and it would scotch a potential situation." Another childhood friend recalled that Michael dated, but didn't have a steady girlfriend. "Most of us didn't. He was more of the rule than the exception." McShane put it this way: "There's a difference between cops and firemen. Cops like to primp and preen. A cop is a ladies' man. Cops get dressed up and look dapper. They sip their drinks as they sit on bar stools. Firemen, on the other hand, love one another best. They have great loyalty and camaraderie. They wear plaid jackets and jeans and sit in the back of a bar and talk to each other as they slug down pints. Michael was a 'fireman'—a guy's guy."

Friends agreed that Michael was well-liked because of his good nature. He was positive and fun-loving. Said Baxter, "He had a twinkle in his eye. Either he knew something or was up to something. He liked hanging out with the guys, same as all of us. As a young teenager, he wasn't as wild as most of us, but when he got older, he let loose." Baxter recalled, "We used to go to this place called Columbia Rock. You can see it from the Circle Line cruise ship as it goes up the Hudson River. Irish was one of only three kids in the neighborhood who would actually jump off it into the river below. It was as treacherous a stunt as what the Acapulco divers do. He even did backflips." In the Bronx, Baxter added, "we called that ballsy, but Mike wasn't a fighter. I never once saw him in a fight."

Growing up, the McMorrow kids recognized that their father had a drinking problem, even though Charles never missed a day of work because of alcohol. On weekends and on days off, he would drink.

And drink. And drink. "Growing up in an Irish-Catholic neighborhood, it was a natural thing to do. Everybody drank," said Meagher.

"Back then," Simpson said, "we didn't have our goals set. A lot of us didn't know what we were doing. We went to college hoping something would fall in our laps and tell us what to do. Some of us were lucky." But as the years went on and all the kids, one by one, started moving out of the neighborhood and into more "sober" lifestyles, Michael's drinking increased, although he always had a job, usually in real estate. According to many friends, most of the time he could hold his liquor, although sometimes, they recalled, he'd get drunk and act crazy. One friend commented, "Michael never moved out of the Bronx—in his mind. He continued the life we lived as kids well into adulthood, long after he should have given it up." The love Mike had for drinking, said Baxter, was something he never outgrew. "He just never left it behind."

Michael recognized that he had a problem and from time to time tried to deal with it by going to AA meetings, but most of the time, he was able to fit his nighttime and weekend bouts into his life. Gene Cizynski, a basketball-playing friend from the Bronx, noted that Michael was a typical BIC—Bronx Irish-Catholic. "He loved life and enjoyed a good time, and drinking was a part of that." A colleague, Matthew Kissil, who worked with him at Sir Realty, praised his ability as a salesman and acknowledged he was a kind and generous person, but he said that sometimes when Michael was drunk, he could be obnoxious and provocative. About a year before the murder, Kissil reported, he had to ask Michael to leave his wedding reception because he had become too drunk.

It seemed that booze had become his nighttime

lover—soothing, available, and enticing. Women had long since paled in comparison, and he didn't seem to mind one bit. "He loved drinking beer, rock 'n' roll, and the Yankees," park friend Tom Parker remarked, "and in all the years he came here, I never saw him take any sexual interest in anyone." Other "parkees" echoed the sentiment. Michael had a routine: he'd work all day, drink all night, and then stumble home. It was a perfectly fine routine for every night of his adult life—except for one.

During the ten years or so that Michael spent his nights in the park, many people warned him about the dangers there, but he shrugged them off, saying that it was safe and that he knew what he was doing. A neighbor, Frank Acquaviva, said he cautioned his friend, "Stay out of the park at night. The demons come out." Acquaviva remembered Michael's reply: "Frank, nothing ever happens." Glenn Golub, Michael's boss at Sir Realty, also warned him about the park. He noticed that Michael's drinking was becoming heavier, even in the three months Michael worked for him, and he feared Michael would end up in trouble. Golub said, "I told him it wasn't safe. It's like a netherworld there after dark." Golub also warned him that if "you keep doing this, you're gonna die." But he said Michael wouldn't listen. According to Golub, it seemed that Michael might have had some kind of death wish. Angel Colon, a handyman in the building where Michael rented apartments, said, "He was just a really nice man. Even the boss liked him. I worked here seven years and I never saw the boss cry. But when he got the call, the tears just came. He couldn't tell me what happened he was crying so much." Colon went on, "Michael just liked to drink, like anybody else. He liked to go out with the other real estate guys after work and have a few. It's just socializing." But Kissil disagreed that it was simply socializing. However, Golub had praise for Michael. He said, "Michael was a little crazy, but no crazier than the rest of us. He had a sharp Irish tongue, but he wasn't physically violent. He was a hardworking all-American guy. Mike was the kind of guy who would have preferred fame to fortune—and I guess he's got some of that now."

Friends surmised that Michael drank in the park not only because it was his favorite place to be, but also because of the anonymity of it. He could drink all he wanted and not break his mother's heart. Margaret would be at home and not know what he was doing. Michael had moved into Knickerbocker Plaza to keep her company and help out with the rent after her husband died in 1982. Theirs was a tidy, inviting apartment with two bedrooms, a living room/dining room/kitchen, and sunny open views to the north and east. Every year, as is required by law, the McMorrows submitted their tax returns. Their rent was based on the income recorded on the form, with the base rent for a two-bedroom apartment in the building being $787.

But Michael went to the park for more than just drinking. Every Wednesday, he played baseball in Riverside Park, and many weekends and evenings he went just to hang out.

Michael was considered a generous and caring person, who adored and took care of his mother. A colleague and friend said, "If you were short before commissions, Michael would help you out. He was always impeccably dressed, wearing cologne, and with his hair done just right." Kathleen Uptegrobe, a neighbor, said that Michael would do anything for anyone, and he was crazy about his mother.

Baxter said that Michael lived up to his nickname

Irish. He stayed a kid at heart, sometimes defying the norms that many people follow. Simpson agreed. "Mike's biggest fault was poor judgment. He wasn't nasty or mean or hurtful to anyone—except maybe himself."

Baxter said that the bond the group formed as kids was unlike any other he'd ever heard of. "We all still stay in touch, thirty years after we moved away. We were all poor back then and we all wanted to be somebody. We had dreams. Some of us grew up to be cops, firemen, filmmakers, journalists, financial analysts, real estate brokers. Mike grew up to be, first and foremost, a character, a funny, wild character, and what defined him, in part, was drinking in the park.

"All he was after was a good laugh," said Baxter. "He didn't take life too seriously."

It wasn't that Michael was a bad guy. He was just a different kind of guy from your everyday forty-four-year-old long-range-planning, suit-wearing, coolly calculating, status-seeking regular Joe.

CHAPTER 17

Located at 100 Centre Street in lower Manhattan on the site that once housed the notorious Tombs prison, the imposing Manhattan Criminal Courthouse appears indomitable and resolute, a stern overseer of the violent world it witnesses. Within its impressive granite and limestone walls, judgments come down, as if from on high—Guilty! Innocent!—causing tsunamis of relief, or despair, to surge through the human beings in custody. The courtrooms within the courthouse are simple and spare, with wood wainscoting, light-wood benches, and Art Deco lighting fixtures. There are no flourishes, no attempts to impress. Here, it is the basics: right or wrong, liberty or lockup.

Into this august building, two women detectives led a dour, handcuffed Daphne early Saturday morning, May 24. She had spent Friday night at the Twentieth Precinct, at 120 West Eighty-second Street, where she met with her lawyer, George Weinbaum. With wisps of blond hair partially covering her face, Daphne looked pale and pained, a determined pout plastered on her face. Dressed in an oversize orange T-shirt under a hooded red sweatshirt and baggy jeans, she was led past reporters who tried to question her about the murder. "Get out of my face!" she screamed as each of her escorts held on tight to one of her arms, while her hands remained cuffed behind her back.

Once inside, Daphne was taken into a courtroom to appear before acting state supreme court justice Ira F. Beal for arraignment—a hearing in which a person is accused of a crime or one in which the accused may either admit or deny allegations that have been made against her or him.

The benches in the back of the courtroom were empty. In the first row sat Daphne's parents, grim-faced with features distorted by pain. Daphne looked anxiously at them. Catherine grasped her husband's hand, but never looked at her daughter. Angelo did, however, glance frequently at Daphne.

Before the proceedings began, Daphne, pressed against a wall, began to cry softly. As tears streamed down Daphne's face, Assistant District Attorney (ADA) Carolyn Streicher spoke directly to the judge. She stated that the prosecution had very strong evidence that linked both teens to "the incredibly brutal murder." She then recounted some specific details. She said that Daphne Abdela had made many statements to detectives detailing how she had seen Vasquez stab, slash, and eviscerate McMorrow. Streicher said that Daphne admitted ordering Vasquez to "gut the body and it would sink because he's a fatty," and then instructed Vasquez to throw the body into a lake. The ADA went on to say that Daphne admitted that both she and Christopher tried to conceal the identity of the victim by burning his identification papers and attempting to cut off his hands. The teen also admitted to having taken money from the victim's wallet.

While Streicher was speaking, Daphne shook her head no. Those in the courtroom were leaning slightly forward, like a flock of geese, necks stretched full-out, straining not to miss a single word.

When Streicher finished, Daphne's attorney, George Weinbaum, addressed the judge. He stated that he had not yet read any statements that the prosecution suggested were made by his client. He asked if he could have all of that text, along with a tape of a 911 call that Daphne purportedly made to the dispatcher. Weinbaum suggested that the prosecution's statements were highly selective, chosen to cast the most negative light on his client and the events of the night.

The judge agreed to Weinbaum's request, and the arraignment came to an end. Judge Beal ordered Daphne to be held without bail at Spofford, a youth detention center in the Bronx. Too young to be sent to Rikers Island, she would have to call a spartan room with a single bed, a desk, and a window her new home. At Spofford, she would be able to look through the wire mesh and thick slats onto the Corpus Christi Monastery, where, ironically, cloistered nuns lived in much the same style.

Outside the courthouse, Weinbaum spoke to reporters. "You'll find this woman to be a sympathetic individual charged with a heinous crime she did not commit." He went on to say that both Daphne and her parents were distraught and that ultimately, when all the facts came out, she would be exonerated. He stated that Daphne planned to plead not guilty to the two charges of murder and two charges of robbery of which she was accused.

* * *

On Friday night, while Daphne was being held at the
"2-0," Christopher was being detained at the "2-4," located at 151 West 100th Street. Early Saturday morning, he, like Daphne, was taken downtown to the
Criminal Court Building for arraignment. Wearing tan
baggy jeans, a green-and-blue-plaid jacket pulled up
above his chin, and a Seattle Mariners baseball cap,
partly obscuring his face, he looked neat and clean.
Police had permitted Christopher's father to arrange
his son's clothes ahead of time, so the teen's face could
be somewhat hidden.

At around 3:00 A.M., the slightly built, clean-shaven
young man, with a fresh cut on his right cheek and a
bandaged left hand, entered the courtroom and sat
down alongside drag queens, thugs, and others who
had recently been arrested and were awaiting their
turn to speak to the judge. However, a short while
before he was to be arraigned, he began muttering suicidal thoughts, and detectives became concerned. "He
was uttering things that scared cops," a source said.
Without Christopher's knowledge—or his parents' or
his attorney's—the detectives took out an order allowing them to remove the teen to Bellevue Hospital,
where he would be put under the observation of a
child psychiatrist. Just minutes before his arraignment,
the detectives approached him and whisked him away.
His shocked lawyer, Robert Fogelnest, raced to find out
what was happening. Like everyone else, he was told
that he would have to wait to talk to Christopher—at
Bellevue.

Once Christopher was admitted to the hospital, he
was cuffed at the ankles to the gurney. After he was
transferred to a room—a four-bedroom suite with

three of the beds empty—he was cuffed to the foot-board of the bed. A police officer was stationed outside the room. Orders were given that the TV was to be kept off so he couldn't see or hear reports about the murder. During the night and for much of Saturday, he alternately dozed and awoke, dazed and bewildered, seemingly unable to understand what everyone else was also at a loss to comprehend: how could a boy who had never been in trouble before have done what he was accused of doing? Workers at the hospital reported that the teen looked despondent as he lay in a sterile room with a guard stationed outside.

When Fogelnest arrived at the hospital, the police officer on guard turned him away. Realizing that there was no chance of a lawyer-client meeting, Fogelnest left, but not before Christopher made one request: "Tell my parents I love them." Soon after, Christopher's parents visited. They brought him family pictures and a letter from his sister, who was attending college. His father reportedly told him to be strong and everything would be okay.

Later, when Fogelnest returned to his office, he was informed that his services were no longer needed. The Vasquez family had hired Arnold Kriss to replace him in defending their son.

Christopher's arraignment was postponed until after psychiatrists had a chance to evaluate him.

CHAPTER 18

On Sunday, May 25, a steady light rain fell as mourners streamed into the wake at the Frank E. Campbell Funeral Chapel on Madison Avenue and Eighty-first Street to say a final good-bye to a friend, a son, a brother, an uncle, a colleague. It was an open coffin surrounded by exquisite and bountiful flowers. The mortician had spent many hours fixing up Michael so he would look like the handsome man that the attendees had known. "Danny Boy" played softly in the background.

Typically, when a body arrives at a funeral home, it's a heart-stopping moment for a mortician. Here is someone's son or daughter or mother or father. He might have been a cherished uncle, brother, or husband. He is someone who had lived, loved, and been loved in return. Here is someone who will love no more.

Funerals are for the living. A mortician's, or embalmer's, job is to make a dead person look as lifelike as possible so friends and family can have a meaningful visitation and possibly some closure. It is the last and often lasting impression they will have of the deceased, so the job must be done well. Family members often bring in photographs to help the embalmer.

Michael's body had been autopsied, so it arrived at a funeral home in a body bag, or disaster pouch. The first thing a mortician does is look at a toe tag or bracelet to make sure that the body is the one that was expected. Then an assessment is begun, with an eye toward cleaning the body of any traces of blood, dirt, or grease. The body might be stiff from refrigeration or from rigor mortis, which usually intensifies around six to twelve hours after death, but gradually declines after twenty-four hours. In order to be able to do their job, morticians might gently flex and contract muscles.

After cleaning the body of dirt and any fluids, an embalmer sets the features. This is done before the body has been injected with embalming fluid, which makes the tissues harden and the setting of the features more difficult. First the eyes are carefully cleaned, and then an eye cap, a convex-shaped device with serrated edges, is slid under the eyelids to help keep the eyes closed completely. To secure the mandible and maxilla, so the mouth is in a closed position, the jaw is wired together with stainless steel or brass wire, similar to what a doctor might do if a person broke his or her jaw and needed the mouth held in place until it healed. The lips are then set so they look natural, using a cream that helps retain the position and prevent dehydration. Sometimes cotton is put into the mouth to bring out the natural look, or a form of denture is used, a horseshoe device similar to a football player's mouth guard, but less bulky. In the dead, the mouth is the most expressive part of the body, unlike in the living where the eyes are, so the embalmer spends a great deal of time trying to create a natural expression on the lips.

During every stage of the process, the embalmer fills out an embalming report that details the condition of the body—any lacerations, discolorations, abrasions, and so on. The report remains part of the permanent record in case a dispute occurs later as to the cause of death or the condition of the body.

The purpose of embalming is to disinfect and preserve the body. To begin the process, the embalmer accesses the circulatory system. A small incision is made on the right side of the neck to access the right carotid artery and the right internal jugular vein. The embalmer raises the vessels by pulling them out and then makes an incision in each. Into the artery, a cannula (small tube) is inserted, which is hooked up by hose to an embalming machine. The machine has embalming fluid in it, formalin, which is formaldehyde, a preservative, along with alcohol and other preservatives and disinfectants. In the first stage of embalming, the formaldehyde-based fluid is circulated by pump through the circulatory system. The second phase requires the removal of blood and bodily fluids by suction, so a six-to-twelve-inch hollow drain tube is inserted into the jugular vein. The other end is outside the body, on the side of the table on which the body lies. Fluid from the tube empties into the drain at the bottom of the table, which sits at an angle of about five degrees. The process can take forty-five to ninety minutes, if the body has not been "disrupted." If it has, and certain areas of the leg or foot or hand, for example, don't respond, the mortician must find another vein (for the return) or artery (for the input) and repeat the process.

An embalmer knows when the process has been successfully completed by looking at the color change of the body. A typical corpse is grayish pink. Formaldehyde wants to turn skin gray, so inside the embalming fluid are buffers to control hues. Active dyes are used that act upon skin color to make it look more "natural." Another way an embalmer knows that the process has been successfully completed is by noting plumped-up skin areas, which before had been dehydrated, or prunelike.

Once the body has been successfully cleansed, the embalmer ties off the ligatures around the artery and vein so no fluid escapes. The cavity—the hollow organs, which include the lungs, stomach, and heart—is now dealt with. A twenty-four-inch-long hollow tube called a trocar is inserted about two inches to the left and above the navel. One end has a sharp point; the other end is open and attached to a hose, which is attached to a suction tube. The embalmer takes the needle and starts moving it around, piercing the organs. Because the tube is clear, the embalmer can see the fluid that is coming out. When the heart, liver, spleen, intestines, bladder—and so on— no longer have any fluid in them, that process is over. Embalmers must pay great attention to removing all fluids from the body, which is called purging, so that nothing seeps out while the body is in the casket.

After the body has been purged, the incisions are sutured closed, airtight, with a baseball stitch, like the kind used on baseballs. Sometimes a trocar button, similar to a thick screw, is used to close the area where the trocar was.

The body is then washed again with soap and water. Typically, a hose is running down the sides of the body to move the fluid. The hair is washed, combed out, and dried.

A little bit of glue, similar to Krazy Glue, is applied to make sure the eyes and mouth stay in position. The embalmer then looks at pictures to try to replicate skin and lip tone, and to highlight a feature that needs to be brought out. Specially manufactured cosmetics for mortuary use—highly concentrated but thinned with emollient cream, to help prevent dehydration— are then applied. The eyes, lips, cheeks, and knuckles are highlighted.

So far, around two or three hours have been spent preparing the body.

The family of the deceased often brings in the clothing that they would like their loved one to wear, and the embalmer takes great care dressing the body.

In some places, after the body has been placed in the casket, the left hand is crossed over the right hand; in others, the hands are placed at the person's side.

Unlike a person who has died a natural death and has not been autopsied, an autopsied body arrives at the funeral home with a Y-shaped incision in it, starting at the shoulders, meeting at the chest, and ending just above the pubic area. Most likely, the body has been crudely stitched back together. The embalmer will open the stitches and pull back the flaps of skin. Inside is the rib cage—a rack of ribs—and underneath it is a bag containing all the internal organs, which had been removed when the body was autopsied. The embalmer takes out the bag before embalming begins.

In cases in which there has been trauma—swelling, discoloration, lacerations—the embalmer must take extra measures to make the body look "normal." Each incision must be cleaned and dried out. Sometimes powder is put in to keep leakage from occurring. If a throat has been slashed, the head has to be isolated from the rest of the body in order for the embalming process to be successful. The left carotid artery might be sought, instead of the right, which has a more direct access to the heart. If the face has gashes on it, the embalmer removes jagged edges of skin, cleans the cuts, and sutures the gash together, with a bridge or subdermal stitch, using a small circular needle, sometimes with dental floss. A special kind of wax, called a restorative wax, is placed on the incisions, like a wood fill or putty, to make the skin look smooth. The wax comes in different colors and levels of firmness and can be used, if necessary, to sculpt a missing ear, nose, or other body part. Any swelling on the body can be treated with a heated spatula applied gently to the area, after it has been moistened so the skin doesn't burn.

Once the organs that were removed in the bag have been cleaned with embalming fluid, they are put back into another bag and placed back in the body. The ribs are arranged correctly, and the body is then closed.

The job is now completed.

"There is tremendous satisfaction in restoring a body so that it looks lifelike," stated Jason Altieri, President of the Commonwealth Institute of Funeral Service. "Being able to use your skills to make someone look like the unique person he or she was brings great pleasure and a deep sense of gratification to an embalmer."

Some of Michael's friends hadn't seen him since grade school or high school in the Bronx; others had seen him over the years at reunions for parishioners of St. Nicholas of Tolentine in the Bronx; and still others remained close to him by almost weekly phone calls. They all remarked on how handsome and peaceful he looked.

The wake was a solemn occasion, with people paying their respects in numbed disbelief. Friend and former coworker Linda Birenbach said that when she saw him in the casket, she could not believe her eyes. She hoped she would awake from this nightmare and see Michael alive. Birenbach knew Michael as a kind-hearted and generous soul, who was energetic and extremely funny. She recalled that he loved to imitate movie stars, including Jackie Gleason, Kirk Douglas, and Jimmy Stewart. He would go "hummina-hummina-hummina" and get an entire party laughing, or he'd posture like Cagney, and everyone would be riveted. He was so good at doing imitations, he could have been a professional, she said. "When I broke my leg several years ago, Michael did all my shopping. He was a kind and brilliant man."

Another colleague, who had worked in real estate with him ten years before, remarked, "You couldn't find a nicer person anywhere. Everyone liked him." Another former colleague said, "He was a real character. It's great to see how many friends he has."

Many of Michael's drinking buddies from the park also came to pay their respects. Ayraton (Gary) Dos Santos called Michael a smart, fun-loving man, who just liked to chill. "He loved life and he loved the park," he said. "It's unreal that this happened, and especially to him. He'd never hurt a fly." A longtime friend from the park remarked that Michael's death showed that bad things can happen to good people. Another buddy said that Michael was honest and generous, but he conceded that he had a drinking problem. One young woman came carrying purple flowers. Another laid a bouquet near the casket, tears streaming down her face.

Nearly everyone mentioned the same qualities when talking about Michael: hardworking, responsible, personable, kind, well-liked, easygoing, and fun-loving. And nearly everyone expressed similar feelings of outrage and disbelief. No matter what had transpired among the three people, the mourners said, nothing could warrant a murder. And, of course, nothing could warrant the viciousness of the attack. Particularly striking to most people was the dichotomy between the peaceful person whom they knew to be Michael and the brutal way he died. It was irreconcilable and unfathomable.

Some mourners called for revenge. They said that the kids who did it deserved to die the same way Michael did. They had no sympathy for the teens. Childhood friend Gus Simpson said, "Nothing justifies murder. There are no mitigating circumstances," and he complained that Michael would probably be put on trial now—not the teens—as often happens in cases like this. Simpson despaired that Michael would not be around to defend himself.

Michael's brother, Charlie, read a prepared statement thanking everyone for coming and especially the police for apprehending the suspects so quickly. "The family is devastated by the loss of our beloved Michael," he said. "The McMorrow family appreciates the outpouring of sympathy and support they have received during this trying time."

All the while, Michael's devastated mother, Margaret, sobbed in a chair. She seemed small, frail, and lost, as if she had somehow come to the wrong place.

She wept and moaned, "I can't believe I'll never see him again."

At the same time that the wake was taking place, some friends from Strawberry Fields set up a shrine around the "Imagine Mosaic." A candle, a red rose, and a picture of Michael were displayed in the center of the tiles. Later in the day, the McMorrow family came by briefly to view the makeshift memorial, as did hundreds of others, not all of whom were aware of who was being memorialized. Yoko Ono stopped by briefly. As she viewed the offering, she was patted gently on the back by her male companion before they walked slowly away.

On Tuesday, at 10:00 A.M., over one hundred mourners came to a funeral Mass for Michael at the lavish marble St. Ignatius Roman Catholic Church on Park Avenue, near Eighty-fourth Street. The church was only a short distance from Loyola, the high school Daphne had briefly attended. It was also the same church where Jacqueline Kennedy Onassis's funeral was held.

Reverend Walter F. Modrys gave the sermon: "In the eyes of the foolish, his passing was utter destruction," he said about Michael. "But we know he is at peace." He went on to say, "Despite cruel tragedy, senseless death, and foolish destruction, nothing can separate us from God's love. Not even this."

Matthew, Michael's nephew, delivered the eulogy. He recalled a trip he took to Central Park with his uncle about ten years before. He and his sister Shannon strolled through the park on a leisurely jaunt, admiring the flowers, feeding ducks and swans, and taking turns pushing one another on the swings. "But what I remember most about that day is James." Matthew recalled that when James saw Mike come into the park, James came over to him, embraced him, and started thanking him profusely. It turned out that Michael had given the homeless man some food and had brought him to a shelter one night. "James credited Michael with saving his life. That was Uncle Mike." Matthew noted that Mike loved and cared about all people. He enjoyed chatting with a young child just as much as with an older person. He talked as easily with a stranger on the street as with an old friend. He treated all people as if they were his own kin. "He understood the real meaning of humanity," Matthew said. "He had this way of making people feel comfortable and relaxed. You knew he wasn't judging anyone, but simply trying to enjoy them."

Eight pallbearers carried the coffin down the steps and into the waiting hearse. A sobbing Margaret, arms intertwined with her daughters, Anne and Joan, followed close behind. Before slipping into the limousine beside her mother, Anne said out loud what many people felt: "It's just such a savage attack. It's unforgivable."

After the funeral, people lingered outside the church, talking softly in groups and consoling each other as they wiped away tears. Many recalled how Michael respected all people and had friends from all walks of life, all races, and all religions, and how cruelly ironic it was that he died in the park that he loved so much.

Before leaving for the cemetery, childhood friend Jack Baxter remarked that Michael had taken care of his mother for the last twenty years, that he'd bring her tea and they'd watch TV together, and that he'd often do the shopping. "She is absolutely devastated," he said, his voice cracking. "No mother should have to bury a child, but Margaret will have to do it and forever deal with the agonizing way he died. It is too cruel." Baxter added, "But those bastards who did it, well, they have to address not me, not Mike's friends or family, but someone else. And sometimes God doesn't have too much mercy."

After hearing about Michael's death, Meagher remembered his childhood buddy as a loyal friend from the old neighborhood: "And I miss him." He said he wished Michael could know how he felt, and so he wrote a note thanking him for their 30-year friendship. Meagher talked of playing the game "What ever happened to. . . ."—a game that allowed them to reminisce about the "colorful characters" from the old neighborhood. "Now I do not have anyone to play this game with anymore," he wrote.

CHAPTER 19

On May 28, both suspects were once again at the Manhattan Criminal Courthouse, in separate courtrooms, for brief hearings to update the status of their cases.

Daphne entered the courtroom dressed differently from her customary homeboy style. Wearing a prim navy blue suit and white blouse, she appeared before the judge like a wholesome young lady on her way to a private-school luncheon. Daphne was accompanied by her new lawyer, Ben Brafman.

Brafman spoke to the judge and asked for more time to sort out the facts. He said that the time would allow him either to oppose the prosecution's evidence or bring other evidence to their attention. He declared that he "would waive the time limits that define how quickly prosecutors must seek an indictment."

After the brief hearing, Brafman spoke at a news conference. He implored everyone to remain calm until all the facts emerged. He stated that it was likely that the teens would mount separate defenses. Supporting his client, he said that it would become apparent that Daphne did not participate in the murder. "When the dust settles and cooler heads prevail, we are very hopeful that Daphne will be vindicated."

One floor below, Christopher, newly released from Bellevue Hospital, looked much the same as he had previously. Neat and clean, he was dressed in dark khakis, a flannel green-and-blue shirt, and white Nike sneakers, with the laces removed. Because of a broken finger, he wore a splint on the third and fourth fingers of his right hand. "There is no doubt in my mind that Mr. Vasquez is fit to proceed," said his attorney, Arnold Kriss. However, Kriss also requested that the juvenile-justice authorities keep up their suicide watch until further notice—simply as a precaution—not because he believed that Christopher was an actual danger to himself.

As Kriss left the Criminal Court Building, he told waiting reporters that he would have no comment on the case. In fact, he went on to say, he was disturbed by the distortions and inaccuracies that had already been reported, particularly statements made that Vasquez had acted in self-defense. "This is a case that will be decided solely in the courtroom. It is the only appropriate place to decide this matter. It is in Christopher's best interest and in the interest of justice."

With two very different clients and two vastly different attorney styles, the stage was set for a richly nuanced and complex drama in which character development and plot would drive the play forward in equal measure, until the climax and ultimate denouement revealed who was the leading character, who played the supporting role, and what was the precipitating event.

* * *

Around a month later, Daphne and Christopher returned to the courthouse once again. This time, they appeared in the same room, only feet from each other. This was the day they would formally hear the charges against them.

As they waited, Daphne, dressed in a black jumper and white blouse, with white ankle socks and black shoes, began crying. Her parents were sitting in the front row, but she did not glance at them. Christopher, too, seemed extremely sad, and he also looked waiflike and vulnerable. Wearing a blue blazer, white shirt, and print tie, he turned his head often to look at his parents— not at the schoolgirl who stood so close. His parents looked back at him, sympathetically and supportively.

Again, the hearing was brief. ADA Carolyn Streicher stated the charges. Each teen, she said, was to be indicted on three counts of second-degree murder and two counts of first-degree robbery. The first count of murder was for causing the death of Michael McMorrow, with intent; the second was for "under circumstances evincing a depraved indifference to human life, recklessly engaging in conduct which created a grave risk of death to another person, and thereby caused the death of Michael McMorrow"; and the third was for "in the attempted commission and commission of the crime of robbery in the First Degree . . . and of the immediate flight therefrom, a participant in the crime caused the death of Michael McMorrow." The two first-degree robbery counts were: "The defendants . . . forcibly stole property from Michael McMorrow, and in the course of the commission of the crime and in the immediate flight therefrom, a participant in the crime caused serious physical injury to Michael McMorrow"; and a participant ". . . forcibly stole property from Michael McMorrow and in the course of the commission of the crime and in the immediate flight therefrom, a participant in the crime used and threatened the immediate use of a dangerous instrument, to wit, a knife."

As she heard the indictment, Daphne cringed, lowering her head and shaking it in disbelief. Her pale milky skin turned a dark red. At one point, she put her hands to her face, but couldn't stop her tears. Brafman put his arm around her shoulder, trying to comfort her, but it did little good. She cried uncontrollably. The Abdelas whispered to each other in French, which, some say, they did so that others would not know what they were saying.

Streicher then stated that, if convicted of second-degree murder, the two teens would face a minimum sentence of five years to life, and a maximum sentence of nine years to life. Upon hearing those words, Daphne put her head down on the defense table. After a few moments, she looked at her father and mouthed, "I love you!" as she broke down in tears. Her father, too, cried, wiping away his tears with a handkerchief. All the while, her mother showed no emotion, as if a wash of numbness had settled over her, making it impossible for her to display any reaction at all.

On the other side of the courtroom, opposite the Abdelas, sat the Vasquez family. Their faces were grim, and they looked tired, as if they hadn't slept for nights. During the entire proceedings, Christopher's facial expression stayed the same: a fixed, vacant mask.

New York State law regulated that the teens be prosecuted as adults because they were charged with intentional and felony murder, but sentenced as juvenile offenders because they were not yet eighteen years old. Mandatory sentencing exists for certain crimes in certain states in an attempt to create uniform punishment, and also to allow, with minimum and maximum ranges, the opportunity for the convicted to display good behavior and thus spend less than the maximum time in prison.

Both teens quietly entered a "not guilty" to second-degree murder.

As Christopher was led out of the courtroom in handcuffs, he slightly smiled at his parents.

Outside, Brafman, speaking to reporters, noted that Daphne's tears were, in part, due to her close ties with her family. He went on to say that she was distraught, as any other person in this situation would be, at being charged with something she did not do. He said that her parents visited her regularly at Spofford. "Daphne Abdela had nothing to do with the murder of Michael McMorrow. Please understand that we're dealing with a fifteen-year-old who is terribly frightened by the process, especially because she knows, and I think everybody else knows, that she did not participate in the murder."

Kriss had no comment.

On October 3, 1997, the teens were once again in court. This time, the judge would decide whether or not the statements made by Daphne to the detectives on the night of the murder could be used in court, or if they should remain sealed. Brafman was adamant in his position that Daphne's statements were rambling, often incoherent, and shouldn't be admitted. However, Judge Michael A. Corriero overruled him.

Documents were then released for public scrutiny: a transcript of what Daphne had told police appeared in the newspapers on October 4, detailing what she called her "night of horror."

In it, she told police that Chris went "nuts," that he "had that look in his eyes. . . . He just flipped out. He took acid and he flipped out. He just kept stabbing Michael. He sliced his throat. We burned his ID to get rid of the evidence. Whatever we didn't burn, we threw in the pond. I have his money upstairs in my room."

While being questioned, she told the police that she could tell them where the body was and then immediately followed that by saying, "I don't know why I'm helping you. I hate cops. I didn't do anything wrong." She admitted to the cops that she told Chris, "You'd better gut him so he'll sink, because he's a fatty."

Later in the evening, while still talking to the police, she returned to her riff about hating cops, saying, "I smell bacon. I smell pork. I don't even know why I'm helping you. I hate cops. I hate pigs. . . ." She also told cops she was afraid Christopher was going to kill her, too.

She admitted that she had been drinking heavily that night. "I drank more than most people can handle," but, she added, she wasn't a murderer. She said she'd done a lot of things wrong, "but . . . Chris did it. Chris had the knife. He gutted him. I was scared . . . I thought he was going to kill me, too. . . . Mike's my bud. . . . I didn't just meet him that night. I used to get LSD off him."

Included in the transcript were details about what was going on in her apartment while she was being questioned by the officers. The document recorded that when her father tried to keep her from talking until a lawyer was present, she screamed at him to get the "f—"

out of there and told him that she'd say whatever she wanted to. She then berated him for calling the police. "You got everybody involved," she screamed. "What was I going to do, sleep in the park with a dead body? Yeah, that's what I'd do! I'd sleep right next to the dead body that Chris killed."

The document recorded that Daphne then offered to show the officers where the body was, but that she didn't do it without reiterating her hatred for cops. She admitted that all three of them were drinking and that the two men started fighting and that Chris took out a knife and stabbed Mike in the stomach. She then led the officers to the Lake at Central Park, where, upon seeing the corpse, she yelled: "Mike, I tried to do CPR. I gave you mouth-to-mouth. I tried to do what I could. I can't believe Chris did this to you. I love you." She then said, "I'm sorry I did this to you—I mean, I didn't help him. Chris did it. . . . I didn't help him kill you. . . ."

After that, she told the officers that she wanted to say a prayer over Michael. She also reported that she had felt his neck for a pulse and, when she was trying to give CPR to Michael, Chris shoved her off him and slit his throat. "I threw up," she stated. She told police that when she tried to give him CPR, she didn't even care if he had HIV. She stated the intestines were yellow, "like in biology books." Going on, she compared the crime to one that took place in *The Silence of the Lambs*. She said that all his insides were out and recommended that the cops see the movie. She told the officers at one point that she wanted to go home. "I wish it were all a dream. I'd close my eyes and you wouldn't be here. That none of this would ever have happened."

Toward the end of the transcript, the document

stated that Daphne was reported to have said, "That dick, he'd better take the heat for this because he knows he did it." When asked by the detectives about a possible motive, Daphne said that Chris was jealous of her relationship with Michael. She surmised that he flipped out after Michael put his arm around her. She told cops that earlier in the day, Chris had "kind of" asked her to be his girlfriend and she had "kind of" said yes.

Detectives reported that during the seven hours they spoke with her, she tried to be tough. She asked the officers if they knew certain cops in the local precinct. She admitted that she had been drinking heavily. She mentioned that she had met Michael at an AA meeting two weeks before.

The document also recorded Christopher's conversation with the police when they came to his house to arrest him. Unlike Daphne, Christopher was tight-lipped and uninterested in talking about the murder. Reportedly, he said nothing about the events of the night. Instead, he spoke about several supermodels, as well as about the Muppets. He told the detectives how much he liked Kathy Ireland, particularly the commercial in which Miss Piggy stole Ireland's potato chips.

CHAPTER 20

Around the same time the Vasquezes dismissed their attorney, Robert Fogelnest, the Abdelas dismissed theirs, George Weinbaum, and immediately hired attorney Ben Brafman. They knew that Brafman's skill—or lack thereof—could mean the difference between a life sentence—if Daphne was convicted of second-degree murder—and parole or even a walk—if she was proven innocent of all charges. The stakes were about as high as they could get, and anything less than a faultless defense would cost much more than money. If wealth didn't bring happiness with it—and it absolutely did not right then—at least it brought huge buying power and great hope, in the form of high-profile attorney Benjamin Brafman.

Brafman, forty-nine, graduated from Ohio Northern University Law School and received a master's degree in criminal justice from New York University School of Law. He came to the Abdelas with a well-earned reputation as a tenacious and winning defender of the rich, famous, and infamous. As a former ADA in Manhattan, he tried twenty-four cases in a four-year period, and lost only one. As a criminal defense attorney, he successfully defended Sammy "the Bull" Gravano, a former Mafia hit man, in 1991. In 1990, he won an acquittal for James Patino, who was charged, along with six others, with the racially motivated murder of a black youth, Yusuf Hawkins, in Bensonhurst, Brooklyn. He won an acquittal for Vincent Basciano, charged along with ten others in 1994 in the "Blue Thunder" heroin-distribution trial, by convincing a jury that his client was discussing illegal gambling, not drugs, during wiretapped conversations. In 1996, he won an acquittal, on federal drug charges, for club king Peter Gatien. He also won an acquittal for a businessman tried as part of the "windows" case, which involved Mob domination of contracts for city housing-projects windows. In 1997, *New York Magazine* named him the city's "Best Criminal Defense Lawyer."

Son of Holocaust survivors, Brafman was an Orthodox Jew who grew up in a strictly observant, deeply religious family. He learned early on the art of charming a tough audience—he worked as a stand-up comic in the Cat-skills. Brafman scheduled cases around Jewish holidays, took Saturdays (the Sabbath) off, and left his office early on Fridays to make it home before sundown. "I figure God will understand if I'm trying to save someone's life and I'm home five minutes late," he once quipped, only to have his brother Aaron, an Orthodox rabbi, remind him that it doesn't quite work that way.

Brafman was widely acclaimed not only for his skill in the courtroom but also for his prowess in dealing with—or, according to some, manipulating—the press. Reportedly, he was recommended to the Abdelas by Stuart Rubin, an experienced criminal defense attorney, who

promoted Brafman as being a virtuoso at bearing up to
the pressure of a media frenzy. A source who spoke on
the condition of anonymity stated that after he takes on
a high-stakes case, he hires a powerful public-relations
firm to spin the story and skillfully orchestrate scenarios that work to his client's advantage, knowing that the
setup will be picked up by a ravenous press and become
part of the public's shared perceptions. And that, as
everyone knows, is worth a great deal—perhaps even
everything—including his attorney fees.

Once hired by the Abdelas, Brafman wasted no
time working the media. "We really don't know yet
what the facts are here. No one knows for sure who
did what—or why. I would only hope that people will
keep an open mind. When things ultimately calm
down, it will be determined that Daphne Abdela did
not participate in the murder. It is my hope that the
DA will ultimately come to the same conclusion."

At the same time, the press—of their own accord
or because of artfully planted seeds of doubt—began
casting aspersions on the man who had been murdered: What was a forty-four-year-old man doing in the
park at night with fifteen-year-olds? Was he after sex?
Did he make a pass at Abdela, so Vasquez felt he had
to defend her honor? Did he make a pass at Vasquez?
Was he some kind of pervert? Was he a drug-dealing
degenerate?

Lawyers following the case surmised that Brafman
may have initially considered two possible defenses:
Daphne was drunk when the murder occurred; and
the killing was justified for one of a variety of reasons,
including self-defense. However, they knew he would
discard both in favor of a stronger tactic: Daphne
would finger Christopher as the killer. She would insist
that he alone did the stabbing and that he alone was

responsible for the murder. She would declare herself simply a bystander—a witness and not an accomplice. And as for her admission to the cops that she had urged Christopher on, even suggesting that he "gut him" because he's a "fatty," he'll "sink," that could easily be explained. She was a confused, hysterical teen, so afraid for her life that she would have said anything. Certainly, those reported words should not be taken as truth.

It was Brafman's job to make sure they were not.

After dismissing Fogelnest, the Vasquezes hired Arnold Kriss to defend their son. In contrast to Brafman, Kriss, fifty, was known to be a man of few words, especially when it came to the media. Cautious and discreet, he was hesitant to disclose any information about a case. For example, even after successfully getting an acquittal in a murder case that former Mayor Edward I. Koch stated, "No one expected him to win," Kriss refused to comment, saying he could not discuss it because the records were sealed. Sealed records or not, most lawyers are only too eager to ever-so-humbly or ever-so-arrogantly discuss the outcome of a case, especially if it shines the spotlight on their own success.

After graduating Brooklyn Law School in 1972, Kriss worked in the Brooklyn DA's Office for four years. He then became a special counsel and deputy commissioner for trials in the police department for several years before going into private practice. Active in politics, Kriss worked on Mayor Koch's first—and only unsuccessful—campaign for mayor, and four years later, he headed Koch's successful mayoral campaign. Kriss's reputation was that of a thorough lawyer who cared deeply about his clients.

Without Kriss having to say a word to the press, savvy followers of criminal cases knew exactly what path he would take for his client. He would say that Christopher had never been in trouble in his entire life. After all, he had been a Boy Scout and an altar boy who regularly went to church and to the supermarket with his mother and grandmother. He had a curfew, which he scrupulously observed, and by all accounts, he was a polite and well-mannered boy. If he had any drawbacks at all, the boy might be considered too quiet, too meek, and not gutsy enough.

Some surmised that Kriss's defense might be one that impugned Michael McMorrow. Michael, Kriss might say, made a pass at Daphne, and Christopher tried to defend her. Michael then got enraged and lunged at the boy. Christopher was simply a teen reacting to, not initiating, trouble—a chivalrous boy acting in self-defense. Kriss would make the case that his client did not set out to find someone to cut up, but rather reacted to something that took place. Besides, Kriss might go on, who said Michael was so great anyway? The defense could argue that Michael was a druggie, a drinker, and a dirty old man who had an eye for teenage girls. Maybe the older man even packed a knife.

Lawyers weighing in on this strategy noted that the prosecution could easily negate these arguments by pounding home the ferocity of the attack and the great number of wounds—many more than a chivalrous stance on Christopher's part would have warranted.

It might help, said several attorneys, to know that Vasquez did not carry a knife around regularly, but perhaps found it nearby. It would also help, they said, to find out that the murdered man had made advances toward Daphne that caused Christopher to feel he had to defend her. He might have panicked, and under the influence of drugs, alcohol, and the urgings of a troubled girl, he had done some things he shouldn't have done.

Considering another scenario, some lawyers thought that Kriss might have his client pin the whole thing on Daphne. Everyone knew she was a loose cannon. Everyone knew she was an angry, rebellious, and provocative young lady. Certainly, it would have been more in her character than in his to kill someone.

But then again, it was possible that Kriss could mount the so-called Prozac defense, one that Christopher's previous lawyer, Fogelnest, had used unsuccessfully in the case of Edward Leary, the subway firebomber. In that case, the defense claimed that Leary did not plan to hurt anyone with his ignited firebombs. Instead, he was made psychotic after taking Prozac, along with other prescription drugs. The jury did not go for it, and Leary was sentenced to thirty-one to ninety-four years. Christopher had been taking Zoloft, an antidepressant in the same category of drugs as Prozac, since he was nine years old. Zoloft, so the argument would go, in combination with beer and other alcohol, might have fueled a psychotic rage with heavy hallucinations. Christopher might not have known what he was doing and therefore shouldn't be accused of murder.

In a newspaper interview, Dr. Harold Koplewicz, a professor of psychiatry at New York University School of Medicine, and director of the Child Study Center, stated that using the Prozac defense would be crazy. "These medicines can't make you do something you weren't going to do anyway. You clearly are going to have certain people with a predisposition for this type of behavior," and those people are the ones who are more given to violence. But to "blame the medicine for this behavior" is wrong. However, in spite of the doctor's belief, in over forty separate cases, lawyers had argued a variation on the Prozac defense, which went something like this: A person cannot be convicted of committing a crime unless intent is proven. If a person is taking a mind-altering drug, he or she lacks the pre-requisite criminal intent.

In making the case against using a Prozac defense, experts cited FDA studies, which showed that Prozac did not lead to violent behavior or suicidal actions or thoughts. Prozac was approved for use a decade ago.

CHAPTER 21

On February 24, 1998, following a request by Daphne's attorney, a conference was set up in Judge Corriero's chambers regarding a possible disposition, or settlement, of the case against Daphne. During the discussion, attorney Brafman revealed that he had reached a plea agreement with a new ADA working on the case, Sarah Hines. According to the agreement, Daphne would be charged with first-degree manslaughter on the condition that she receive the maximum penalty for a juvenile convicted of that crime under New York State law—three years and four months to ten years in jail—and she would not be required to testify against Christopher at his trial.

A plea bargain establishes that a defendant may, "with the permission of the court and the consent of the prosecutor, enter a plea of not guilty to less than the entire indictment (to less than each and every count as charged), to dispose of the indictment completely, provided that the plea includes at least one offense charged or a lesser included offense."

According to the law, a person can be found

guilty of manslaughter in the first degree under two conditions. The first is if, with intent to cause serious physical injury to another person, he or she causes the death of that person. The second is if, with intent to cause the death of another person, he or she causes the death of such person under circumstances that do not constitute murder because the person is acting under the influence of extreme emotional disturbance. Extreme emotional disturbance is defined as behavior for which there was a reasonable explanation or excuse, the reasonableness of which is to be determined from the viewpoint of a person in the defendant's situation under the circumstances as the defendant believed them to be.

The major difference between second-degree murder and first-degree manslaughter is intent: in the former, there is the intent to kill; in the latter, there is no homicidal intent, but as a result of physical harm, a death occurs. Manslaughter in the first degree is considered a class B felony.

Lawyers following the case closely said that Brafman's move to enter into a plea agreement was a savvy one. They remarked that Daphne would probably not be a credible witness on the stand—she had changed her version of events many times between June and November 1997, when she was being interviewed by detectives. At first, she said she was simply a witness. Then she admitted to helping Christopher cover up the crime by telling him to gut the body so it would sink and by helping him destroy Michael's identification papers. In September, she admitted to detectives that she was more than an innocent bystander, stating that she witnessed Christopher and Michael in a serious struggle, with Chris brandishing a knife, and that she helped Christopher by kicking Michael's feet out from under him.

Former prosecutor Ed Hayes, weighing in on the plea deal, stated that the prosecution would not have given Daphne the deal if there had not been a weakness in their case against her. He surmised that they did not have enough evidence against her. For example, forensic work might show that fingerprints on the knife found in Christopher's apartment—the alleged murder weapon—belonged to him.

Some lawyers believed that because of Daphne's race, gender, age, and background, she would probably get manslaughter anyway, so why not cut a deal and avoid the chance—small as it was—that the jury could find her guilty of murder?

Brafman spoke out about his reasons for making the deal. He stated that going to trial would run the risk that Daphne could be convicted of murder—even though he firmly believed she was innocent of that crime—and thus face life in prison. Even if he mounted the best defense in the world, a jury might still find her guilty— juries are notoriously unpredictable—and he reiterated that Daphne was simply a witness, not an accomplice. Brafman didn't want to risk a trial, because any defendant, even Daphne, could antagonize the jury with his or her words and demeanor.

Brafman also stated that it was the responsibility of a lawyer to suggest a plea bargain, regardless of how close two defendants might be at the beginning of a case—even if it was at the expense of a friendship or a love relationship.

ADA Sarah Hines also spoke out about the plea bargain, stating that, in her opinion, it was a "fair and just resolution." She said that she had discussed it at length with the McMorrows and that they fully understood why it was brokered. Hines didn't make any further comments, saying that the case against Christopher was still pending.

Unlike Hines, neighbors of Christopher's had plenty to say. They were outraged with the plea bargain. They felt that Daphne had cut a deal of a lifetime and was getting off easy because of her high-priced lawyer. Instead of Daphne possibly having to face life in a women's lockup, she would now serve only several years in a juvenile facility. They were concerned that Christopher's more humble background would spell disaster for him. "Because she has money," said Frank Greene, a next-door neighbor, "she'll be out in no time and [Christopher will] get shafted. What's good for one is good for another," he added angrily. Another neighbor wondered why Christopher would have to take all the blame when it was documented that Daphne was there all the time. He felt that they should go on trial together. Also angry was Glenn Golub, Michael's boss, good friend, and the person who identified the body from police photographs. He said the plea bargain was "absolutely absurd." It was absurd that Daphne could be out in 2½ years. He was convinced that Daphne could not learn a lesson in that short amount of time. One neighbor had a strong word for Daphne: She was a "bitch," and said that Daphne was not off the hook yet. "She will have to answer to someone else" one day.

On March 11, 1998, Daphne returned to the courtroom of Judge Michael A. Corriero in state supreme court to formally enter a guilty plea to manslaughter in the first degree, in accordance with the agreement that had been arranged the previous month. Outside the courthouse, reporters were assembled, hoping to interview the families of the teens.

Justice Corriero, fifty-four, became the first judge in New York City to specialize in juvenile-offender law cases, in 1992. He was Manhattan's only Youth Part judge. The Youth Part was a court set aside within the adult court system to deal with only the most serious and violent crimes committed by youths—the cases of juveniles, thirteen years old and over who were being tried as adults for murder, as well as all juveniles over fifteen years old who were being tried as adults for a variety of felonies.

The judge's courtroom was an oasis in the midst of the criminal justice system. It came into existence through the direct intervention of Corriero, who, in 1991, wrote a seminal paper detailing why juveniles should not be treated the same as adults, even if they committed similar crimes. His belief went against the current of the time, which supported a "get tough" policy in response to a few high-profile juvenile murders. However, enough professionals agreed with the judge's belief, citing overcrowding of detention facilities, long trial delays, and increased costs of detention, that the youth division was established.

It was Judge Corriero's conviction that adolescents could benefit from rehabilitation—education and special attention—and he meted it out in the form of mandating services to deal with the mental, emotional, and physical needs of the juveniles who appeared before him. It was in Corriero's hands to send a youth he considered appropriate for rehabilitation to an alternative program, or even to let him or her go on probation. If defendants were willing to plead guilty and the judge deemed them worthy, he could enroll them in a youth-offender program on the spot, where they would be required to go to school, keep a strict curfew, and report back to the judge once a month so the judge could monitor the progress being made. However, for those whose records were particularly violent—a youth, for example, charged with assault with a knife and attempted sexual abuse of a woman, and whose former charge was for grand larceny—Corriero might send them back to a detention facility in the Bronx, to await another appearance or a trial, depending on the crime.

After the court was called to order, Judge Corriero asked Daphne for her plea. She quietly entered a plea of guilty to manslaughter in the first degree. He then asked her if she would like to address the court. She replied that she would.

Standing at the front of the courtroom in baggy, khaki pants, a huge maroon sweater, and uncombed hair, Daphne, still fifteen, began reading from a prepared statement. In a deep, husky voice, she stated:

"On May 23, 1997, I participated in the assault that caused the death of Michael McMorrow. . . . At some point during the struggle between Mr. McMorrow and Christopher Vasquez, I struck Mr. McMorrow and caused Mr. McMorrow to fall to the ground, by kicking his feet out from under him which caused him to fall backwards. At the time I took this action I saw that Mr. Vasquez was using a knife in his assault on Mr. McMorrow. . . . My actions were taken by me to aid Mr. Vasquez and to cause serious physical injury to Mr. McMorrow."

She paused and then added her final statement: "I never intended for Mr. McMorrow to be killed and I am truly sorry that he died."

All during her brief speech, Michael's mother, sisters, brother, and nephew cried openly. The family
had been escorted into the courtroom by Detective
Mooney, who had been with them while they were in
Sarah Hines's office earlier that day, listening to the
prosecution's justification for the plea deal. They had
been brought into the courtroom through a back
door to avoid the swarm of reporters waiting to get a
word with them. Across the aisle from the McMorrows, Mr. Abdela looked heartbroken. Mrs. Abdela
showed no emotion. The rest of the row was empty.

Daphne returned to her seat at the table with her
lawyer, who then addressed the court. He said that in
all the years that he had been a criminal lawyer, some
twenty or so, he couldn't recall handling any case as
tragic as this one. He said that today he was concerned with trying to save the life of Daphne Abdela.

At the conclusion of the proceedings, Judge Corriero
spoke to the people gathered in the courtroom. In a
voice slow with sadness, he said, "A friend of mine described the walls of a courtroom where children are sentenced as walls that weep. Today, I think the walls are
weeping. They weep for Mr. McMorrow. They weep for
Miss Abdela. And they weep for their families." After
that, Judge Corriero added a statement of encouragement. He said that Daphne had taken the first step in
turning her life around by admitting her guilt. With the
right treatment, the judge added, we can hope she has
a bright future.

Daphne was taken out of the courtroom in handcuffs and driven back to the Bronx, where she was still
being held without bail in the Spofford Juvenile
Center. On her way out of the room, she smiled and
waved at her parents.

Outside, when reporters, congregated on the steps,

asked the Abdelas to comment on the proceedings, they refused. For the first time, it looked as if Catherine was fighting back tears. Brafman stated: "She's a young kid who did something bad. . . . She's not an urban terrorist who goes out wreaking damage."

Later that day, in the apartment that Michael had shared with his mother, the McMorrow family gathered. Although Daphne's apology brought partial closure, Michael's sister Joan said that it was still an impossible thing to understand. "We're pleased it's partly over, but it will never bring Michael back. It should never have happened." She went on to say, "Daphne admitted that nothing Michael did that night brought it on, and that's important because Michael was such a nonviolent person. We were glad she admitted to what happened that night. We appreciated the apology. My mother will miss him very, very much and will never get over him." Joan said that she really didn't have any specific feelings about the plea agreement. Her family, she said, was grieving deeply and even feeling some pain for what the Abdela parents might be feeling. "Nothing can heal our heartache."

CHAPTER 22

On April 2, 1998, Daphne returned to the court-room of state supreme court justice Michael A. Corriero for sentencing.

SUPREME COURT OF THE
STATE OF NEW YORK
COUNTY OF NEW YORK PART 73

THE PEOPLE OF THE STATE OF NEW YORK:
Indictment No. 4943/97
-against- :
Charge: Mans. 1
DAPHNE ABDELA, : Defendant.

111 Centre Street
New York, New York 10013
April 2, 1998

BEFORE:
HONORABLE MICHAEL CORRIERO, J.S.C.

Daphne Abdela in fourth grade, first row, far right,
displaying a peace sign.

Daphne in fifth grade, in center, wearing white shirt.

Daphne in sixth grade, in back row, fourth from left.

Daphne Abdela with friends

Daphne in center, with friends.

Michael McMorrow at St. Gregory's School. *(Photo courtesy of Joan McMorrow)*

Michael posing before taking his highly regarded "sweet jump shot," at All Hallows High School in the Bronx. *(Photo courtesy of Joan McMorrow)*

A relaxed and dapper Michael in a three-piece suit.
(Photo courtesy of Joan McMorrow)

Cops drag the mutilated, floating body of Michael from the Lake at Central Park, on May 23, 1997.
(*Photo courtesy of Juan Gonzalez*)

Long shot of the gazebo where Michael was killed. Boaters enjoy a lovely spring day, as a police van with detectives and police officers search the area. (*Photo courtesy of Dan Brinzac*)

Under heavy police guard, Christopher is led away from the 20th precinct on Friday May 23, 1997. *(Photo courtesy of Dan Brinzac)*

Daphne with attorney George Weinbaum during her arraignment in Criminal Court, 100 Centre Street, Manhattan, Saturday afternoon, May 24, 1997. She was ordered held without bail. *(Photo courtesy of Rex USA/New York Post, Jim Alcorn)*

Catherine and Angelo Abdela, Daphne's parents, leave
Manhattan Criminal Court, May 24, 1997.
(Photo courtesy of Rex USA/New York Post, Jim Alcorn)

Patricia Reidy and Angelo Vasquez, parents of Christopher,
leaving Manhattan Criminal Court, surrounded by reporters.
(Photo courtesy of Rex USA/New York Post, Don Halasy)

From left to right: Commissioner Howard Safir, Mayor Giuliani,
and Parks Commissioner Henry Stern speak at a press conference
to report the arrest of two suspects in the Central Park stabbing.
(Photo courtesy of Rex USA/New York Post, Don Halasy)

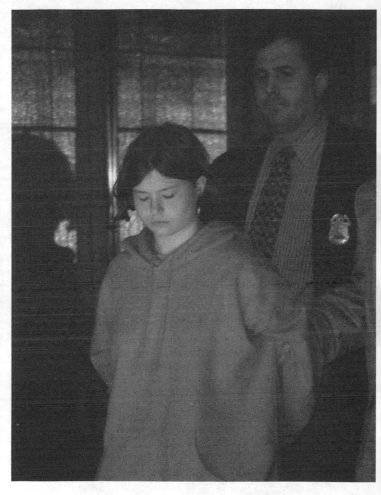

Daphne with police officer, May 25, 1997, before an arraignment. *(Photo courtesy of Dan Brinzac)*

Michael's mother, Margaret McMorrow, attends Michael's wake on May 25, 1997. *(Photo courtesy of Dan Brinzac)*

Margaret McMorrow is supported by her daughters, Joan and Anne, as she arrives at the funeral mass for Michael. The funeral service took place at Saint Ignacius of Loyola Church in Manhattan on Tuesday, May 27, 1997. *(Photo courtesy of Rex USA/New York Post, Luiz C. Ribeiro)*

Margaret McMorrow with her grandson, Matthew McMorrow, on a bench dedicated to Michael's memory, in Strawberry Fields, Central Park. *(Photo courtesy of Rex USA/New York Post, Michael Norcia)*

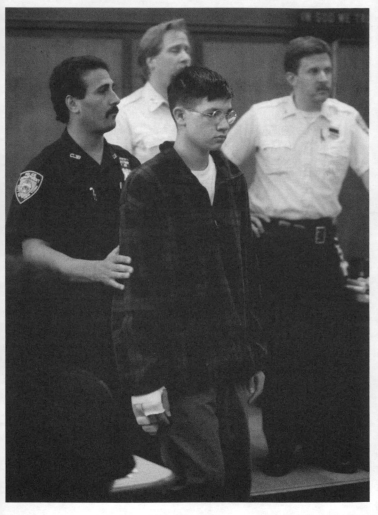

Christopher with his hand bandaged, in court, before being taken to Bellevue Hospital after he was heard muttering suicidal statements. *(Photo courtesy of Reuters)*

Michael's brother, Charles, speaks to the press on May 25, 1997, about the family's grief and the atrociousness of the crime. At far right is Matthew McMorrow, Michael's nephew.
(Photo courtesy of Dan Brinzac)

Christopher, center, showing no reaction as the verdict is read by jury forewoman Leonore Bode. Christopher was found guilty of manslaughter on Friday, December 4, 1998, in the courtroom of Judge Corriero. Margaret McMorrow weeps, second from left. Patricia Reidy, Christopher's mother, is at right.
(Photo courtesy of Associated Press)

New York Post cover December 15, 1998, expressing outrage at Christopher's manslaughter verdict.

New York Post cover, January 22, 2004, showing Daphne and a note she penned and left on the bench in Central Park dedicated to Michael. The note was left a few days after her release from prison.

Daphne dressed up, as she appears in court on May 28, 1997.
(Photo courtesy of Reuters)

APPEARANCES:
(For the People:)
ROBERT MORGENTHAU ESQ.,
District Attorney,
County of New York
BY: SARAH HINES, ESQ. and
RICHARD PLANSKY, ESQ.
Assistant District Attorneys
(For the Defendant Abdela:)
BY: BENJAMIN BRAFMAN, ESQ.
Clarence Ballard, Jr.
Senior Court Reporter

In a hushed but tense courtroom, the clerk spoke first: "Number three on the calendar, Daphne Abdela. May we have your appearances, please?"

Brafman stood and stated, "For Miss Abela." Hines stood and remarked, "Sarah Hines for the people." Plansky stood and stated: "Richard Plansky for the people. Good morning, Your Honor."

Judge Corriero said, "Good morning, everyone. The defendant ready for sentence, Mr. Brafman?" To which he answered, "Yes, Your Honor."

The judge asked if the people wished to be heard on the issue of the sentence, and Hines replied yes. She then rose and spoke to the court.

"The murder of Michael McMorrow on May 23, 1997, was a horrifying, terrifying, and tragic event in the life of this city. It was particularly tragic for Mr. Mc-Morrow's family members, a number of whom are here in court today." As she scanned the courtroom, she could see Michael's mother, sisters, brother, and nephew.

Hines continued by stating that the murder was also tragic for all New Yorkers. Even jaded New Yorkers, she said, were shaken by the gruesome details of the case. She paused before continuing. "People were further shocked to find two 15-year-olds charged with committing such a crime."

Hines reminded the court that Abdela had pleaded guilty on March 11, 1998, to manslaughter in the first degree, after admitting that she had participated in the assault that led to Michael McMorrow's death. In discussing the how and why of the plea, Hines told the courtroom that the sentence was $3\frac{1}{3}$ to ten years—the maximum authorized by New York law for a defendant of Daphne Abdela's age convicted of manslaughter in the first degree.

Hines stated that the decision to take a plea from this defendant for manslaughter in the first degree was reached after a long and thorough process of deliberation. She said the DA's office considered all the facts of the case, as well as the legal issues that would arise if the case went to trial. She mentioned that she was grateful for the input of the McMorrow family as they analyzed these issues. "From our dialogue with the McMorrow family, I think that the family members understand the reasons for the plea and, in general, support it."

She then mentioned by name the people from the McMorrow family who were in attendance in the courtroom: Michael McMorrow's mother, Mrs. Margaret McMorrow; Michael McMorrow's two sisters, Anne McMorrow DeWindt and Joan McMorrow; Michael McMorrow's brother, Charles P. McMorrow; and Michael McMorrow's nephew, Matthew.

Hines continued by saying that she had spoken briefly about the impact of the crime on the city. She would now like to introduce Anne McMorrow DeWindt to the court. DeWindt, she told the court, was the representative of the family and would give a victim impact statement on behalf of the McMorrows.

A victim impact statement gives the victim of a crime—or in the case of death, the family members of the victim—the opportunity to speak during the sentencing or parole hearings of the convicted. The statement gives voice during the decision-making process to the person or persons most directly affected by the crime and, in doing so, raises the status of the victim at the same time as personalizing the crime. It can also aid the victim in emotional recovery: being able to confront the offender has been said to help in the recovery process. The statement also gives a person the opportunity to tell what financial and psychological impact the crime has had on the victim (if alive) and the extended family, with the hope that this information will be used in the sentencing phase.

The first victim impact statement in the United States was made in 1976 in Fresno, California, even though making such statements was not yet law in that state. In 1982, President Reagan's *Task Force on Victims of Crimes, Final Report* recommended that "judges allow for, and give appropriate weight to, input at sentencing from victims of violent crime." By 1997, forty-four states allowed victim impact statements during their official proceedings.

Anne walked to the front of the courtroom and stood next to Hines.

She said, "How senselessly and viciously he was killed . . . It is beyond our comprehension how anyone can participate in such a cruel and unconscionable act of violence. The uncivilized disrespect for human life demonstrated by Miss Abdela warrants the maximum punishment allowed by law for the crime for which she is convicted."

"Anyone involved in the taking of a human life in such a senseless and brutal manner must be punished."

Spent, Anne took her seat. Many in the courtroom were wiping away their tears.

Judge Corriero, obviously affected, thanked DeWindt for her remarks. He then asked ADA Hines if she wished to add anything. Hines responded, "No, Your Honor." The judge then asked Brafman if he wished to say anything on behalf of his client. He said he did and stood up to address the court.

"Your Honor, I think this is a most difficult moment for all of the participants in this truly horrific case. I don't think that there are any people who have been involved in this case on either side in any capacity who have anything but sadness in their heart as a result of the enormity of the tragedy that has not only befallen the McMorrow family, but two other families as well.

"In a brief moment, with Your Honor's permission, Miss Abdela will rise to read a painfully eloquent, remorseful statement that she herself has written.

"Because this is a negotiated plea with an agreed upon sentence, I will not belabor the issues of the case, and confine my remarks, Your Honor, to brief statements which I think the case warrants, and that Miss Abdela and her family deserve as well.

"From the very beginning of this horrible episode, I think it is important for everyone to understand, including the McMorrow family in their grief, that despite the actions that Daphne took that cause her to be here on this day, she at no time intended to cause the death of Michael McMorrow. I do not say that as an excuse. She has entered a plea, and she's prepared for sentence.

"But I think the record should reflect that shortly after Mr. McMorrow was stabbed, Daphne Abdela tried unsuccessfully to keep him alive by administering CPR in the dark in the park. That is not a justifiable defense to the crime that she participated in. But it is an indication that we are dealing with a young person who understood and understands that gravity of the offense, and in her own fashion tried desperately to keep life from ending for Michael McMorrow.

"She is also the person who first called the police and notified them of a death in the park. And while her statements to the nine-one-one operator attempted in some respects to conceal her own participation in the event, it was as a result of that call that the police came to Daphne Abdela's apartment. It was then that Daphne Abdela took them to the park to locate the body of Michael McMorrow.

"By pleading guilty, as confirmed in the probation report, Daphne Abdela has, I believe, taken a first extraordinary step with great difficulty on the road to hopefully rehabilitation. And by accepting responsibility for her role in this offense, I think she also has demonstrated to the court, to the general public, to her family, to herself, and also respectfully to the McMorrow family, that she is truly sorry for the actions that she participated in, and truly sorry that Michael McMorrow's life was ended as a result of these actions.

"In her own words, both to the Department of Probation and the statement she will soon read to the court, she indicates how she would like to be able to go back in time and undo her participation and bring Michael McMorrow back. The question now arises as to what about the people who participated in this offense, what do we do with them? And how do we try and fashion a disposition that is consistent with the interest of justice and consistent with Daphne's lesser culpability despite the horrific nature of the crime. I think this disposition is an appropriate disposition under the facts.

"A three-and-a-third to ten-year sentence is the maximum sentence under the law for a juvenile on a manslaughter plea. And manslaughter is an appropriate disposition, I submit, because Daphne Abdela did not intend to cause the death of Michael McMorrow. And I hope that the public, the McMorrow family and the press understand why this is indeed an appropriate disposition.

"I would also hope for the sake of the Abdela family and for the sake of Daphne, as she tries desperately to cope with the years ahead, that there is a refrain from referring to her as either a murderer or a butcher. I don't think it advances anyone's best interests, because A, they are inappropriate characterizations, and B, with her plea, I think she has acknowledged some degree of acceptance of responsibility, which is a big step in this case.

"Daphne Abdela, for those of us who have come to know her outside the horror of that night in Central Park, in Daphne Abdela we recognize a very intelligent, precocious, smart, talented young woman with enormous potential. And that is why, sir, I believe that a sentence that combines punishment with a hope of a future for this young woman is an appropriate disposition.

"Unfortunately, as a general proposition, when horrific crimes involving juveniles surface, and are on the front pages of the media nationwide, the knee-jerk reaction is, build more prisons and put the offenders away forever. And I think in an enlightened society, in a civilized society, we should hope to be able to do better, to fashion treatment and sentences that secure the public, punish the offender, but hopefully plan a future for our youth that does not only include in-

carceration. I know how hard Your Honor struggles
with this issue on a daily basis. And I do not envy the
position of this court in cases where young people
stand before Your Honor and where Your Honor, I
think, recognizes that despite the horrific nature of
the crime, there is genuine worth and genuine talent
and future and hope and promise in the eyes and
heart of these children regardless of the nature of
their crime.

"I anticipate that one day we will all again be proud
of Daphne Abdela. I am hopeful that she will use the
period of incarceration productively, that she will
study and continue to receive treatment for her alco-
holism, for the emotional distress that brought her to
this period in life.

"I would like to mention for the record, in fairness to
them, that Daphne's parents, Mr. and Mrs. Angelo
Abdela, who are present in the courtroom, have, in my
judgment, done everything humanly possible as responsible parents for Daphne throughout her life and
during this period demonstrated enormous support
and a great deal of class under extraordinarily difficult
circumstances.

"On the day that we took the plea in this courtroom, Your Honor, on behalf of Daphne and her parents, we extended heartfelt and most sincere and
genuine expressions of sympathy and condolences to
the McMorrow family and true and honest, sincere
regret on behalf of the entire Abdela family. We
repeat those sentiments today. And I urge them to understand in their grief, if it is at all possible, that there
is another family grieving as well, grieving for their
own child, who in a sense has also been taken from
them, and grieving as well with the knowledge that

they will live with the sadness of Mr. McMorrow's
death for the rest of their lives as well."

At the end of his remarks, Brafman thanked the
court for their attentiveness. He thanked Miss Hines
and Mr. Plansky and the other members of the district
attorney's office who, he said, "have aggressively pur-
sued their responsibilities in this fashion, and yet also,
I think, recognized that the disposition with a manslaughter plea was truly in the best interest of the
public at large, the criminal justice system, the family
of the victim, and perhaps most important, Daphne
Abdela as well."

The judge then addressed Daphne and asked her if
she would like to make a statement. "Yes, Your Honor,"
she replied.

Daphne stood up and, hunched over, began
reading.

"There is no one to blame for this tragedy. There
are no scapegoats on whom I can pass the blame,
except for myself, for being at the wrong place at the
wrong time, but also being there with the wrong individual as well."

The McMorrow family audibly gasped. *Did she really
say there was no one to blame? Did she really say that she
blames herself only for being in the wrong place at the wrong
time and for being with the wrong person? Is that the responsibility she takes for the murder?*

"I cannot say I will never drink again because I do
not know that this is guaranteed for certain. Addic-
tions are strong, fierce, powerful, and persistent."

Daphne continued by saying that God had granted
her the serenity to accept her situation. She understood that she could not change Michael McMorrow's
fate.

"Each and every one of us in this courtroom today

has made mistakes in life," Daphne told the court. "This is the punishment for my error."

"I can never say in a million words how sorry I am that this occurred and how much I wish I could have prevented any of this from happening."

The judge looked quizzically at Daphne, most likely wondering exactly where she was going. The McMorrow family looked visibly disturbed at having to sit and listen to her personal beef with the media.

"The way in which the media operates, claiming to have no established ideology, no racial, gender, or class bias, is false. How the media reports on crime is determined by class and racial background of the victim and victimizer. Wealthy victims receive the attention while the typical low-income victims remain another number in an ever-growing statistic.

"It is funny how the struggle of African-Americans, Latinos, women, the poor, unemployment, nuclear power, arms spending, and multi-million-dollar corporations' mistreatment of the environment never receive the front page. Instead, gossip of the rich-and-famous fill the first pages of so-called informative, worth-reading newspapers.

"Everyone is entitled to their own opinion and has a freedom to express it. Please, let us not allow these people to lie to the public any longer. So, when you write about my life or, rather, my newly invented life, please write Daphne Abdela, the outspoken fifteen-year-old, said, 'I'm sorry, and I hope you can find it in yourselves to forgive me for striking Michael McMorrow and sweeping his feet out from under him.'"

The judge looked stunned. "You can sit down for a moment now. You can sit down," Judge Corriero said harshly, looking angered and unnerved.

After a moment, he looked out at those gathered in

the courtroom and locked eyes with Mrs. McMorrow. "I'd like for a moment to directly address Michael's mother, Mrs. McMorrow.

"From all that I've heard and seen, Michael was a very fortunate young man, fortunate to have a mother whose feelings at this difficult time so overwhelm her that she is incapable of considering life to continue to have value. All I can say to you is that Michael would not want it that way, that he would want you to share the warmth and love that you had for him with his nephew, with your other children, so that they, too, can share in the spirit that you gave to him, the life that you gave to him. And there's nothing, absolutely nothing, that I can do to bring Michael back, to change that night that's brought us all here together, a night that took place in a special part of this city, a place of beauty, a place where we would take our loved ones, a place where we would enjoy our relationships. So, please, accept the only thing I can give you: the understanding that I, on behalf of authority in society, have tried to make every effort to deal with the very complex and difficult issues in this case in a way that takes into consideration your hurt and your concern. And the ultimate resolution of this case is an imperfect one, does not meet or can never fill the void that's in your life, but I can assure you that it was arrived at after careful and thoughtful consideration. So, please accept my condolence in this regard. And know that Michael would want you to continue and to share the love that you have with your other children, who are with you today."

He paused for a moment, and then continued: "I'd like to speak to Daphne's family, Mr. and Mrs. Abdela. All that Mr. Brafman tells me about you is that you have done everything humanly possible. You shared your love and attention and affection with Daphne. It is very difficult raising children in our world because this is a world that we adults create. It's a world that we shape for our children. It's a world where violence seems to be common, everyday experience. There's only so much we can do. And hope eventually that our example will lead our children to know right from wrong, to make the right decisions. Ultimately it is their individual choice that controls the situation.

"Please also know that in considering the ultimate disposition and recognizing that our juvenile justice system is inadequate because we, as humans, are generally inadequate, that we have made every effort to try to blend a result here that takes into consideration the enormous loss of the family of Michael McMorrow with the hope that Miss Abdela, who has acknowledged her responsibility, will someday emerge from prison a more mature, more responsible, more understandable person."

The judge then joined Brafman in thanking Hines and Plansky for their professionalism in a very difficult case. "And this disposition is well reasoned, and based upon the sound understanding of the law, and in the highest traditions of this district attorney's office." The judge also thanked Brafman by saying, "You succeeded in the accomplishment of this result, not solely because of your capabilities as a lawyer, but because it was there. It was there. And it was what the facts required, what the legal issues required. But I'm grateful to all counsel for the professional way in which a very difficult case has been partially resolved." The judge then spoke directly to Daphne.

"Miss Abdela, you participated in the loss of a life. In society and our culture, there is no greater crime, no greater crime. You are fortunate in the sense in terms of the consequences that you will have to pay. From everything I'm told about you, you are a very bright young woman.

"I must tell you that in listening to your remarks, especially those indicating your remorse, that it's apparent to me that you have a grasp of the enormity of what you did. But it's also apparent to me, although I understand perhaps your anger at the portrayal of you in the media, but it's apparent to me that you do have anger. What I would hope that you would be able to do during the time that you spend confined, that you learn to take that anger, the energy that produces that anger, and to control it, to tame it, to live your life for two people, just not for yourself, but for the life that you took. And when you're angry, you must learn to tolerate that anger twice as much. And when you work, when you're tired at night, you work beyond that. You work twice as hard. And that you learn to forgive twice as much.

"Being an adolescent, a child, is of course very difficult. And certainly you have touched upon all of the problems that parents dread. But you owe your parents a responsibility, an obligation.

"Mr. Brafman again indicated to me that he has never met parents who have exhibited such great concern and devotion to a child. And I've seen them here on each occasion that you have been brought out in handcuffs and seen the anguish on their faces. You have a responsibility ahead of you. Someday you will emerge from prison. And it is my hope that the words that you expressed today will find meaning in a life well spent, a life dedicated to making up for participating in the loss of another life."

Now everyone who had intended to speak had

spoken, and it was time for Judge Corriero to formally read the sentence.

"The sentence of this court will be a maximum sentence of ten years' imprisonment with a minimum of three years four months."

Daphne showed no emotion as the words were uttered and her immediate fate sealed.

After the sentencing, Brafman walked over to the McMorow family and said that he would like to extend his condolences. They accepted, and as Margaret walked away, she commented to Joan on what a nice man he was.

Some people always look for the good, Joan said later about her mother, even in the face of absolute evil.

Shortly after, Sarah Hines took on another assignment. As a result, she would not be associated with the case, if any other issues would later arise that needed to be litigated. In July 1998, she was replaced by a new prosecutor.

CHAPTER 23

The DA's office was not open to a plea bargain for Christopher, as it had been for Daphne. The attorneys were convinced that Christopher had committed the crime, and they thought they had a good case against him. Typically, in a case with two or more defendants, the most culpable does not get a plea deal.

Pretrial proceedings were held during September and October of 1998 in Judge Corriero's courtroom. In attendance were ADAs Matthew Bogdanos and Richard Plansky; Christopher's defense attorney, Arnold Kriss; and Daphne's defense attorney, Ben Brafman.

Bogdanos was now the new lead prosecutor, having taken over this position from Sarah Hines. Known as relentless and untiring in the hundreds of cases he had prosecuted as an assistant district attorney in Manhattan since 1988, Bogdanos had other impressive credentials. He held both a master's degree in classics and a law degree from Columbia University, in New York City, and a second master's degree, in strategic studies, from the Army War College. He was also a competitive boxer and a classics scholar. Although some people called him "significantly challenged" in the bedside-manner and social-graces departments, Bogdanos was, nevertheless, a riveting and eloquent prosecutor who would do anything to bring bad guys to justice. Good-looking, solid, and a lean-and-mean machine, he was laser-focused and eloquent, a prosecutor a defendant might justifiably fear.

(Several years after the trial, as a consequence of the September 11, 2001, terrorist attacks, Bogdanos was recalled to military duty, as a Marine Corps Reservist colonel. His charge was to head counterterrorist operations in Afghanistan and later in Iraq, where he served several tours of duty. While in Iraq, he was determined to get to the bottom of what happened to the antiquities that had been stolen from the Iraq National Museum in Baghdad during the United States invasion. In his customarily thorough and relentless fashion, he uncovered and documented many eye-opening facts, which he detailed in his book, the highly regarded *Thieves of Baghdad*. Royalties from the book are being donated to the Iraq Museum.)

On September 3, 1998, during the pretrial hearing, Bogdanos stated to Judge Corriero that he had been meeting with Daphne in jail at Spofford. She had intimated that she wanted to testify at Christopher's trial. Her motivation was to clear her conscience. She wanted to get right with what went down so that when she was released from prison, she would be able to go on with her life. She said, said Bogdanos, that she believed in the "cleansing power of confession." Bogdanos stated that prosecutors would continue to meet with her, but as of now, she was leaning toward testifying, in defiance of her lawyer's advice.

An angry Brafman asserted that he would do

everything in his power to dissuade Daphne from testifying. In his opinion, if she testified, she would reverse the emotional progress she was making in jail. Furthermore, he feared that she might be coerced into saying something on the stand that might jeopardize her standing with the parole board. He stated firmly that even if Daphne was to be subpoenaed by the prosecution, he would advise her to invoke her Fifth Amendment right to remain silent so as not to incriminate herself in any way.

Corriero emphasized that Daphne was a "pivotal witness to both sides" and that her testimony would be of great importance. He told Bogdanos that he would give the DA's office every opportunity to convince Daphne of the potential magnitude of her testimony.

At each hearing during those months, the two sides proved so contentious that Corriero had to admonish them to act civilly or risk derailing the proceedings. He told the lawyers that he had never seen so much personal animosity between two sides in a case before—about major issues, as well as petty matters. Citing one particularly rancorous interchange, he pointed out that when Bogdanos asked for a trial delay, Kriss accused the prosecutor of trying to ruin his practice.

One of the major issues over which the two sides clashed was whether or not to allow into evidence some of the statements Daphne made on the night of the murder, particularly those in which she placed blame squarely on the shoulders of Christopher. The defense wanted to cast doubt on the accuracy of this statement by describing Daphne as a "drunken liar," which Kriss called her in pretrial hearings.

On October 1, Corriero stated that an edited part of Daphne's confession, including the statements in which Daphne admitted to having kicked Michael's feet out from under him, while Christopher stabbed him repeatedly, could be submitted. Kriss was outraged, and once again questioned the validity of Daphne's statements. He maintained that she was too drunk that night and couldn't be counted on to give a truthful version of the events. Corriero told Kriss that he could challenge the veracity of Daphne's statements during the trial.

CHAPTER 24

A trial date of November 9, 1998, was set—nearly one year and six months after the murder was committed. Christopher was to be tried as an adult by a jury of twelve men and women and sentenced as a juvenile by Judge Corriero.

The day before the trial began, one newspaper proclaimed that the teenager who was accused of the "mutilation murder of a middle-aged drinking buddy in a drunken rage" might need a miracle not to get life in prison.

Everyone waited to see if miracles really do happen.

SUPREME COURT   NEW YORK COUNTY
        TRIAL TERM   PART 73

THE PEOPLE OF THE STATE OF NEW YORK:
Indictment No. 4943/97
-against- :

Charge: Murder 2
CHRISTOPHER VASQUEZ, : Defendant.

111 Centre Street
New York, New York 10013
NOVEMBER 9, 1998 et seq

B E F O R E:
HONORABLE MICHAEL CORRIERO
Justice of the Supreme Court and a jury

A P P E A R A N C E S:
(For the People:)
ROBERT MORGENTHAU ESQ.,
District Attorney,
One Hogan Place
New York, New York 10013
BY: MATTHEW BOGDANOS &
RICHARD PLANSKY, ESQS.
Assistant District Attorneys

(For the Defendant)
ARNOLD KRISS, ESQ.
123 Williams Street
New York, New York

Anna L. Bogier, R.P.R.
Senior Court Reporter

The first day of the trial was a cold, drab Monday morning. The windowless courtroom was filled to capacity. The media, interested observers, and the extended families of the Vasquezes and the McMorrows were in attendance. The McMorrows sat on the left-hand side facing the judge; the Vasquezes on the right. Not a sound could be heard. It was as if everyone had agreed ahead of time that small talk was out of place.

Nervous anticipation was palpable, as was a slightly acrid scent, the smell of fear.

Members of the McMorrow family had been escorted into the courtroom through a back door in order to avoid the press, who had positioned themselves outside the main courtroom doors. Christopher, wearing a tie and gray flannel jacket, looked small and meek at the defense table. His face showed no expression. His body was stock-still.

Seasoned courtroom observers believe that opening statements can make or break a case. If done skillfully, these persuasive arguments can resonate in the jurors' minds throughout the proceedings, predisposing them to view the events as truth—whether or not during the trial, the attorneys prove that those events actually took place. On the other hand, a poorly crafted opening argument or one, for example, that promises to prove something beyond a reasonable doubt—but which ultimately doesn't deliver—can cause jurors to negate even some of the most compelling testimony. Like a person yearning to be wooed, a jury craves to be won over, persuaded, and ultimately convinced—but if along the way, they discern dishonesty, either in the form of exaggerations or outright falsehoods, their fury is ferocious and unbridled, like a lover deceived, and they punish the evildoer by turning fervently in the other direction.

Judge Corriero entered the courtroom. Everyone rose respectfully, then sat down. He immediately began the proceeding, speaking in a straightforward, yet earnest, manner. He reminded the jurors that during the jury-selection process, he had told them that if they were selected for this jury, there would be two judges in this courtroom. At this moment, he went on to say, there were, in fact, two judges. "I am one. I am the judge of the law." He told the jurors that they were required to follow the law as he gave it to them, whether they agreed with it or not. Elaborating on this idea, he stated that the jurors should not bring to court any preconceived notions of what they believed was the law, or what they thought the law should be. "You must follow the law as I give it to you."

He continued by asserting that they were also judges in this courtroom. They were the judges of the facts. It would be up to them to decide exactly what took place in the early-morning hours of May 23.

He paused for a moment. Then he reminded the jurors that they would be deciding the facts of the case, in the same manner as they should expect him to preside over this trial—"fairly, impartially, objectively, without fear, without passion, without sympathy, without prejudice."

Pointing out that this case had received some notoriety, he urged the jurors not to be intimidated by the press. He told them that together, they would make sure that justice was rendered in this case. And what did he mean by justice? Justice meant that whatever verdict they rendered, they based it on the law as he gave it to them and on the facts as they found them. Only they, he said, would decide the guilt or innocence of the defendant based on the evidence. "You and you alone are the sole and exclusive judges of the facts."

The judge then explained the meaning of evidence. He stated that evidence was the testimony of witnesses under oath, as well as any physical exhibits that were introduced during the course of the trial. Evidence was also any stipulations or agreements that may have been entered into between the lawyers with respect to the facts in this case.

Things that were not evidence, he pointed out, were, for example, statements that were made by lawyers during the jury-selection process or in the course of opening or closing remarks. Dramatic input from a lawyer, he asserted, "doesn't add one thing to evidence. The mere asking of a question (by a lawyer) about a certain subject matter, the way in which the question is phrased, or the dramatic input of the lawyer with respect to the question adds nothing to the evidence."

Turning his attention to the lawyers, he urged them to make any objections during the trial that they wished, because objections were their responsibility and because it was important for them to bring to his attention any concerns that they have about evidence being offered in violation of the Rules of Evidence.

The judge then focused on the jurors and asked them to suppose that a lawyer asked a witness a question and a lawyer made an objection to the question.

"My responsibility," he said, "would be to either sustain the objection," which meant that the witness should not answer the question, or overrule the objection, which meant that the witness may answer the question.

The judge also pointed out that if he was not quick enough on a objection and a witness answered a question before he had a chance to rule, he would instruct the jurors to disregard the answer. He told the jurors that the answer would be struck from the record, and although they may have heard the answer, they must not use that information in arriving at a verdict. He emphasized that they should not factor that answer in when determining the guilt or innocence of the defendant. "You must disregard it entirely."

The judge continued by reminding the jurors that anything that they saw or heard outside of the courtroom was not evidence, and must therefore be disregarded. Also, during a trial, he pointed out, there would be items, physical objects, and documents that might be marked for identification. "If a lawyer wants to ask a witness to clarify a point or wants to ask a witness about something that is contained in a document . . . , in order to identify that document for the record, we will mark 'it for identification.' Now that document may or may not ultimately come into evidence. If it doesn't come into evidence, then you can't consider that document or anything about it in the context of the deliberations in the case."

He reminded the jurors once again that this case would certainly be reported in the media. He told the jurors not to read or listen to anything about the case during the proceedings. If any jurors accidentally read something touching on this case, he asked them to bring it to the court's attention because he needed to know whether or not this information was affecting them in any way.

Corriero asserted that it was up to the jurors to decide which of the witnesses to believe and how much of any witness's testimony to believe. It was also up to them to decide when a witness was telling the truth and when a witness was lying, or when a witness was simply mistaken. All of these things, he pointed out, were the responsibility of the jury.

Corriero explained that opening statements would follow. Opening statements, he pointed out, were simply outlines of what the lawyers claimed the evidence would reveal as it unfolded during the course of the trial. Opening statements were designed to give an overview of the case because the case would come in piecemeal. The lawyers, he said, would use opening statements to give an overview of the charges and the evidence.

The judge told the court that the district attorney would make his statement first and that the burden of proof rested with him. "He must tell you what he expects to prove and how he expects to prove it—through what witnesses and exhibits, because the defendant is presumed to be innocent of the charges against him. The defense has no burden to prove anything to you."

After the DA made his case, said Corriero, the defense would make his opening statements. When he had completed his remarks, it would be up to the DA to present his direct case. What that meant was that the district attorney would call witnesses to sustain the charges that had been brought against the defendant. After the prosecution presented its direct case, the defense would have the opportunity to cross-examine the witnesses presented in support of the direct case. Then the defense was given the opportunity to call witnesses; although, because the defendant was presumed to be innocent, there was no responsibility on the part of the defense attorney to call any witnesses at all, "but if the defense calls witnesses, then he is bound by the very same rules that the prosecution is bound by in support of the testimony of the witnesses." When a witness had finished testifying on direct examination, said Corriero, the prosecutor had the right to cross-examine that witness.

Corriero then told jurors what his definition of a trial was. "A trial is kind of [a] controlled friction between two adversarial parties, direct examination, cross-examination, and it's through this process that we believe the truth will emerge that twelve people can agree on what happened."

Corriero said that to decide the facts in this case—whether a witness was being truthful or not, for example—jurors should use common sense and reason. Everything that was done in this courtroom should be based on these two concepts.

After the defense had called witnesses, said Corriero, if he chose, the DA could present any "additional evidence in the form of rebuttal, and then we'll turn to the defense again . . . and at the conclusion of all the evidence . . . I will give the lawyers a final opportunity to summarize the evidence from their point of view."

He reminded the jurors that since the district attorney had the burden of proof, he would go last. The defense attorney would be called upon first to summarize the evidence and to suggest the reasons why the defendant was not guilty. The prosecution would suggest the reasons why the defendant was guilty based upon the evidence. "If you find that any argument that is urged by either of them is reasonable, logical, based on the evidence as you recall it, then you're free to adopt that reasoning in the course of arriving at your verdict."

Concluding his remarks, the judge said that at the end of the trial, he would define the crime with which the defendant had been charged and would give guidelines to help in determining the credibility and the reliability of the information that had been given to them in the form of testimony under oath and physical exhibits introduced during the course of the trial. He told the jurors that their verdict had to be unanimous. "Focus on the issues," he said, "and I'm sure that you will render a verdict that speaks the truth."

When the judge finished speaking, it seemed as if a little more air had suddenly filled the room—as if all the people in the courtroom had been holding their collective breath and now let out a sigh of relief. As difficult and heart-wrenching as the trial might turn out to be, at least it was beginning, and the terror of anticipation would finally come to an end.

"We turn now to Mr. Bogdanos," Corriero stated, "on behalf of the people of the state of New York, to make his opening remarks."

Bogdanos wasted no time. He strode to the front of the courtroom and immediately began laying out his case. Standing tall and looking directly at the jury, he began, "On May 23, 1997, Michael McMorrow was forty-four years old. He was just one week shy of his forty-fifth birthday. He was a good-humored, gentle man. He lived with his eighty-one-year-old mother on Second Avenue between Ninety-first and Ninety-second Streets."

Michael McMorrow, Bogdanos went on to say, "wasn't going to invent a cure for cancer. He wasn't going to write the next Pulitzer Prize–winning novel, but he got up for work every morning, had his cup of coffee, kissed his mother good-bye, and then he went to go to work at Sir Realty. He was a salesman at a real estate company on Seventy-sixth Street, just off Central Park West."

Bogdanos then described a man who, he said, was subject to the frailties of the human condition. "Mr. McMorrow drank, including drinking a lot, daily." That night, he "had a blood alcohol level of .31, three times the legal limit, so you know that he was drunk, very drunk." He also "succumbed to the vanity of middle age and he had worn a hairpiece." The ADA told the jurors that when McMorrow drank, he became even more jovial than usual and often made pronouncements about the madness of the world, "the madness of modern-day society." He would look at you, said Bogdanos, as he was making a toast and ask you if you were part of that madness. He mentioned that although

McMorrow went to work daily, and although he played in a weekly softball league on weeknights, most other nights, Michael McMorrow could be found in Central Park drinking with people that he met there.

Bogdanos stated that most of the time, Michael drank with buddies in Strawberry Fields, right around Seventy-third Street. He would enter the park, said Bogdanos, from Central Park West, at Seventy-second Street, pass the "Imagine Mosaic," and sit down on the grassy expanse. "Most nights, you could find Michael McMorrow and his friends, or it's more appropriate to say acquaintances, and they were his acquaintances from all walks of life, all colors, all shapes, all sizes." Bogdanos pointed out that however different in appearance and background the group might be, they all had some things in common. Each and every one of them liked to drink. They liked to talk about modern-day society, and they liked to watch the sun. "This is what Michael McMorrow did on most nights. It's what Michael McMorrow did on Thursday night, May 22, 1997."

On his last morning alive, Bogdanos told the courtroom, McMorrow kissed his mother good-bye, went to work, and afterward walked to Strawberry Fields, where he met up with his drinking companions. That night, they were drinking their beverage of choice, Guinness.

The ADA then switched his attention to the teens. "Over on the other side of town, literally and figuratively, were two youngsters, kids, whatever, people, two 15-year-olds, Christopher Vasquez and Daphne Abdela, two 15-year-olds from private schools with too much time on their hands."

Bogdanos went on to say that at around eight-thirty that evening, while McMorrow was already in Strawberry Fields having his first beverage of the night, the teens were at Blockbuster, renting a movie. He told the jurors that they would see a video in a little while from the surveillance camera at Blockbuster. It would show, he promised, how the two conducted themselves just hours before the murder. But what it wouldn't show, he stated, was what they ultimately did that night. Then, Bogdanos stated poignantly, and with sorrow in his voice, "Fate, circumstance, and sheer random chance brought all three of them together in one night of absolute horror."

The attorney then summarized the events of the evening, stating that at around nine o'clock, the teens Rollerbladed into the park and went directly to Strawberry Fields. Once there, "a look of recognition passed between Daphne and Michael. It appears that they may have met at an Alcoholics Anonymous meeting. Yes," Bogdanos went on to say, "yes, you'll learn that Miss Abdela, at the age of fifteen, was already on her way toward being an alcoholic."

After he let that statement sink in, he continued by pointing out that at around 10:00 P.M., Daphne left Strawberry Fields to buy some beer. As she skated off, she ran into a police officer at the entrance to the park. "She falls; she's already well on her way to another drunk." She hit her head on the pavement, and the officer asked her if she was okay, if he should call an ambulance. She declined, and after a minute or two, she continued on her beer run.

Bogdanos stated that soon after Daphne returned to the park, a police officer, Fernando Losada, who was on scooter patrol, went into Strawberry Fields to make sure that no one was drinking out of an open container. Of course, most of the people were, so he gave them a warning. "If you stay, I'm going to confiscate your beer, or if you go, you can keep it."

A no-brainer. All of the approximately twenty people who had been gathered on the lawn dispersed as soon as they could get themselves together. Some exited the park through Seventy-second Street; some walked south, some went north. Some were going home, and some, perhaps, were on their way to the next watering hole.

As McMorrow walked to the northern end of Strawberry Fields, Bogdanos stated, he took a path that led down to the drive, where he could continue on to the East Side, where he lived. He was heading home.

However, said Bogdanos, staring directly at the jurors, "he never makes it home because right behind him, following right behind him, is Christopher Vasquez, and behind Mr. Vasquez is Daphne Abdela, and in her hands is a bag with beer, so the three of them, at about eleven o'clock, leave together, just the three of them."

Then, taking his time and emphasizing each word, Bogdanos stated, "Mr. McMorrow is never seen alive again." Alive, then dead. A life. A life no more. Stark, dark reality.

The ADA then stated that he was able to piece together what happened that night from several sources: the forensics, the recovery of the murder weapon, the autopsy, and the statements made by Daphne. However, he declared, there was one thing he would never be able to figure out—*why* it happened. No one, he suggested, would ever be able to say why.

Bogdanos then recounted each and every knife wound to Michael's body, pausing dramatically between each blow. In the extended and repeated silences, the words turned into sensory images, and many in the courtroom were brought to tears by the sheer horror and revulsion of the details—broken nose; fractured ribs and sternum caused by ferocious knife stabbings; over five slashes across the face, so "viciously that the medical examiner can't tell you how many times across his face and eyes."

He then stated that after Daphne kicked Michael's feet out from under him and Michael fell on the back of his head, Christopher took a knife, and with three more slashes to the neck, severed the man's jugular vein—not his artery—so there wasn't a lot of blood. Michael was still alive, and Christopher was not yet done. Pointing to the defendant, Bogdanos stated that Christopher then inflicted at least seventeen more stab wounds to Michael's abdomen before he gutted him so that his intestines came out of his stomach. But still, declared Bogdanos, Christopher was not done.

The ADA described how Christopher tried to cover up his crime by attempting to sever Michael's right wrist. Yes, he said, Christopher tried to cut off Michael's hand, but he was unsuccessful. Why? Certainly not for lack of trying, but because the knife wasn't up to the task. "Christopher was, the knife wasn't," and so the two of them—Daphne and Christopher—"push Mr. McMorrow into the lake, where he later died faceup in that murky water."

Bogdanos then told the jurors that during the course of the trial, they would see a photograph—and he apologized that they had to see something so gruesome, but, he said, it's the evidence. He also apologized ahead of time for the fact that he was going to show them a video of the crime scene. Again, he added, "it's the evidence. It's what he did and it's what will be proven. . . ."

Continuing, Bogdanos stated that in order to further cover up his crime, Christopher took the man's wallet and burned any identification. As a result, when McMorrow was found, he didn't have any identification on him whatsoever. He was a John Doe until the police were able to identify him as Michael McMorrow by "a couple of business cards that remain at the crime scene for detectives to find halfway."

After describing in detail the grisly act, Bogdanos reported that the teens then Rollerbladed away, "leaving Mr. McMorrow faceup in that water right by the gazebo, blood everywhere."

The lawyer mentioned that the detectives who went to Christopher's apartment saw a white bloodstained sock on the floor of his bedroom and under it, a shirt with a bloodstain on it. Under that was a pair of pants with a bloodstain on them. Inside the pants, Bogdanos pointed out, the detectives found a knife, which showed no trace of blood because it had been wiped clean—later, after DNA testing, it was revealed to have a microscopic spot of blood on it "consistent with a mixture of Michael McMorrow and Christopher Vasquez." Bogdanos stated that Christopher had "an injury consistent with a punch on the right side of his face. It seems that Michael McMorrow got one shot in before he was murdered." And, said Bogdanos, Christopher also had an abrasion on his right hand, "consistent with a punch, where he punched Mr. McMorrow." Bogdanos went on to tell the jury about the two 911 calls, about the officers arriving at the Majestic, and about Daphne taking them to the body.

Bogdanos concluded his opening remarks by declaring that no one single piece of evidence would convict the defendant, but rather it would be the accumu-lation of many pieces of evidence that would do the job: the knife in the defendant's bedroom, the fact that the defendant was following Mr. McMorrow at 11:00 P.M., the fact that the two teens were Rollerblading away from the murder scene shortly after screams were heard by police officers, the fact that the defendant had injuries consistent with a fight, the fact that the defendant was covered in blood and that his blood was at the crime scene, and the admission by the co-defendant of her own guilt and her statement that Christopher was the person who did the killing as she assisted "by kicking [Michael's] feet out from under him causing him to fall backwards, as the defendant stabbed again and again . . . Michael McMorrow."

Bogdanos stated that at the end of the trial, he would return to sum up his argument and to ask the jurors to return a verdict of guilty to murder in the second degree. He went on to explain that there were two separate counts of murder for them to consider. One, under an intentional theory, stated that the defendant intended to cause the death of Michael McMorrow—that his conscious aim or objective was to do that. The second murder count, under a depraved indifference to human life theory, stated that the defendant committed murder, although it may not have been his conscious aim or objective. The ADA pointed out that that would be a question for the jurors to decide: what was Christopher's state of mind at the time he murdered Michael McMorrow? But no matter what Christopher's state of mind might have been, Bogdanos asserted, "we should make it absolutely clear on this. I will ask you to return a verdict of guilty of murder against Mr. Vasquez, and I shall do that for one reason, and one reason alone." He paused, looked directly at the jury, and then made his final, dramatic utterance: "Because he is."

Bogdanos remained lock-eyed with the jurors for a few seconds longer, before returning to his seat at the table. He had given it his best shot and hoped that the jury would come to see things his way. He desperately wanted to win this case, not only because he believed he was on the side of the truth, but because if he did, perhaps the McMorrows would one day be able to sleep through the night, if not peacefully, then at least upon awakening, find some small comfort in the fact that justice had been served. Admittedly, this was a meager consolation, but it was the only one he could offer, and the only one they could hope for.

Without wasting any time, Corriero asked the defense to come to the floor and begin his opening statements. Arnold Kriss took his time before beginning, possibly to give the jurors the opportunity to clear their minds and focus afresh. He asked the jurors to sit back and listen carefully to what he was going to say. He promised that his version would be the one they would accept as the truth.

After praising the jury for agreeing to serve, he noted that a lot of people tried not to serve, stating that many individuals "stepped back," whereas "you, ladies and gentlemen of the jury, stepped forward." He said that it would be their presence in the courtroom over the next several weeks that would make the jury system work and come to a fair and just verdict. He then told the jurors that they were intelligent, questioning people and that they had a commitment to justice. "This is a New York jury, a smart jury. And this case requires an intelligent jury to come to a judgment." He then acknowledged how difficult his own role would be—to defend a person that the assistant district attorney had just said "committed a terrible crime, either by himself or with somebody." He urged the jury not to accept what the prosecutor had said as the truth. Even though the prosecution might be "well-intentioned," what they said might not be factual. Even if they truly believed it was, Kriss stated, that didn't mean it was. He reminded the jurors that they had to do something that was required by the court. "They must prove beyond a reasonable doubt that Christopher Vasquez took Michael McMorrow's life." The burden never shifted to the defense, he said. Never at all.

Kriss reminded the jurors that even the most articulate and intelligent opening was not evidence. Evidence, he stated, would come from witnesses. It would come from direct questions asked by the prosecutor and by himself in cross-examination.

The attorney firmly stated that the facts of the case did not support the charges of murder that were brought against Christopher. The facts, he told the jurors, would tell a different story. "The facts," Kriss said slowly and deliberately, "will point clearly to Daphne Abdela as the perpetrator who took the life of Michael McMorrow" and that it was she, not Christopher, who covered up the crime. It was she who pointed the finger of blame at Christopher, but, according to Kriss, that scenario was simply not true.

At the prosecutors' table, the two ADAs looked stunned. They believed that Kriss was going to use an EED defense—the boy was suffering from "extreme emotional disturbance"—and they were prepared to counter that with details from the psychiatrists' reports, allowable under an EED defense. They had no idea the defense was going to put the blame squarely on Daphne. Now, all they could do was hear Kriss out and think fast and strategically how to counter his argument.

Kriss again reminded the jurors that he did not have to prove beyond a reasonable doubt that Daphne was the murderer. After all, he was not an assistant district attorney. As a defense attorney, he stated, "all I have to do is raise a reasonable doubt.

"This is a case of murder," declared Kriss. It was an act of violence that not only ended Michael McMorrow's life, but one that continued even after he was dead. It was brutal and horrific. But, he said, what must be answered was *who* committed this act. *Who*, beyond a reasonable doubt, did it? Did Christopher Vasquez, a then-fifteen-year-old, do this? Kriss stated emphatically no.

The defense attorney reiterated that there were two counts of murder that would be considered in the case. However, he added, regardless of which count was being considered, each must be proven beyond a reasonable doubt. "Just because the prosecution in its opening stated that Christopher Vasquez did this crime, that doesn't mean he did. If there is one reasonable doubt—not two or three or four—and that doubt is based on evidence or lack of evidence, you, the jurors, must find Christopher not guilty." It took only one reasonable doubt.

Kriss told the jurors that there were no eyewitnesses to the crime. But, he said, the crime scene would speak volumes, even though it was not a living thing. "It's science. Science will tell you certain things that happened down there." He urged the jurors to pay close attention to the criminal scientists who would come and testify. They should listen carefully to the medical examiner, who would be a "very, very important witness." She, Kriss stated, would tell the cause of Michael McMorrow's death.

"Regrettably," Kriss went on to say, "Michael died of multiple stab wounds," but sympathy must be kept out of the courtroom. "Because these wounds are so shocking . . . it had to [have been] done by someone who was so out of control who intentionally inflicted [some] wounds on a dead body." He called the act "so diabolical. So wanton. So inhuman. . . ." He declared that the evidence would clearly point to Daphne Abdela as the murderer—alone—and that she—and not Christopher—covered up this crime by placing Michael McMorrow into the Central Park Lake.

"In murder cases," Kriss said, "there's always a theory why someone is killed—generally, greed, jealousy, hate, random acts of violence, hostility to explode in a person and cause the death of another individual." And although the prosecution did not have to prove motive, as jurors "you will also be able to consider the lack of motive on the part of Christopher Vasquez to commit this murder, and this is an important consideration." His client, he said, had no prior relationship with Michael McMorrow and no feelings of hate or any other emotion toward the man. None whatsoever. There was absolutely no proof, he stated again, that before the date of the murder, Christopher knew Michael, either directly or indirectly.

Kriss portrayed Christopher as a normal teenager—one who went to school, came home, and went out to enjoy himself after his studies were completed. On the day of the murder, Kriss said, Christopher attended classes at Beekman, then went home, just like any other teenager. He changed his clothes, put on a baseball cap, "a blue-and-white soccer shirt and baggy jeans" and wore "shoes called sketches [*sic*], carried a beeper." But, declared Kriss, Christopher was "also a not-so-normal teenager—he never missed a curfew unless he had permission to stay out with his friends."

Kriss told the jurors that Christopher's mother would be a witness, part of the defense, and that she would state that on the afternoon of May 22, she continued to beep her son to come home for dinner, but that Christopher didn't respond. She became extremely upset, even frantic. Kriss mentioned that Christopher had never missed responding to a page before. "Ms. Reidy will tell you how, when she hadn't heard from

Christopher, she called the Abdela household—and the phone records will support this—and that while phone calls were being made in and out of the Vasquez and Abdela households, here's what was happening. Christopher and Daphne, we know, went to Blockbuster—a video of the store will show this—but the two never watched the video they rented. Instead, they went to the park. Two witnesses in the park that night, Bradford Harriman and Victoria Donnelly, both friends of Michael's, would be taking the stand later and testify that Daphne asked for drugs and acid and that she offered to buy beer for a group of people, which included Michael." Kriss stated that other witnesses would testify to Daphne's aggressiveness at a deli toward two men "who had nothing to do with Central Park, who had nothing to do with Michael McMorrow, who had nothing to do with Daphne Abdela or Christopher Vasquez, just two New Yorkers just like yourself, just like myself, going out to get a newspaper, a pack of cigarettes, beer, whatever it may be." Kriss declared that when Daphne rolled up on her Rollerblades to buy beer, she challenged the much bigger and older gentleman who was in the store. "She challenged an adult that she didn't know." The jury would also hear, he promised, how Christopher attempted to calm "the raging Daphne."

Kriss mentioned that Officer Losada, who saw Christopher and Daphne skating in the park earlier in the evening, thought that Daphne was a male, as did Manuel Guzman from Blockbuster Video, as did another witness from whom the jury would hear later. "Officer Losada will tell you that Christopher's demeanor was calm, and several witnesses would reinforce that Christopher was just there [as a] nonentity." Kriss told the jurors that a videotape would show the secluded gazebo. The video, he promised, would give them a sense of what the place looked like and of what happened there, and, he emphasized, a picture was worth a thousand words. What happened at that lake? he asked. "That is where the forensics and the criminologists will be of help." The evidence would show, Kriss promised, that Christopher did not participate in or aid in causing Michael's death. He admitted that yes, Christopher was there, but that, he said emphatically, did not mean he committed any crime. Being there—before, during, or after a murder—did not make a person guilty of a crime.

Evidence would show, and evidence would raise a reasonable doubt, stated Kriss, that Christopher did not kill Michael, and evidence would also show that "Daphne Abdela did this murder, even though there was no eyewitness. This was a case of following the blood. The evidence would show that Daphne had Michael's blood all over her major Rollerblade wheel. It was also on her ankle supports. Mr. McMorrow's blood was up there," said Kriss. "And nowhere was there any of Mr. McMorrow's blood on Christopher's Rollerblades . . . and if Christopher committed this bloody crime, there is no doubt that Michael McMorrow's blood should have been there on his Rollerblades." But there was none of McMorrow's blood on Christopher's Rollerblades when Detective Gannon recovered them from Christopher's apartment.

Kriss paused and then addressed the jurors directly: "Ladies and gentlemen of the jury, this is a terrible crime. But this is an up-close-and-personal killing. Face, neck, chest. Those are all the antemortem [or] predeath wounds. Just that alone, forget about anything else, just think about that." He remained silent for a few moments letting the jurors form an image in their minds of a killing that took place up close. "You've got to get up to somebody so close over their body and do this," he said, "and thus the blood should be on the Rollerblades of the killer. On Daphne's, yes; on Christopher's, it was not."

Kriss mentioned that Dr. Alandy, the state's medical examiner, would tell the jury that when the wounds were inflicted on McMorrow, he was flat on his back. There was not one cut on McMorrow's forearms or hands. In other words, there were no defensive wounds on Michael. As a result, the perpetrator—the real murderer—would have to have been up close to the helpless body in the defenseless position, and with her Rollerblades on his body, slashed and cut at him while he was defenseless on his back. Kriss maintained that there could not have been any wiping off of blood from Christopher's Rollerblades because the DNA would have still shown some traces— and, he said, it did. It showed that only the blood of Christopher was on his Rollerblades. So, he asked, how could he have been up close to Michael McMorrow and yet have no blood on his blades?

Kriss stated that DNA would show that the two men did not engage in a struggle or fight, as evidenced by there being no scrapings under the fingernails. There was no DNA of Michael's found under Christopher's fingernails—Christopher's hands had been bagged on the night of the murder to preserve evidence—nor were there any scrapings of Christopher's DNA under Michael's fingernails, which were checked the next morning during the autopsy. However, he went on to say, as incredible as this might sound, Daphne's hands were not bagged—never, even after she was arrested and was in custody. So, he said, science cannot tell us whether or not she engaged in a struggle with Mr. McMorrow, but science had clearly shown us that Christopher and

Michael emphatically did not engage in a struggle. "That much we know."

Kriss pointed out that although Christopher sustained injuries—a cut to his finger and another to the area of his right ear, a buckle fracture to his little finger, and a laceration to his right shoulder on his upper back—the jury should not draw any conclusions as to how those injuries were sustained until the facts of the case came out. There would be a reasonable doubt, Kriss declared, as to whether or not McMorrow and Vasquez had any physical confrontation at all that night. The cut on Christopher's left index finger was bleeding so profusely at the lake site that he dropped blood on the path, on the sidewalk, and on top of the path, and he continued to bleed in Daphne's apartment, after leaving Daphne's house, on his way home, on the clothes that Daphne had given him, and which he wore home, and in his own apartment. Kriss promised that the significance of this blood trail would be apparent soon. "Wait until the end of the case" to decide whether the injuries were sustained in a fight or in another way altogether.

Kriss affirmed that the jurors would hear time and time again from the ADA about how Christopher wielded the knife and how Daphne kicked Michael's legs out from under him, causing Michael to fall. He pointed out that Daphne had told this version of events when she pleaded guilty to the crime of manslaughter in the first degree. But he begged the jurors not to take her statement at face value, but instead "determine whether it's reliable, whether it's truthful, whether it's factually possible that this struggle took place as she stated to this court, to Judge Corriero on March 11, 1998."

Then, in one razor-sharp, unambiguous sentence, Kriss gave his version of what happened at the Central

Park Lake. "After Daphne coldly murdered Michael McMorrow, she then pushed him into the lake."

Kriss urged the jurors not to "be fooled because Christopher Vasquez is a male that he did this. . . ." He described Daphne as five feet four inches or five feet five inches tall at the time, and weighing approximately 150 pounds. "She was tough, so tough, she challenged the adult males right in that convenience store. . . . She's so tough she added her nickname, ZED, *Z-E-D*, with some object on her leg. The evidence would demonstrate she was physically capable to do this [murder] by herself and push this poor man into this watery grave by herself. . . ." He asked the jury to think about this: If she *merely* kicked Michael McMorrow's legs from under him and didn't have any blood on her, why was she in the tub with Christopher? And why, if she had no blood on her and all she did was kick Michael's legs out from under him, why would she put her clothes in the washing machine? "I can understand Christopher's clothes, but I don't understand Daphne's clothes being washed by her." He stated that there would be testimony from the doorman at 115 Central Park West that he saw Daphne entering the apartment with blood on her hands and that there was nothing remarkable about Christopher's appearance. There would also be testimony from a porter at the Majestic who thought he saw two males Rollerblade into the lobby—but that he later learned that one was a female, and that person was, in fact, Daphne Abdela. And, Kriss said, there would be testimony from others who saw the chunky girl in the baggy pants that night who also thought she was a boy.

Kriss told the jury that the knife that the police officers found in Christopher's apartment might have been

Christopher's, but they were in the pants given to him by Daphne. Daphne gave Christopher a clean set of clothes to wear home, clothes that he did not have on while he was in Blockbuster, which can be seen in the video. "You must determine beyond a reasonable doubt whether it was Christopher Vasquez who wielded this knife or Daphne Abdela. The mere fact that [the prosecutors] say it, it ain't so. This is New York. Prove it to me."

Kriss concluded his opening remarks by stating: "The evidence will show that Christopher Vasquez was only a follower that night, being led around by the pit bull Daphne Abdela. The evidence will also show that Christopher was the dupe, the jerk, the one who, because of Daphne's efforts, now sits before you charged with murder in the second degree." He said he hoped the jury would "not only find that Daphne Abdela is the individual who did this diabolical, willful, and vicious act by herself, [but] also find, with this reasonable doubt or doubts, that Christopher Vasquez is the wrong person who is on trial for Michael McMorrow's murder."

In one last forceful remark, he declared: "Ladies and gentlemen of the jury, when the foreperson rises at the end of this case, the only verdict, the only just verdict, the justice in this case, the verdict that should and will be [is] that Christopher Vasquez is not guilty of the crime or crimes of murder in the second degree."

And with those words, Kriss thanked the court and sat down.

When Margaret McMorrow was called to the stand, all eyes turned to the frail eighty-two-year-old woman who had lived with her son. She rose unsteadily and walked to the witness-box, her legs heavily Ace bandaged and barely strong enough to carry her there.

Her eighty-two years showed like a curse. Asked by the prosecution to recall what took place on that Thursday morning, she said that she had awakened at her usual time, had a cup of coffee with her son, and then kissed him good-bye, as usual. She was then asked the names of her children and she replied in her lilting Irish brogue: "Joan, Anne, Charlie," and then, through sobs and with her hands covering her eyes, she stated, "Michael. Michael is gone." Tears streamed down the faces of some of the jurors.

That day, several witnesses were called to testify, including a police officer, a few Central Park regulars, and a video salesman from Blockbuster. Each one described Daphne as mannish, combative, belligerent, and brutish. They characterized Christopher as quiet, meek, and a follower.

After the first day of testimony ended, the jurors were led out of the courtroom. Once the door behind them was shut, chief prosecutor Bogdanos wasted no time speaking to Judge Corriero. He was livid. He said that in his opinion, Kriss had come dangerously close to being unethical by switching blame for the murder from Christopher to Daphne, and by saying that Christopher was merely an innocent bystander. Bogdanos contended that Kriss knew only too well that on the night Christopher was taken to Bellevue Hospital for evaluation, the boy had told four psychiatrists a different version of the events from the one Kriss had just posited in the courtroom. Bogdanos implied that since Kriss had read the interviews, he was on morally thin ground by pinning the murder on anyone other than Christopher.

Kriss immediately objected to Bogdanos's bringing up the psychiatrists' reports, stating emphatically that the judge had already ruled them "off limits." Corriero stopped the discussion at that point and said that he would ask the jurors the next day if they had read or heard about the reports.

The trial was covered by all the New York City newspapers. DEFENSE TACTICS ROCK "BABY-FACE" SLAY TRIAL, read the headline in the *Post*. The article detailed how a Manhattan courtroom "erupted in rancor yesterday" after Christopher Vasquez's lawyer, Arnold Kriss, switched blame for the murder of McMorrow from Christopher to Daphne. The article pointed out how several people—a cop, a video salesman, and several Central Park drinkers—all testified that Daphne was a "mannish, aggressive brute," and that Vasquez was her meek follower.

EX-GAL PAL BLAMED, read the *Daily News* headline. The article stated that lawyers for the former altar boy charged that the boy's "raging pit bull rich-kid ex-girlfriend" was the person who committed the murder. It stated that Daphne was up to at least her Rollerblades in blood. The article reported that Bogdanos, on the other hand, asserted that Christopher was the murderer and he did the killing with a folding knife, which, he admitted, wasn't up to the task of cutting off the victim's hand, but the boy was.

DEFENSE IN CENTRAL PARK CASE SAYS FRIEND WAS THE KILLER, read the *Times* headline. The article went on to report some of the gruesome details of the case. It noted that the killing shocked the city not only because of its brutality, but also because of the young age of the defendants.

CHAPTER 25

On the second day of the trial, November 10, employees of the Majestic took the stand, as did Officer Lee Furman. All gave details about the teens in the washroom. In gripping testimony, Furman described the two rubbing each other and washing each other in the tub, less than a half hour after the murder. Furman labeled Christopher the more aggressive of the two, "more confrontational and cagey," the one with a "fresh mouth and feisty demeanor." He described how after Christopher was fully dressed, he got right up in Furman's face, only an inch away, and screamed, "I'm not a wiseass. I'm not afraid of you." He said that Christopher was "very arrogant." Furman said that Christopher yelled, "Leave her alone; she didn't do anything" when the officers were escorting Daphne out of the utility room. In summing up Christopher's manner, Furman described him as having "a real wiseass attitude."

When asked to describe the bruises on both the teens' bodies, Furman stated that Daphne didn't have any abrasions that he could see, except for one on the back of her head. Christopher, on the other hand, Furman testified, had cuts and bruises all over his body—most visibly on his face, hand, and upper leg.

Furman reported that even though the tub water was a reddish blood color, he didn't think anything serious had taken place. The prosecutor asked him if the color of the water could have been caused by rust, to which he answered, "It was a blood color." Daphne, Furman stated, had assured him that the two had gotten injured Rollerblading and he believed her. "I just thought they were fooling around" in the tub.

After testimony for the day ended, the prosecution and the defense continued to jockey for position. Kriss stated to Judge Corriero that he wanted the jurors to hear all the statements Daphne made to the officers, because if they did, they would see that what she said was at odds with the forensic evidence. He wanted the jurors to hear how she had claimed that Michael McMorrow had given her a sliver of LSD two weeks before the murder and that she had hallucinated that she was driving a car through trees in Central Park. He also wanted jurors to know that while she was talking to police, she was highly intoxicated and had admitted that she suggested to Christopher to eviscerate him "so he'll sink because he's a fatty." Corriero said he would listen to arguments on those issues on Thursday, when the trial would resume.

As the McMorrow family were leaving the courtroom, Steve Dunleavy, longtime columnist for the *Post*, introduced himself and asked if he could have a brief interview with them. They agreed. The next day, his article appeared in the paper. He reported that "there was a bloodbath at the Majestic apartment building." He stated that two families sat eight feet apart in the courtroom "tensed as if every muscle was [*sic*] a piano wire." Dunleavy reported that Michael's brother, Charlie, told him that the murder was "like a bad episode out of *Law and Order*," and described his brother as having been "filleted like a fish."

Michael's mother, whom the columnist called "Maggie" in the newspaper, told Dunleavy in her "thick Irish brogue from County Leitrim," how much she missed her son. She recalled that he was always around, laughing and joking. "Oh, I miss him so."

Joanie, Michael's younger sister, told Dunleavy that she tried not to look at Christopher, but that she accidentally did sometimes, and "it makes you sick to your stomach." Describing her brother, she told Dunleavy, "My brother was one of a kind, oh, he had a lot of fun, loved a beer and was sometimes his own worst enemy. But I will never forget a television report that put *him* on trial. They gave the impression that Mike made a pass at Vasquez in the park that night. And that led to the disgusting way he died. . . . Well, if you knew Mike, you knew that wasn't him."

Dunleavy agreed, and reported that he did, indeed, know Michael, who had "poured more than two or three beers for me at a midtown saloon"—that Dunleavy frequented—"and there were more than two or three ladies he charmed."

Dunleavy went on to say that this wasn't "a ghastly ghetto gutting." Both the Vasquez family and the Abdela family gave all they could to their children. He admitted that it was hard not to feel the pain each family must be feeling. Then he went on to describe a third family—the McMorrows—who "struggled to get out of the poverty of Ireland, were lucky to get out of the poverty of the Bronx," but will forever be "bankrupt because there was a body in a lake that could hardly be recognized."

Dunleavy's article wasn't the only one to appear in the *Post* that day. Another column's headline read: BABY-FACED BUTCHER BLOODBATH. It showed a picture of each baby-faced teenager and detailed how Christopher and Daphne were "caught literally red-handed after the slaying of a drinking buddy. . . ."

Before the trial resumed on Thursday, November 12, the judge made several rulings that affected what could and could not be admitted as evidence during the trial. Corriero said he would allow jurors to hear the account that Daphne read in court on the date she pleaded guilty, as well as some of the conflicting statements she made about the murder. However, he denied Kriss's request to allow the jury to hear that Daphne called the cops "pigs" several times, that she reported that McMorrow had given her LSD weeks earlier, that she had stated that Christopher was "flipped out" on LSD on the night of the murder, or that she had told cops about her alcohol rehab treatments and her drug use. Corriero would also not allow the jurors to hear any information about Daphne's past violence toward family members and toward a boyfriend, calling all those statements hearsay.

In one statement that Daphne had made to the cops about a month after the murder, she stated that two weeks before the murder, Michael was swaggering up a path in Central Park, singing and talking to himself. She knew he was drunk. She gave him a beer, and he gave her and some friends rolling papers. Then, she said, she and Michael talked about drinking, about their families, and Michael spoke about being Irish. Then, according to Daphne, Michael talked about cocaine and LSD while they all were smoking and drinking. Daphne admitted to Michael that she had never taken LSD and asked him if he had any. He obliged by giving her a sliver. Daphne told the officers that she began hallucinating, imagining that she was driving a car through the trees. She admitted becoming paranoid and leaving the park, afraid that a person who had asked her for a cigarette was an undercover cop. Daphne also reported that she hadn't seen Michael again until the night he was killed.

Kriss strongly objected to some of Corriero's rulings, stating that many of the details—her violent outbursts and her drug and alcohol use—could help prove that it was Daphne—not Christopher—who mutilated and killed McMorrow. Kriss believed that if the jurors knew those things about her, they would see that her statement that she merely kicked out McMorrow's legs from under him, while Christopher wielded the knife, might not be the whole truth, or even part of it. He felt that her statements would "unmask" her as being a not credible witness.

The prosecution vowed to continue to fight the admission into evidence of the police statements.

CHAPTER 26

On the third day of the trial, Officer Furman continued his testimony, stating that Daphne was defiant and antagonistic when they arrived at the Abdela duplex. When her father came into the kitchen during the interrogation, Daphne told her father "to get the 'f—' out of here." Furman also reported that he saw some blood on her wristwatch and that the officers in the apartment had found Christopher's beeper and wallet in her room.

After Officer Furman completed his testimony, Officer Lawrence Moran took the stand. He testified that Daphne led him, other officers, and Mr. Abdela to where Mr. McMorrow's body lay floating in the lake, and that when she saw the body lit by Moran's flashlight, she screamed, "I tried to save you! I loved you! We were buds!" Moran stated that Daphne was extremely upset, crying, and looking around for someone to hold her up as she nearly fell to the ground when her knees buckled beneath her.

Moran's testimony was then briefly interrupted when Bogdanos asked Michael's family if they

wouldn't mind leaving the courtroom. He stated that
the graphic account that Moran was about to give, detailing the state of the body, might be too upsetting
for them. They left and testimony continued, with
Moran giving a detailed picture of Michael's mutilated body floating in the lake.

The next day, when Moran's testimony was reported in the papers, columnists called it "sympathetic to Daphne and a heavy blow to Christopher,"
because Moran had painted Daphne as vulnerable—
not a mannish thug—when she saw the corpse.

On November 13, the fourth day of testimony, a
video and photographs were introduced as evidence.
The photos were enlarged, in full color, and displayed
on a huge felt board. Both the video and photos
showed the butchered body of Michael. As the twelve-
person jury looked at the display, one woman juror
wept openly. Others grimaced. It was the first time
that photographs of the corpse were displayed,
adding dramatic and explicit details to the description the jurors had heard only in words up until that
time.

Before the photographs were displayed, Michael's
family members were once again asked to leave the
courtroom. "Ladies and gentlemen," Corriero told
the upset jurors, "these photos are in evidence to
show you the nature of the wounds in this case, and
certainly not for the purpose of inflaming you."

Detective Hal Sherman, from the police Crime
Scene Unit, was then called to the stand. He stated
that when he looked at the corpse at 3:00 A.M., he saw

wounds all over the man's torso. He added that the intestines had been removed. "A large portion of fat and other substances [were] coming out of the stomach." Sherman continued by giving specific details about the body, the crime scene, his work at the crime scene, and about the evidence he collected.

Several jurors were visibly upset listening to his testimony.

On November 16, the fifth day of the trial, the autopsy report of Dr. Maria Luz Alandy, the acting first deputy medical examiner, was admitted into evidence. Alandy stated that McMorrow was not yet dead when his forehead, eyelids, cheeks, and throat were slashed, time and time again, and that he was still alive when his jugular vein was sliced with a knife. Alandy stated that the cause of death was a knife wound that pierced McMorrow's heart and lungs and severed his aorta.

The doctor went on to testify that McMorrow was most likely on his back when the knife was thrust into his chest, seven times, one thrust ultimately causing his death. After he was already dead, Alandy went on to say, fifteen of the sixteen slashes to his abdomen were delivered.

On the sixth day of the trial, November 18, DNA expert Lawrence Quarino, a forensic scientist with the city medical examiner's office, was called to testify. He stated that on both sides of the four-inch blade of the folding knife owned by Christopher, there was the mingled blood of Christopher and Michael. He went on to say that none of Daphne's DNA was found in the blood on the knife. Quarino said that McMorrow's DNA could have gotten on the knife if he had merely touched the implement. Quarino testified that traces of blood were found on Daphne's right Rollerblade, and that they came from McMorrow. He posited that they could have gotten there when, as Daphne admitted in her plea bargain, she kicked the "bleeding man in the thigh," so he would fall.

Kriss, in an attempt to deflect blame from Christopher, raised the issue of how a bloodstained knife could have gotten into the pocket of the jeans lent to him by Daphne, which he wore home from Daphne's apartment that night after his pants had been washed in her washing machine. He also raised doubts about how, if Christopher had stabbed McMorrow over thirty times, there was no blood on the shirt he had worn that night. In response, Quarino suggested that any blood on Christopher's shirt could have been washed away in the washing machine.

Ending the day's testimony was Christopher's friend and fellow student at Beekman, Aryana Fernando, who testified that Christopher started packing a knife for protection after he had been beaten up by a gang on the subway. She said that he told her that "if it ever happened again, he'd have protection." She admitted, however, that he didn't say it with any anger or hostility in his voice.

On November 23, Judge Corriero once again blocked much of Kriss's attempts to admit Daphne's statements and past actions. He ruled as inadmissible details that Daphne was so violent and aggressive in the weeks before the murder that she "grabbed and slapped" her father, who then called the cops. He also ruled inadmissible statements from Elk Hotel doorman Haresh Patel that Daphne had raced out of a hotel room on Forty-second Street, which she was sharing with her purported twenty-seven-year-old boyfriend, "Max," with blood on her fist, screaming, "I'm going to kill him!"

"You know those statements are hearsay," Corriero angrily stated to Kriss.

On November 23 and 24, Kriss put several witnesses on the stand who testified about Daphne's aggressive behavior. It was the first time jurors heard witnesses speak about her violent actions on the day of the murder. One witness, Paul Carhart, a clothing sales-man, stated that a few hours before the murder, while he was making some purchases at a local deli, Daphne entered the deli looking for a fight. He said he was scared of her and quickly left the store. "It's no exaggeration to say she was obnoxious, rude, confrontational," he said. "She was belligerent. She wanted to get into a fight," said Carhart. Another witness, Mr. Clauson, corroborated Carhart's statements by testifying that he saw Daphne accost someone in the deli. The witness stated that Daphne screamed at the stranger that he was an alcoholic and asked him if he wanted to fight her. He didn't take her on, and nothing further occurred.

Carlos Magriz, a surprise defense witness, testified that earlier in the day, at Carl Schurz Park, "Daphne pulls out a black folding knife and says, 'If you want trouble, I'm going to give you trouble.'" Magriz also stated that Daphne threatened a chess-playing man for no apparent reason and that he, Magriz, grabbed the knife from her and only gave it back when she calmed down. At that point, Magriz said, she put the knife back in her pocket, but he admitted that she wasn't easily tamed. He said that Daphne spoke directly to him, to Vasquez, and to others, urging them to "get somebody," but that only Vasquez was game. He reported that Daphne said, "I'm going to get somebody before the night is over—I'm gonna kill somebody."

Detective Robert Mooney was called to the stand and, prompted by Bogdanos, described what he considered Daphne's admission of her role in the murder. He stated that Daphne, after long interrogation sessions conducted four months after the murder, finally became quiet and then admitted that she helped in the McMorrow murder. She stated, "I hit him." Mooney reported she made the admission with her head down, staring at the floor. Mooney went on to say she was crying uncontrollably. This, according to Bogdanos, should have convinced jurors that Daphne's statements all along—that she only kicked the man's feet out from under him during the murder—were a true account of what happened that night. Bogdanos, in trying to emphasize the credibility of Daphne's statements, was at the same time attempting to place the blame of the killing squarely on Christopher's shoulders.

On November 25, Dr. Louis Roh, deputy medical examiner of Westchester County, took the stand as a medical expert. He was called on behalf of the defense. Roh brought into question Daphne's account of how she kicked McMorrow's feet out from under him with her in-line skates. He stated, "The rollers are straight. These three spots (on McMorrow's thigh) are not in a straight line." Roh's account was at odds with the previous week's testimony by the city's acting deputy medical examiner, Dr. Maria Luz Alandy, who had stated that the three thigh bruises on Michael could have come from Daphne's Rollerblades. Roh was trying to shore up the defense's point of view that

Daphne may have had more to do with the murder than she admitted to, in March. Roh's testimony suggested that if Daphne had been lying about kicking McMorrow's feet out from under him, then she may have had a much greater involvement in the murder.

Roh stated that he believed McMorrow was on his back, already unconscious, when he was stabbed over thirty times. He came to this conclusion because there were no indications of a struggle or that Michael had tried to defend himself. There were no wounds on Michael's hands or arms.

However, under cross-examination, Roh admitted that McMorrow would not have had any self-defending wounds if he had been too drunk to defend himself, or if he had had his hands in his pockets.

The disagreement between the two medical experts, Alandy and Roh, was crucial particularly because Daphne would not be testifying in the trial. Up to this point, jurors knew of only Daphne's version of what had taken place that night—that a very crazed and drunk Christopher, wielding a knife, was Michael's attacker, while she merely kicked the victim's legs out from under him.

On Monday, November 30, the tenth day of the trial, jurors heard part of a tape of Daphne's "chillingly casual" 911 call reporting a body in the lake. Jurors heard that the only time during that call when Daphne's monotone voice revealed any emotion was when the operator asked her if she was male or female. Daphne reportedly responded angrily, "I'm female!"

On the tape, Daphne stated, "Go have your boys check out Central Park and drain the river. You'll find a body. You can't miss it. You can't miss it." All during the call, Daphne's radio was blaring in the background. At one point, she invited the cops to come to her house so she could talk with them about the body. Kriss introduced the tape, hoping that it would show the lies that Daphne had made to the 911 operator. He felt this should taint everything else she said, including her statement that Christopher committed the murder. On the tape, she lied: "I didn't know what it was at first. Then I saw it was a body, and I freaked out and left." Jurors also heard her say, in another lie, according to Kriss, that she thought it was a man, but she didn't know for sure. She "saw that [expletive] floating, and was like, what?"

A second tape was also admitted as evidence. On the tape, which had been recorded about a month after the murder, Daphne left a message for her friend Diana Bass Choate, stating that only she and Chris truly knew what took place that night, and she hoped the truth would be revealed. If not, "the real killer, he or she, will, you know, if they're not punished down here while they are alive, then on Judgment Day, they will get what they deserve." He or she, Kriss repeated. If she had nothing to do with the murder, suggested Kriss, why wouldn't she have simply said, "he" will get what "he" deserves?

As his final witness for the day, Kriss called Christopher's mother to the stand. Patricia Reidy reported that during the entire cab ride home from the Abdelas' on the night of the murder, Christopher didn't speak a word. He only cried. "He was leaning his head against the window . . . just staring." At that point, she admitted, she had no idea what had happened. She felt her son was upset because he knew that he was going to be punished for missing his curfew.

After Reidy left the stand, Kriss rested the defense's case.

In a surprise move, Bogdanos called Gerardo Vasquez, Christopher's father, to testify. Christopher showed no emotion as his father walked to the front of the courtroom and took the stand. The older Vasquez, hair in a ponytail and cracking gum as he spoke, denied the prosecution's contention that he had given Christopher a miniature replica of an army knife that he had supposedly used while in the service twenty-five years ago. "I was not a paratrooper," Vasquez stated. "I was a foot soldier. The only knife I was issued was a bayonet." He said that he never had an original Army K55 knife.

After the day's testimony, Bogdanos said he might bring Christopher's father to the stand again tomorrow because "hope springs eternal that he might tell the truth."

However, he did not call him back to testify.

After both attorneys concluded their remarks, Judge Corriero called the lawyers into his chambers. He said that he was considering offering the jurors the option of a manslaughter charge, but only if they first found Christopher not guilty of murder.

The prosecution was outraged. They feared that with this option, some jurors might think about Christopher's age and seek the lesser charge, rather than pay attention to the cold, hard facts. If they did, and found Christopher guilty of manslaughter, Christopher could face as little as *no* prison time. "You're trying to endow the jurors with the wisdom of Solomon in letting them cut the baby," complained

Bogdanos to the judge. "We don't let jurors cut the baby!" shouted the attorney.

The judge listened to both sides' reasoning, and after a heated debate, he stated that he was persuaded by Kriss to offer the manslaughter after concluding that Christopher could have stabbed McMorrow without intending to kill him. He stated that he thought it reasonable that the jury could decide that Vasquez's accomplice was more "responsible and more culpable" for the slaying than he. He went on to say that the jury could find that since McMorrow's blood was found on Daphne's Rollerblades, and not on Christopher's, that Daphne was more responsible and culpable.

Corriero concluded his remarks by saying that the jurors must first consider the two murder charges. If they concluded that Christopher was not guilty of murder, then they could consider the manslaugher charge.

CHAPTER 27

Closing arguments began on December 1.

Defense attorney Kriss began by telling the jurors that they would soon be hearing persuasive and unequivocal arguments in defense of his client. Interjecting a bit of humor, he also said he would do something he had never done before. He would bend down several times during his closing, not simply for exercise, although, he stated, he would probably enjoy doing so, since he'd been sitting down for a long time during this lengthy trial—just like the jurors—but also because the transcripts were on the floor. He would need to refer to them and read from them, so he hoped the jurors would excuse him.

Kriss stated that he would be pulling together a lot of things, but he reminded the jurors that the burden of proof did not rest with him, but it rested squarely on the shoulders of the district attorney's office. "I am going to try to convince you there's a reasonable doubt in this case. That's all I need to do." He said that he would represent his client as best he could, as persuasively as he could, so that it would be reasonable and logical for the jurors to come to the right conclusion.

Standing directly in front of the jury box and looking squarely at the jurors, he reiterated what he had said in opening remarks on November 9—that they were a New York jury. He explained that that meant that they were smart and intelligent, but even more than that, they were also street-smart, which counted for a lot in his mind. He urged the jurors to take all the time they needed to sort through all the evidence and then, ultimately, return a verdict of not guilty "to each and every charge the judge gives you." Why should they do this? he asked the jurors. Because, he believed, there was a reasonable doubt concerning Christopher's involvement in this case.

He then told the jurors that after he completed his argument, he would be forced by law to sit down, which was fine with him "because once you make your argument, you should sit down." He said that he could not get up and argue again, after Mr. Bogdanos made his summation, because the rules of the court didn't allow that. But the rules did allow him to object, which, he said, he intended to do whenever appropriate, because that's what good lawyers did.

Keeping the tone light, he said that the premise under which he was working was that the people had not succeeded in proving the defendant's guilt beyond a reasonable doubt. "That's a big statement to make," he said. "The people of New York are pretty big. We're the people of the state of New York."

Kriss stated that he had read the transcript of the trial over and over and over again and found that he was unable to find one reasonable doubt. That's right, he said, he couldn't find one reasonable doubt. Pausing, he then said, "I found, I think, more than twelve." He was hoping, he added, that he'd find only twelve, one for each juror, so he could go up and down the row, presenting one for each person. But, he said, there were way more than twelve. He offered to give some of the doubts to the alternates.

Kriss began his case by stating reasonable doubt number one: Daphne Abdela. He stated that this reasonable doubt was not a "little" reasonable doubt. It was a big one. However, he went on, before detailing why Daphne was reasonable doubt number one, he said he would first like to tell the McMorrow family that his heart went out to them. He paused and scanned the courtroom to lock eyes with the family members. He then stated that although it hurt him deeply, seeing their grief, he couldn't allow that kind of sentiment to come into the courtroom. The jurors, he said, must think about the evidence and try to put aside the "aggravation, the hurt, and the upsets that go on in your hearts before you show up at your job and you have to just do your job." He again stated that Michael McMorrow "should not have died that way." It was a terribly tragic and unfair way to die.

It was his firm opinion, he declared, that Daphne Abdela was the killer and that she should bear the responsibility for the way Michael died. He reminded the jurors that Daphne was fifteen years old, five feet five inches tall, weighing around 150 pounds, and that she had an alcohol problem for the past three or four years. He told the court that she had been treated for substance abuse and alcohol before May 22, 1997. She was a troubled young lady, he maintained. She had a short fuse, which, he believed, "burned very bright" on the night of the killing. Kriss said he was bringing in this information to help the jurors evaluate Daphne, since she never made an appearance in the courtroom and because "a lot of testimony in this case depends on one or two things that Daphne Abdela said." Kriss stated that if the jurors found her statements to be non-sense or unreliable, they should throw them out.

He went on to say that he wanted the jurors to know a little about Daphne. Here were some facts. Daphne was in Central Park on the night of the murder. She was at Blockbuster. She and Christopher were together most of the early evening, into the night, as well as in the early hours of the next morning. However, "mere presence, mere presence with somebody who eventually commits a crime, does not make a person who is with the person who committed the crime guilty." Based on history, Kriss stated, the explosion was going to happen, and it was an explosion of one person, one Daphne Abdela.

Kriss then recounted how the day of the murder began at Carl Schurz Park. He reminded the jurors of the testimony of Carlos Magriz and two others, Adam and Paul. All three, he pointed out, stated under oath that Christopher had never hung out at Carl Schurz Park before, and that Daphne was a regular there. "This was Daphne's place," said Magriz. Kriss repeated some of Magriz's testimony that at one point during the afternoon, Daphne jumped up and threatened to beat him up. Kriss reminded the jurors that Carlos was six feet tall, 280 pounds. The two started slap boxing, testified Magriz, and he knocked Daphne down. Did she care? asked Kriss. No, she simply got up and started in all over again. Magriz eventually tired of her ineptness and told her to stop, but she wouldn't, until finally he landed a good one. Daphne fell down again, and this time, she got up and walked away. According to Magriz, all the while, Christopher was just there.

Not doing anything. Magriz reported that one kid named Steve put Christopher in a headlock, and Christopher did nothing. He just allowed it to happen. Magriz said that Christopher was simply "bystanding." He was just standing there, doing nothing.

But that was not Daphne, Kriss declared forcefully. She tried to pick a fight with a forty-year-old man in a deli. Christopher didn't. Again, all Christopher did was stand there. Magriz also testified, Kriss reminded the jurors, that at Carl Schurz Park, Daphne said to him, "Look, look, I have a beef with this guy. Come settle it with me. Come help me out." And Magriz reported that he went to take a look, but he told her he wanted no part of it. "A forty-year-old?" Forgetaboutit.

All that day, maintained Kriss, Daphne was ready to fight, to get down. He reminded the jurors that Magriz also testified that Daphne pulled out a black folding knife and showed it to him. He took it and started playing with it and eventually gave it back to her. Christopher was still standing there, "bystanding." He never took the knife. He never played with the knife. He never showed any interest in the knife. He just stood there, watching the activities.

But that was not Daphne, Kriss stated again. Hostile, angry, and agitated, she was bored and "down to fight." Then, according to Magriz's testimony, she said, "Come on, let's go. I'm going to get somebody tonight. Before the night's over, I'm going to end up killing somebody. Come on, let's go. Let's hang out."

He reminded the jurors of Daphne's actions at Blockbuster. According to Manuel Guzman, she was loud and hard to miss. In fact, he believed she was a boy. On the video showing the teens at the store, Kriss reminded the court that at one point, Daphne was sprawled out on the floor. Aberrational behavior? he wondered. No. Her actions seemed totally in character. She was wild. She was uncontrollable. She did whatever she wanted. Kriss pointed out that after the two teens went to Daphne's building, the doorman testified that Christopher stood some twenty-five feet back. Doing nothing. Just standing there. *Bystanding*.

Kriss then brought up the testimony of Victoria Donnelly and Bradford Harriman. "A bone-chilling description of what Brad Harriman felt about somebody he'd never met before, Daphne Abdela." Daphne had a weird attitude, said Harriman, going up to the people in the group, who were not interested in her at all, and asking if anyone had any LSD. He then reported that Daphne sat down next to Michael McMorrow and planted two kisses on his cheek and put her arm around him. According to Harriman, Michael seemed to have recognized her, but seemed taken aback by her "forward approach and aggressive attitude." And again, Kriss asked, "Where was Christopher? He was just standing there." *Bystanding*.

Kriss recounted how Daphne told Christopher to "stay here" while she went to get some beer, which he did for a while. But then, he reported, Christopher got anxious and impatient and went after her. In describing Daphne, Harriman said, there was something that put a person on guard when she was around. "You knew that she was up to something that you had no idea what it was."

Again and again, Kriss reiterated that all the while that Daphne was acting out, Christopher was simply a piece of the scenery, a mere presence at a location. Doing nothing. *Bystanding*.

Kriss pointed out that when Daphne went on her

beer run and was stopped by Officer Losada on her way out of the park, she told him her name was Alex. The officer thought she was a boy. Kriss pointed out that Daphne looked and acted so tough that many people that day thought she was a boy. To police officers later, she declared she hated cops, had gotten kicked out of school, and hated her parents. "Pretty brazen stuff," declared Kriss, for a young lady to say to police officers. "This fuse is burning; it's lit; it's moving."

Kriss asked the jurors to think back over all the days of the trial and see if they could find one witness who ever placed the knife in Christopher's hands. Although the knife belonged to Christopher, Kriss said, a gift from his grandmother, no one ever actually saw him with it. If you believe any of the witnesses, stated Kriss, Daphne was one scary kid and one capable of using the knife. Christopher, though, was not.

Kriss repeated details about the run-in at the deli, in which Daphne confronted an older man, a salesman at a men's store. Again, Kriss pointed out, here was a fifteen-year-old taking on an adult who was six feet tall and weighed 175 pounds, "and who had the good sense to walk away" even after Daphne exploded in anger and continued to challenge him. Christopher, the deli man reported, was simply standing there, low-key and very polite. *Bystanding.*

Up to this point, Kriss asked the jury, did Christopher do anything "that sounds like he's going to have an eruption to kill an adult? Does he sound like a person who's about to commit one of life's most deadliest sins, murder?" He urged the jurors to look at Christopher—to take a long, careful look—and use their common sense and be the judges. Do you think, he asked them, that Christopher would commit such a crime based on what you have seen and heard about him up until eleven o'clock thus far? Or, he wondered, is this bystander someone who may have witnessed or may not even have witnessed the murder? Common sense should tell you, declared Kriss, that what runs through the entire issue was Daphne's seeds of anger.

Which, he said, brought him to reasonable doubt number two: the crime scene. In going over the photos, the testimony, and the video, Kriss declared, there was a reasonable doubt here, too. Before he delved into the details, Kriss began by casting doubt on Hal Sherman's testimony, saying that the crime scene detective did not take enough samples, even though Sherman had said he liked to err on the side of taking too much. In fact, Kriss stated, they found a total of one droplet of blood near where the killing presumably took place, even though Christopher had cut his finger badly and was bleeding profusely. Now, he asked the jurors, if Christopher had helped throw Michael into the lake, wouldn't there be droplets of his blood there? There were plenty of blood droplets up on the park bench, and there were blood trails all the way up to the edge of the park and on the way to the Majestic, but there were none where the body was rolled into the lake. Reasonable doubt, to be sure. "The crime scene spoke," stated Kriss.

Acknowledging that Christopher had gotten a bad cut on his finger, Kriss suggested that that in no way suggested that the teen was involved in a murder. A cut finger did not even prove Christopher had a fight with McMorrow. The cut could have been self-inflicted—Christopher could have pierced his finger opening a can of beer, for example. There were lots of ways a person could cut a finger. In fact, Kriss

stated, there was no DNA of Christopher's and
Michael's anywhere together. "We know there's no
combination, no mixture. We know Christopher did
not have his hands on Mr. McMorrow's body because
there's no DNA from Michael McMorrow over there
(where Christopher's blood was found)."

Kriss went on to say that the abrasion on Christopher's face most likely came from a fall, as did an abrasion on his right leg. "You don't get punched in the
right leg and get an abrasion." He urged the jurors to
use logic and see that it wasn't Christopher who was
fighting with Michael.

Reasonable doubt number three, stated Kriss, was
the prior relationship between Daphne and Michael,
and the fact that there was no prior relationship between Christopher and Michael. That alone, he declared, should give you a reasonable doubt. And, he
reminded the jurors, although the DA didn't have to
prove motive—that Christopher, for whatever reason,
killed Michael—you should consider lack of motive in
your deliberation. Christopher had no prior relationship with the man. He had no motive to kill him.

Another reasonable doubt: the testimony of Aryana
Fernando, a friend of Christopher's, who had never
seen him with a knife, had never heard him threaten
anyone with a knife, even after he was mugged on the
train. Kriss pointed out that Fernando's testimony was
just one more piece of information to weigh: Christopher was a meek kid who never could have done this.
It defied logic. Christopher didn't even want revenge
from the kids who mugged him! How could this kid,
who showed no kind of homicidal anger in his entire
life, reach the level of rage to murder? On the other
hand, Kriss suggested, when you're fifteen years old

and you walk up to—and punch—an adult, that's "big-league stuff."

Another reasonable doubt: state of mind. Kriss reminded the jurors of Dr. Alandy's testimony, in which she said that it depended on the state of mind of a person as to how much strength he or she could have in a given situation. So, Kriss contended, consider the state of mind of Christopher and the state of mind of Daphne. If you're in a rage, like Daphne Abdela was, think of the adrenaline surge that was going through her body. Think about her rage, about her fuse that was burning, about her explosive behavior. Daphne, Kriss declared, had the strength to throw McMorrow into the lake.

More reasonable doubts. There was no blood of Michael's on Christopher's Rollerblades. Christopher's blood was on his skates, but none of McMorrow's blood was there. "Not on the sides, not in the wheel well, not on the wheel guard, not on the wheels, not on the laces, nowhere. Nowhere. Not a drop, not a smidgen." Kriss suggested that if Christopher had been the murderer, blood should have been on his Rollerblades. Both kids were wearing Rollerblades, he said, yet there is no DNA of Michael's on Christopher's. But on whose Rollerblades is there the blood of McMorrow? The DNA showed that it was Daphne Abdela's, he declared. And how did she get it? he wondered out loud. Kriss asked the jurors to imagine something. Imagine that Daphne Abdela were on trial right now for murder. Would you have enough evidence, beyond a reasonable doubt, to return a guilty verdict against her, based on many things, but right now, based alone on the DNA evidence on her Rollerblades? "I submit to you, you probably would." And that was reasonable doubt number six.

Reasonable doubt number seven, declared Kriss: the

"debris of a plea allocution," which, according to him, should be thrown out and disregarded, because "it's a bogus document . . . a bogus statement." Kriss stated that not one allele of DNA was found under Michael McMorrow's fingernails that could be attributed to Christopher. And if there were a struggle, if the two had engaged in a fight, where is the exchange of DNA? And even if there were no struggle, wouldn't the assailant's hands have to have been in such close proximity to the body that the fingernails would be touching the blood and some would have come off, something would have managed to get under the fingernails of Christopher from Michael? "It had to get there," said Kriss because Michael was brutally and savagely cut. According to Daphne's plea allocution—if you believe her—it was not "a little random act" that supposedly Christopher had with Michael. It was "a major situation."

But, Kriss continued, guess what? With all the chiefs, the detectives, the sergeants, and the captains—a whole crew, all the top brass—nobody, not one person, had the foresight or the wherewithal to seek a court order to take fingernail scrapings from under Daphne's fingernails! She was in custody. She was going nowhere. Just like Christopher. He was in custody. He was going nowhere. Yet, they bagged his hands. They didn't bag hers. So, Kriss asked the jury, wouldn't you like to know what was under her fingernails? He suggested that they all knew what was inside of her, but they didn't know what was under her nails. "She was charged with murder. We got blood on her Rollerblades. We got her in her apartment in an aberrational behavior, walking around, smoking cigarettes, up and down, talking spontaneously, not shutting up." But, and here was the crux of reasonable doubt number seven, nothing in Christopher's fingernails linked him to Michael—even though Daphne said Christopher was the murderer—and, furthermore, there was no bagging of Daphne's hands. A reasonable doubt, to be sure.

Reasonable doubt number eight: according to Angelo Goetze, doorman at 115 Central Park West, he saw blood on Daphne's hand. He said it was on her fingertips, on the top portion of her hand. Now, if she did nothing but kick his legs out from under him, asked Kriss, where did the blood come from? Reasonable doubt.

Reasonable doubt number nine: why, if Daphne did nothing, did she get in the tub with Christopher? Why did she lead him to the washroom? Imagine, he asked the jury, to assume for a moment that Christopher *is* the murderer. "You wash him up." Yes, that's logical. "But why was she getting washed? Why was she getting undressed" if she did nothing?

Once upstairs in the apartment, Daphne washed both hers and his clothing in the washing machine. Kriss wondered why Daphne had to wash her own clothes if they didn't have any blood on them. She gave Christopher a shirt, pants, and "she gave him the knife to take home, except he didn't know he had it.

"The bottom line is that knife, you can find was put there by Daphne," he said, and he declared that he would tell the jurors how they could know that. He said that when Christopher left Daphne's apartment, he left his wallet there, but "he has the presence of mind to take his knife . . . and put it in his pocket?" Absurd!

"Don't you usually take [your] wallet?" he asked.

Kriss pointed out that Daphne berated her father in language Kriss did not care to use in the courtroom, but which jurors heard in testimony. She was angry that he had called the cops and reported her missing. Why was she angry? Because if her father hadn't made the call, she wouldn't now be in the awful position of having to figure out how to get out of the mess she's in. But, Kriss suggested, because her past actions showed her to be manipulative and cunning, you could be assured that she would prove to be quite good at it.

Reasonable doubt number ten: Officers Furman and Moran. Kriss pointed out that Moran's conduct on May 23, 1997, "at about twelve-thirty in the morning, should make every New Yorker cringe, cringe." Kriss asked the jurors to think about this: He's a cop. He heard screams. He zipped around in his radio car, but didn't get out of it. Maybe the person was simply an extremely disturbed person. "Where does it say sick people don't have any right to have the police find them and help them?" But he didn't get out of his car. He didn't walk around to check the distance between the West Drive and the lake, where he heard the screams coming from. To further compound his inefficiency, stated Kriss, and here "is the most offensive" thing he did, was that upon hearing there was a body in the lake, this four-year veteran said, "I thought it was a garbage bag. No big deal."

Moran, Kriss stated, conceded that even if it were a garbage bag, such an item wasn't often found, if ever, in the lake. "I think he said it never happened when he was on duty." But, Kriss stated, Moran did nothing about it. Maybe it was just a garbage bag, but maybe, Kriss posited, it was a body!

Kriss then pointed out that once again, in Daphne's apartment, Moran bumbled. But, he said, injecting a bit of humor, at least "he's consistent. Consistency is wonderful." Daphne, in charge, led the officers upstairs to the laundry room, where clothes were in the dryer. She took them out, one at a time, very slowly, holding each one up. "She kept taking [them] out." He asked the jury to think about this: didn't Moran think about safeguarding . . . I mean this is a contamination nightmare? "Assuming [the stuff] was of evidentiary value, they didn't give it a chance. . . . It's a disgrace."

And Furman, too, stated Kriss, was to blame for bumbling the case. In his memo, said Kriss, Furman stated that he found jeans and underpants. But there were no underpants found later. Furman stated under oath that Christopher was "arrogant and confrontational." However, Kriss pointed out, that when Furman spoke to Detective Mooney about the case, and had him report every detail he could think of, Furman never once mentioned that Christopher got up in his face. Never once mentioned that he was confrontational or arrogant. "Don't you think that's important if you're going to build a case against an individual who committed a violent crime?" Kriss suggested that perhaps the cops had gotten together, in Bogdanos's office, and tried to get their story straight in an effort to convict his client!

The work of the police, Kriss reiterated, was so inept that nobody even took Daphne's alcohol level when she was in custody! Nobody bagged her hands! Nobody, it seemed, was the least bit interested in doing professional police work on her.

But consider this, Kriss pointed out. When the cops went into Daphne's apartment after her 911 call, she was eating macaroni and cheese. Kriss suggested that that "is an example of the callousness, coldness, the calculatedness of a killer." According to her testimony, she just witnessed a murder—and she's calmly eating mac and cheese? Furthermore, Kriss declared, she "acted out" against her father upstairs. She knew she was in deep trouble and had to find a way out, had to find "a fall guy." So what did she do? "Christopher Vasquez, my friend, stabbed Mr. McMorrow." That's what she did. "The Chris chant was rocking and rolling from the time the cops get in the house."

When the police followed Daphne to the crime scene, Kriss suggested, it wasn't unreasonable for them to conclude that this fifteen-year-old girl could have done the killing. In fact, he said, at that point there was really nothing at all to connect Christopher to the killing. But when they got to the lake, "Kate Winslet would be thrilled. This is not a *Titanic* performance, but an Academy Award performance." She was hysterical, distraught, and highly emotional. She was crying. Everyone was comforting her. And all this, asserted Kriss sarcastically, because Chris did it?

Kriss asked the jurors to think about Central Park and how the cops had to solve this fast because this was going to be big news in no time. So here they've got a witness, they've got a body, and they've got some bloody clothes. Well, then, case shut. "If Daphne says it's so, it must be so."

When Detective Gannon showed up at Christopher's house, stated Kriss, he put him under arrest. "The decision was made" and on "whose basis, whose intelligence, whose information, was it made? Daphne Abdela." That alone, said Kriss, was reasonable doubt.

Reasonable doubt number eleven: let's make a deal, or the plea bargain, which elaborated on reasonable doubt number seven, said Kriss. The deal was made after Daphne was arrested, not six months later. "This [case] was moving." Daphne was arrested on May 23. She was in the DA's office, around June 19, less than a month after the crime, "probably through very good counsel." Kriss suggested that Daphne knew she was in deep trouble: she was arrested, was facing a charge of murder in the second degree, she had acted out all night in the police's presence, and she was in jail. So how can she get the pass card? "Well, if you're a princess, you go to the DA's office and you become 'Queen for a Day.'" But, Kriss declared, Daphne wasn't simply queen for one day. Her reign lasted from June to November 1997, and most likely up to March 11, 1998. "She saved herself, but she didn't do it honestly."

Kriss stated it would be too painful to go through the testimony of the assistant district attorney Sarah Hines, which allowed Daphne to plead guilty with no strings attached, to go one down from murder two and plead guilty to manslaughter in the first degree, to get a sentence of three years and four months to ten years, and then to say good-bye. There were no conditions, no quid pro quo. Kriss suggested that Daphne could have been made to testify, but the prosecution didn't think it a good idea. Manslaughter one and she's out of here. "It's mind-boggling," declared Kriss.

Kriss questioned whether anyone else in the world would have made a judgment on somebody's life, or on one's own future, based on what Daphne had said. Is her word reliable? Kriss suggested it was not. There was nothing believable in Daphne's statements that could "cause you to render a guilty verdict in [Christopher's] case, nothing at all." Kriss stated that the science and the facts were at odds with what Daphne said. Her plea of guilty was "her ticket from a life sentence." Her version of events was unreliable. Therefore, stated Kriss, this was a major reasonable doubt. "She's unbelievable. She's a liar."

Reasonable doubt number twelve: the knife. There was DNA of Michael's on the knife, which, Kriss suggested, could have come from when Daphne picked up her Rollerblades, got some DNA from Michael on her hand, transferred it to the knife, and then planted the knife in Christopher's pocket. But the cops never swabbed the knife handle—so no one knew what fingerprints might have been found. They didn't swab it, so that made it a reasonable doubt as to who wielded the knife. Blood on it could have gotten there any number of ways.

Judge Corriero then sustained an objection brought by Bogdanos, who felt that reasonable doubt number thirteen, concerning difference in lifestyles between the two teens' families, had no relevance to the issues of the trial.

Reasonable doubt number fourteen: the Diana Bass Choate tape. Kriss urged the jurors to recall two tapes that were brought into evidence: Daphne's 911 tape telling of the body in the lake and Daphne's call to Diana. He said he was sure that they could recall hearing a different Daphne on each call. On the Choate tape, which was made from a cell at the Spofford Juvenile Detention Center, Daphne was "wistful." Kriss suggested that she had had some time to think about what had gone down, and in a moment of vulnerability, her guard came down and her guilt surfaced. On the tape, she mentioned a "killer," not "killers." Kriss directed his attention to the jurors. "One killer. He or she." If it were Christopher, she would have said to Diana, "Christopher's got to face Judgment Day. He did it, yet I'm the one here. He's the killer." The tape also suggested that there was only one killer—not two, not that the two acted together. And, he submitted, it was the "she," not the "he," who did the killing.

Kriss reiterated that Christopher was simply "the dupe of a wealthy teenage girl." He was "the rich kid's fall guy." Kriss reminded jurors of testimony that had come out in the trial, and that on the day that the murder took place, Daphne had been brandishing a knife and swearing she would kill somebody before the day was done. Kriss characterized Daphne as a troubled girl with a short fuse. "You can smell that gunpowder about to go off."

Kriss then concluded his remarks by saying that this was any parent's worst nightmare. It's a tragedy for three families. However, he urged jurors to think about their responsibility, not about the feelings of the families. Kriss stated that the prosecution was asking the jurors to take a leap of faith, to say that the DA's office had proven, beyond a reasonable doubt— and without an eyewitness—that an individual was guilty and should be convicted of murder.

Kriss mentioned that he would not be able to respond to the closing arguments that Bogdanos would be making, but he trusted that the jurors would reach the right verdict. "The fate of a human being is in the hands of twelve strangers." Both the prosecution and I, he stated, were trying to get you to see things our way. We had different styles, but Kriss cautioned, no matter how hard the prosecution argued, no matter what he believed, beliefs "can't substitute for evidence. And if you have a reasonable doubt and even though this is a murder case with notoriety attached to it, you've got to stand up . . . and you've got to stand by your convictions." He urged the jurors to look deeply into their minds, their hearts, and their consciences and unanimously come to the "right, proper verdict in this case."

Kriss then rested his case, more than three hours after he began.

The judge then told the jurors they could take a much-needed lunch break, and with that, they filed out of the courtroom.

CHAPTER 28

After the jurors returned from their break, the judge called on Bogdanos to begin his summation.

Bogdanos forcefully laid out various scenarios that could prove Christopher guilty. Bogdanos asserted that if Christopher stabbed Michael McMorrow, he's guilty of murder in the second degree. If Christopher stabbed Michael McMorrow at the insistence of Daphne, he's also guilty of murder in the second degree. If the two teens committed the act together, once again, Christopher would be guilty of second-degree murder. If Christopher participated in the murder that caused the death of Michael McMorrow, Christopher would be guilty of murder in the second degree.

The case, he said, was simple: Three people went to the lake. Two people came back. One was dead. So the question was, who did it? And with a resounding voice, he declared, "Both."

Bogdanos remarked that the defense stated that there wasn't enough evidence to convict Christopher of murder in the second degree. "Sure there is," said Bogdanos. Contrary to the defense's notion that no witnesses were present, Bogdanos declared that there were plenty of witnesses. Michael McMorrow, for example, was one. He was a witness to what Christopher did. The defendant's knife was another witness, Bogdanos declared, as was the defendant's blood, along with the injuries to all three people.

Bogdanos stated that he would illuminate these witnesses and show how each one should convince the jurors beyond a reasonable doubt as to what happened—that the defendant is guilty of the crime of second-degree murder.

The ADA then promised that anything he offered as evidence to support his claim would not "be bathed in partial light," as the defense's arguments were. He would not, for example, quote only half a sentence, pick only one small piece of a whole. If he quoted from a conversation that took place in the cab with officers, for example, he would not quote only the words he liked. He would quote all the words, the full truth. Referring to statements that Kriss told the jurors were said in the cab, Bogdanos declared that these were the actual words: "Chris, that dick, he better take the heat for this. He knows he did it." Kriss, Bogdanos stated, only said half of that. He left out the most important part: "He knows he did it."

Bogdanos asserted that he would take a little over an hour to prove his case, and he would rely only on the evidence. He reminded the jurors to cast aside whim, speculation, and conjecture "if it is not based on evidence."

He mentioned that over the past few weeks, the jurors had probably built up sympathy for the family of the victim. However, he urged them to put those feelings aside, stating that they would not help them in their deliberation, nor would they "bring Michael McMorrow back."

Patricia and Gerardo, Chris's parents, were not responsible for the crime, Bogdanos maintained. There was nothing they could have done that would have prevented Christopher's actions that night. Bogdanos stated that Christopher's parents were not on trial. Christopher, however, was, for his actions—and "no one else."

Bogdanos then urged the jurors not to fall "prey to the trap of appearances," and to set aside any feelings they might have based on the boyish look of Christopher. Even if they looked at the table where Christopher was sitting and said to themselves or others, "He doesn't look the least bit like a criminal," they must discard those sentiments. "What does a criminal look like?" asked Bogdanos. "How tall? How old? I don't know." He urged jurors to focus only on the facts.

And what are those facts? he asked. Pointing at the knife, he said, the first fact was the knife. This knife was the defendant's knife. Bogdanos stated that Christopher had owned it for several years, and about five weeks before the murder, he began carrying a knife after having been mugged on the train.

Another fact: on May 22, Miss Abdela and Mr. Vasquez went to Carl Schurz Park at around four o'clock and they stayed together for the next four hours.

More facts: They went to the Majestic, tried to get to the sundeck, were told they couldn't go, so instead went to Daphne's apartment. They went to Blockbuster, where they remained for a half hour. They left at around 8:30 P.M., "not apart for one moment." Everything the two did that night, they did together. Those were the facts.

Another fact: they met Michael McMorrow at the park.

Here is where the defense and I have a disagreement, maintained Bogdanos. The defense wanted you to believe there was some kind of relationship between Daphne and Michael. But was that speculation based on evidence? he asked. "Of course not." There was no evidence of any kind of a relationship—only, perhaps, a brief encounter at an AA meeting, Bogdanos stated.

Another fact: Daphne walked up to Michael, put her arm around him, kissed him twice on the cheek, and then a little later, left to get beer.

Another fact: Christopher was growing more and more impatient, even in the few minutes Daphne had gone to get beer, so he Rollerbladed after her.

Facts: Daphne Rollerbladed up to where Officer Losada was sitting in his car. She fell, hit her head, and received a cut. After going to a grocery store, where she met up with Christopher, the teens encountered two men: Mr. Carhart and Mr. Clauson. On the way back to the park, they once again met Officer Losada and returned to Strawberry Fields. They drank some more, and then Officer Losada dispersed the crowd, at which time Daphne, Michael, and Christopher "walked off together down that fateful path toward the gazebo." Michael was in the lead, followed by Christopher, followed by Daphne.

Fact: Mr. McMorrow was never again seen alive.

At 12:30 A.M., Officer Moran testified, he heard two screams coming from the area of the lake. Around fifteen minutes later, he saw two people coming up behind his marked car, which had its engine and lights off. The two were Daphne and Christopher, and they stayed behind the car for about five minutes before calmly Rollerblading away.

Fact: The teens then went into the Majestic. The two together. Every single second. Never apart. "Never more than an arm's length or two away from each other the entire night. Everyone who testified to this said the same thing."

Fact: At around 12:50 A.M., the two went to the Majestic washroom and got into the tub, "stripped down naked and washed each other." Together. Together some more.

Fact: The police arrived at the Majestic in response to a 911 call made by Daphne's father, saying that she was missing. The officers went to the washroom, found the pair together—still together—and then, after they got dressed, the pair went back upstairs to Daphne's apartment. Christopher's mother picked him up soon after.

Fact: Within a minute or two after Christopher left for his home, Daphne picked up the phone and called 911. Again, the police arrived. Shortly after, Daphne showed them where the clothing was that they had been wearing, as well as her watch, which had blood on it. She turned the watch over to the officers, along with the clothing taken from the dryer.

Fact: When detectives arrived at Christopher's apartment, a knife was found in his pants pocket in his bedroom. But whose pants were they? Who gave him those pants? Bogdanos asked. On the knife was human blood, he stated, a mix of Christopher's and Michael's DNA. This was all uncontradicted fact.

More facts: Michael McMorrow's mutilated 210-pound body was found in the lake with seven knife wounds to the face, three to the neck, one to the left clavicle, seven to the left chest, sixteen to the abdomen—fifteen of which were postmortem. His wrist was almost severed. His hairpiece, glasses, identification, and wallet were all gone. Only one business card remained. All that, he said, were the facts.

Fact: Christopher's blood was everywhere at the

crime scene: north, south, east, west. Miss Abdela's was nowhere. Christopher had nine separate fresh injuries that were not there when Officer Losada saw him at 10:35 P.M.

Fact: Miss Abdela didn't have one scratch on her anywhere. Not one. Not an abrasion or a laceration or a contusion or an incised wound. Nothing. And the defendant? He had nine separate visible injuries.

These were the facts, declared Bogdanos, and nothing that any lawyer stated in this courtroom could change those facts.

And what did those facts indicate? Bogdanos asked. "These facts indicate one thing and one thing alone. Three people went to the lake; two came back. Who killed Mr. McMorrow? Both of them. Who stabbed Mr. McMorrow? Christopher Vasquez."

Bogdanos declared that he would prove how "overwhelming" the evidence was that no one else but Christopher stabbed Mr. McMorrow. Bogdanos asked the jury to set aside Daphne's plea allocution, as if it never existed, and pay attention only to the evidence, and here it was. The defendant was carrying the knife. Bogdanos reminded the jurors that Christopher had been beaten up on April 14, and after that, he missed approximately three days of school, and when he went back, he had a black eye. He had told one of his best friends, Miss Fernando, that he was now carrying a knife so that if anything like that ever happened again, he would have protection. Miss Fernando observed that when he said it, however, he didn't seem upset or angry. This, stated Miss Fernando under oath, seemed strange. What this suggested, said Bogdanos, was "the calm before the storm. But for that beating on April fourteenth, Michael McMorrow [would be] alive today. But for that beating, there would be] no knife at the gazebo that night. But for that beating, there [would be] no one at the gazebo willing to use that knife."

Fate, suggested Bogdanos, hung on a thread. Lives turned on that kind of timing. And, he surmised, that was how Mr. McMorrow's life ended—because a man decided to carry a knife for protection after April 14.

He told the jury that this individual, Christopher, was interested in Daphne "as only a fifteen-year-old can be interested. You saw him walk up behind her and hug her at Blockbuster in the video. Everything you have seen and heard told you that Christopher was interested in and wanted, desired, Daphne. So, they were together all day, and as soon as Daphne began to be interested in someone else, in Michael McMorrow by putting her arm around him, and kissing him twice in front of Christopher, Christopher reacted." According to Brad Harriman, Christopher became silent and sullen and withdrew from the group. Daphne excluded him, told him to stay while she got beer, but he didn't listen because he wanted to be near her. He couldn't stand being apart from her. That night, everything Christopher did was to impress Daphne. "Sadly," he added after a long pause, "everything about this case also shows that he succeeded."

He asked the jurors to keep one snapshot of the two in their minds, even though it wasn't an actual photograph. Two naked fifteen-year-olds in a bathtub in the Majestic. "They have, the two of them, committed an indescribable act and there are the two of them washing the blood off each other.

"Everything you need to know about the relationship between those two, the dynamic between those two and why those two acted the way they did that night, can be captured in that one moment of the two of them in that tub." He urged the jurors to keep that snapshot in their minds "to help in understanding why he did what he did at the gazebo and why she did what she did afterward to help him cover up. . . ."

Concerning the injuries to Michael, Bogdanos stated, firstly, there was a laceration on the back of his head, one inch from the top, which, Dr. Alandy told you, was consistent with the ring that Christopher wore that night. No one else that night wore a ring. The cut didn't come from a fall, but from being struck by the defendant. And, Bogdanos went on, concerning the contusion to the area below Michael's front lip—that was consistent with the back of the defendant's right hand. Bogdanos then told the jury to consider the stab wounds, and asked the jurors if they noticed anything odd about them—one to the left clavicle, seven to the left nipple area, three to the left abdomen, and ten postmortem to the left abdomen area. If you were facing Mr. McMorrow, Bogdanos surmised, all the wounds would have been done by the right hand, correct? Christopher Vasquez was right-handed. But these wounds told something else, he posited. They told you that what was done that night to Michael was not a one-person job. "It took two—one with the knife and the other helping, kicking, tripping."

And here are other things that the DA's office knew: Michael was dead before he was pushed into the lake—there was no water in his lungs; his heart had stopped pumping and he had stopped breathing, so he was dead. So here was 210 pounds of dead-weight, and no, he wasn't "rolled" into the lake. There were rocks in the way, several feet high, which one person, Bogdanos claimed, could not have managed to get McMorrow over.

"No," said Bogdanos, "the death, the murder of

Mr. McMorrow, was a two-person job, and disposing of the body was also a two-person job."

He asked the jurors to think about what the defendant's injuries suggested about the crime. Bogdanos told them to think back on the 2,808 pages of the testimony in the trial and find anyplace where there was any indication that the laceration on Christopher's knuckle could have come from opening a bottle, as the defense claimed. None of the experts who testified suggested the cut could have come from opening a bottle. The cut, said Bogdanos, could only have come from one way. And here was how it happened: when McMorrow was found in the lake, his right wrist was almost severed. It was hanging over a rock, out of the water when the body was found. "That's where he [Christopher] tried to sever the wrist. . . . There is only one way this wound [to Christopher's finger] could have been inflicted, and that is as he was holding down Mr. McMorrow's wrist with his left hand, the right hand of the defendant had the knife . . . and sliced down on his [own] finger. That's how it happened."

It was the only possible explanation, Bogdanos suggested. Not just the only logical and reasonable one, but the only possible one. Christopher cut his finger after Michael was already in the water as he tried to sever the dead man's wrist.

All the other injuries the defendant suffered added to this. They indicated that Christopher was in a fight, in a struggle with someone. And it wasn't Miss Abdela. Why? Because she didn't have a scratch on her. So, Christopher was at the gazebo with two others. He was in a fight. He was not in a fight with Daphne. The only person he could have been in a fight with was Michael McMorrow. Christopher's injuries told the truth: that

Christopher was in a fight with Michael and that he stabbed him to death.

Even if Attorney Kriss was correct in labeling Christopher a bystander, stated Bogdanos, he certainly wasn't a bystander at the gazebo, even if one believed he was a bystander before. How do we know this? he wondered aloud. We know this because when Officer Nichols took Miss Abdela away, Christopher screamed, "Leave her alone. She didn't do anything," and then, said Bogdanos, according to Officer Furman, Christopher got up into his face, got confrontational, and told the officer that he wasn't a wiseass and wasn't afraid of him. So, suggested Bogdanos, after the gazebo, in his first encounter with anyone, he was "still feeling that rush, still in the same state of mind as he was in the gazebo when he murdered Michael McMorrow."

Bogdanos continued by repeating what he had said earlier: the crime scene was a witness to the murder and to the guilt of the defendant, and he would continue to show why. More facts: Forty-seven separate blood samples were recovered from the asphalt, the park bench, and from swabs. He reminded the jurors that Detective Sherman mentioned he had never taken so many separate samples. In fact, he had never heard of anyone taking so many. So the question, Bogdanos stated, was not how come he took so many, but how come every single one that had been DNA tested exhibited the defendant's blood? One hundred percent of them.

The trail of blood, said Bogdanos, was the defendant's blood. And according to Detective Sherman, the blood was everywhere, "exactly where the murderer's blood drops should be," said Bogdanos. But, he added, those aren't my words, "those are Dr. Alandy's and

Detective Sherman's, that every drop of blood is just where it should be in the scenario."

Bogdanos stated that the defense was trying to suggest that something happened other than what really happened with the blood. The defense asked the jurors to assume things, said Bogdanos, but "I am asking you only to follow the evidence." The evidence was clear: Michael McMorrow was standing up, at some point. This was known because the stab wound to the left clavicle was a scalloped wound, which, as Dr. Alandy indicated, happened as the victim and the assailant "were moving in relation to each other." So, Mr. McMorrow was standing. There was an antemortem wound to the abdomen. And here was how it took place: As Mr. Mc-Morrow was standing, perhaps he received some slash wounds to his eyes and other parts of his face, temporarily blinding him. The next stab wound was to his left clavicle, as the knife was in the defendant's right hand. The tip of the knife bent as Mr. McMorrow tried to grab the defendant. Then there was another stab wound in the left abdomen, at which time Daphne approached Mr. McMorrow and hit him once on the arm. McMorrow pushed her off and she fell to the ground. She then kicked him two times in the right thigh, bruising him, and then she swept his legs from under him. McMorrow fell, at which time the defendant pounced on top of him, stabbing him seven times in the chest, with six of the wounds penetrating his heart.

That, said Bogdanos, was what happened, and that was exactly what the crime scene showed.

Then Bogdanos took aim at Dr. Roh, who, he said, was paid $4,000, but never examined the body, never examined the murder weapon, and yet came up with an opinion that the knife that had been introduced as evidence wasn't the weapon that was used to kill

Michael! Dr. Roh never went to the crime scene, never looked at the Rollerblades, or talked to Dr. Alandy, who performed the autopsy, but, instead, took all his information from his employer: Mr. Kriss. According to Bogdanos, Dr. Roh simply collected his $4,000 and walked. "How dare he, how dare he walk in here without having done one bit of investigation . . . even the court had to cut him off on two separate occasions, saying, 'Doctor, aren't you changing, aren't you [incorrectly] pointing on your head where the wound is to [McMorrow's] head?' How dare he do that."

Bogdanos stated that the crime scene revealed that Christopher, the murderer, with his helper, Daphne, killed Michael McMorrow and then tried to cover it up. And then, as Christopher was trying to destroy evidence, thinking he was covering up the crime by tossing things in the lake, what he was really doing was leaving evidence: lots of blood.

The ADA pointed out that only one item of clothing hadn't been put in the washing machine, and that was Daphne's green vest that. It was the same vest that everyone at Strawberry Fields attested she had worn. It was the same vest that was seen on the video from Blockbuster. And the officers found it alone on a chair in Daphne's room, unwashed, just lying there, with blood and dirt all over it. So, asked Bogdanos, what was missing from that item of clothing that was worn all night by Daphne? After DNA testing, there was no blood of Michael's on it. Not one drop. Why? Simple. "Because she didn't stab him." Her Rollerblades had blood on them, as well they should. And the blood was exactly where it should have been because she kicked Mr. McMorrow, sweeping his feet out from under him. Of course she would have blood there: "He was bleeding from having been stabbed." But there was no blood on her vest, which would have had blood on it if she had stabbed him.

The only place where there was DNA from Michael was on the knife. And lo and behold, said Bogdanos, there was also DNA of Christopher's on it! None of Daphne's. There was a reason for that. "*It* murdered Michael Mc-Morrow in the hands of Christopher Vasquez."

Bogdanos conceded that yes, the defense was correct: Daphne was a pit bull and therefore she must have committed the crime. "She did, she did do it, she's guilty, that's why she's in prison." But, he went on, the defense also wanted you to believe that she must have done it alone. "That is not possible." The defense also wanted the jurors to believe that the more one disliked Daphne, the more that would erase evidence against Christopher. "The more criminal she is, the less criminal he is?" No way, asserted Bogdanos. Daphne was a killer, and that's why she was in prison. And so was Christopher, and that's why he was here, in court. Bogdanos wondered if, after listening to the defense, jurors were supposed to conclude that Miss Abdela did it alone, because some people called her aggressive. But, Bogdanos pointed out, although she was loud and belligerent and boisterous, she didn't actually engage in any violent behavior that entire day. She didn't do anything to Mr. Carhart other than yell at him. She didn't do anything to Mr. Clauson other than yell at him. The same thing at Carl Schurz Park. She was loud. She was obnoxious. She yelled at a person playing chess. "Did she do anything to him? No. Did she touch him? No."

Bogdanos stated that Daphne was all bark and no bite, like an empty barrel that made the most noise. Obnoxious? Yes. Loud? Yes. But violent? No. Simply because the defense wanted to bring in past violence didn't mean that that day or that night, Daphne engaged in any violent actions.

This was not a trial, said Bogdanos, of the people against Daphne Abdela. That was over. She was convicted. This, he reminded the jurors, was a case against Christopher Vasquez. And even if one added up all the bad behavior by Daphne, it still didn't explain what happened at the gazebo that night. Bogdanos conceded that Daphne was "callous" in her 911 call. But, so what? She was bitter in her call to her friend Diane Bass Choate, fearful of Judgment Day. But, so what? Bogdanos pointed out that when Kriss recounted what Daphne had said on the taped call to her friend—"the killer, her she" will be punished—Kriss failed to mention the other parts of the conversation: "Well, you know if they are not punished down here while they are alive, then on Judgment Day they will get what they deserve." Bogdanos declared that in that one sentence, Daphne was telling Miss Choate the truth: *they* will be punished, *they* will get what they deserve. In other words, they *both* did it.

And when the forensics came back, way after Daphne admitted to exactly how she kicked McMorrow's legs out from under him with her Rollerblades on his right thigh—sure enough, there were bruise marks that incontrovertibly matched up with her account. She had told the truth! Blood was also on the bottom of her Rollerblades. She didn't know the state was testing them, stated Bogdanos, but sure enough, when the DNA evidence came back, the blood matched exactly where it should have been, according to her account. Again, she told the truth. And the blood on the back of her vest, which was in custody, was exactly where it should have been if she had been lying on her back, kicking Michael. Truth again. And what was going on while Daphne was kicking Michael?

Christopher was stabbing him. "She can't do two things at once. . . . It's a two-person job." One person, he stated, can't be lying on her back and stabbing someone at the same time. There had to have been a second person for that. And the plea allocution was not a plea allocution bargain, as the defense would like the jurors to believe, Bogdanos went on. The evidence was there: she pleaded guilty to the crime that Miss Hines, as the assistant DA in charge of the prosecution, believed was just and right. Daphne was in prison for manslaughter in the first degree, and she received the maximum sentence.

Bogdanos reminded jurors of Detective Mooney's statements about what took place between Daphne and him when he first interviewed her. At every point during their interview, Mooney stated, he left the room to seek confirmation for what she had said, and at every point, he discovered that she had, in fact, told him the truth. She admitted that she hit Michael. "I hit him. I was coming back from the bushes and I saw Michael had his left hand on Chris's shoulders, on Chris's right shoulder, and Chris had a knife in his hand and he was stabbing him and I skated up, behind him, and I struck him." She told Mooney that she then struck Michael from behind. She even got up and demonstrated to Mooney how it all took place, telling him that with her forearm she hit him on the back, on the victim's right shoulder, and the victim shrugged her off and she fell down backward. Still, all during this, the defendant and the victim were engaged in a deadly struggle, with the defendant stabbing Michael, and Michael holding on to the defendant. Miss Abdela told Mooney, Bogdanos reminded the jurors, that while she was lying on her back, she lifted her feet and kicked Michael with the bottom of her Rollerblades, on the back of his right thigh, which didn't seem to affect Michael at all, so she swept Mr. McMorrow's feet out from under him with her Rollerblades, which caused him to fall down backward. She told Mooney that Christopher then jumped on top of the downed man and continued to stab him. All that, Bogdanos told the jurors, had been corroborated by experts at the trial.

It is clear, he said to the jurors, that Daphne admitted to Mooney what the forensics had conclusively and independently shown. He told the jury that they may not be happy that Daphne was allowed to plead guilty to manslaughter in the first degree for assisting Mr. Vasquez. But, he urged them to set aside those feelings because they had nothing to do with this case. "It will not change what either of them did." But, he stated emphatically, there was a difference between the person who actually did the stabbing and the person who assisted. They both killed Michael, but Christopher murdered him. "We should be clear on this."

Bogdanos pointed out that the people did not have to prove every single fact: was he lying down, standing up, sitting? No, the DA's office did not have to prove how or why, but *who*. Jurors, he suggested, might ask themselves over the course of the trial, *why*? Why would a fifteen-year-old have done what he did? He responded by saying that there was never a good reason why a person would kill, so "stop looking for one." The law, he stated, did not place the burden of figuring out and proving *why*. He urged the jurors not to impose that burden on themselves, either. It was not their duty to determine why.

Summing up his arguments, Bogdanos stated that the court would give the jurors four charges: murder in the second degree under two separate theories (intentional and depraved), manslaughter in the first degree, and manslaughter in the second degree. Bogdanos stated that he would not go into detail about each, knowing that His Honor would be doing that. But he wanted to point out some things that he felt jurors should understand.

The question of whether the murder was intentional or depraved turned on the state of mind of the defendant at the gazebo. If the defendant's conscious aim or objective, when stabbing Michael McMorrow, was to kill him, then he is guilty of murder in the second degree. If instead, the defendant was acting with depraved indifference and callous disregard for human life—but it was not his conscious aim or objective to kill the man—then that was murder in the second degree under the depraved theory.

Those were two counts that the judge would give you, Bogdanos stated. And those were the only two reasonable interpretations of the defendant's actions. "Either he intended to kill Mr. McMorrow with the aid of Miss Abdela, or he just had an absolute callous disregard for human life."

Bogdanos pointed out that the jurors would also hear details about two lesser charges, manslaughter in the first degree, which differed because the intent in that case was "to cause serious physical injury." However, Bogdanos stated, Mr. McMorrow's body told the jury that "this was not manslaughter." What the two teens did was not with the intent to cause serious physical injury. "It was with the intent to kill him. That is murder."

Another count the jurors would be given, stated the ADA, would be manslaughter in the second degree, meaning that when the defendant did this act, he acted recklessly. "I'm submitting to you that any verdict of manslaughter in the first degree or manslaughter in the second degree would not be justice in this case."

Bogdanos asserted that no reasonable view of the

evidence could show that the defendant did these things, but did not intend to kill Michael McMorrow. "Any verdict of less than murder, I submit in this case based on these facts, is a compromise." Bogdanos said that he looked up the definition of compromise and found it to mean "to surrender that which you hold." He told the jurors that His Honor would soon instruct them that it was improper to surrender a conscientiously held belief. In other words, it was wrong to compromise. So, for example, he stated, if the jurors considered the charges and found the defendant guilty of only manslaughter in the first degree, the jurors wouldn't have done justice for anyone, even though "it will make everyone happy." Christopher's family would be happy, realizing he wasn't convicted of murder; the victim's family would understand that the defendant was being made to pay for his crime. But this was wrong. Bogdanos reiterated that this crime was not one that was intended to cause serious physical injury. "Thirty-four wounds before death . . . do not indicate anything other than an intent to cause death. And that is murder."

Bogdanos began winding down his summation with these words: "I'm asking you now to return a verdict of guilty, as to Mr. Vasquez, and I'm asking you to do that because it's the just and right thing to do. Forget about what happened to Daphne Abdela. . . . This is the trial of Christopher Vasquez for the death of Michael McMorrow. I'm asking you that on your oaths, you do justice in this case."

Bogdanos stated that it had been claimed that everyone wanted to go to heaven, but that nobody wanted to die. He stated that he felt that everyone wanted justice done by other people, at another place in time. But, he said, this was the time, this was the place, and the jurors were the people to do justice based on the evidence that they had seen and the oaths they had taken. He urged them to tell Christopher Vasquez that for what he did on that date, he was guilty of murder for having stabbed Michael McMorrow to death. "He is guilty."

Here were two final thoughts, said Bogdanos, before sitting down. He told jurors that around the court hallways, there's a saying that every prosecutor gave two summations: the one the prosecutor actually gave and the one he planned on giving the night before. But, he suggested, there was a third one, the one when you wake up weeks later and bolt out of bed in a "cold sweat at four in the morning and you think of all the things you should have said or should have done that would have made your job easier." He begged the jurors not to allow that to happen, not to allow anything that he or Mr. Plansky did, or failed to do, alter their verdict. "Base your verdict on the evidence, your oaths, and the law, on that and nothing else." Then, he stated, you will indeed have done justice. And justice, he pointed out, meant coming to this conclusion. "At the hands of Christopher Vasquez, Michael McMorrow was murdered. He died faceup in the half-light of that Central Park that he loved so much. One can hope that he didn't see it coming. One can hope that he didn't suffer long. And one can hope that he died quickly. But no one knows that he did."

And with those words, he thanked the jurors and sat down.

The long trial had finally ended, with both sides feeling they had given it their best shot. Juries are known to be unpredictable, and by all accounts, this verdict could touch the extremes of what was possible: guilty of murder, or innocent of all charges.

Time would tell.

CHAPTER 29

On December 3, after a full day of deliberation, jurors asked the judge to once again explain the charge of manslaughter. Court watchers surmised that this could mean one of two things. Either the jurors were confused about what they had been instructed to consider by the judge, or they had already ruled out a conviction of murder and were now considering first- or second-degree manslaughter. If convicted of manslaughter, Christopher could receive a shorter sentence than Daphne.

People watching the case closely felt that the jury was coming close to a verdict, because they asked Judge Corriero if they could continue their deliberations until 10:00 P.M. The McMorrow family, heavily supporting eighty-two-year-old Margaret, and the Vasquezes were called back to the court, just in case a verdict was reached.

However, no verdict was handed down that evening, and the relatives of the defendant and of the deceased returned to their homes. The sequestered jury would reconvene in the morning.

257   BABYFACED BUTCHERS

weary—almost to the point of numbness. Christophe

CHAPTER 30

On December 4 in New York City, temperatures are typically around 40 degrees. On that date in 1997, when Yankee tickets went on sale, the temperature was a chilly 41. However, on December 4, 1998, the thermometer hit a record high of 73 degrees in the afternoon. Air conditioners, rather than heating systems, were turned on, and people on the street could be heard saying: "Let it snow!"

However, even if it had been snowing on that day, things would have been hot in the jury room. It was on that day that the jury, composed of three men and nine women, reached its verdict after thirteen hours of deliberation.

The McMorrows and the Vasquez family were called back to the courtroom. As they waited for the jurors to enter, they talked quietly and nervously. Unlike when the trial began, everyone seemed to have something to say. Reporters chatted and made predictions. The Vasquez family sat nervously whispering in the front rows. The McMorrows talked anxiously with one another. Both families appeared distraught, worn-out, and weary—almost to the point of numbness. Christopher sat at the defense table, looking small, bewildered, and vulnerable—as he had during the entire trial—dwarfed by an oversize gray flannel jacket. With acne and rimless glasses, he looked like the skinny, dorky kid who was always in the back row of a classroom, a person who couldn't be a menace even to a cockroach on his desk. If looks alone told destiny, it would be hard to fathom him as guilty.

After calling the court to order, Judge Corriero asked the forewoman if the jury had reached a verdict. Lenore Bode stood proudly and stated yes, they had reached a verdict. The judge asked Christopher to stand, which he did, along with his attorney.

Bode then proceeded to read the verdict in a strong voice.

"We the jury have found Christopher Vasquez guilty of first-degree manslaughter."

As soon as Christopher heard those words, he looked at his parents and smiled a small smile. The Vasquez family tried to put on a strong front for their son, but Patricia was unable to keep it together and wept openly. It was, of course, a victory of sorts, although they had hoped Christopher would have been acquitted of all charges.

Mrs. McMorrow trembled and then broke down in sobs, with her daughters trying to comfort her. They were overwhelmed with emotion, also, and burst into tears. Theirs were tears of sorrow. No one was going to pay for Michael's death.

Five jurors openly wept. One juror, after looking at Mrs. McMorrow, put her head in her lap and sobbed.

In effect, the verdict meant that neither Daphne nor Christopher was considered guilty of intentionally murdering Michael McMorrow. No one was deemed responsible for the killing.

During the entire trial, the two families—McMorrow and Vasquez—had been in attendance every day, sitting only a few feet apart across the aisle from one another. Neither had been able to look at the other. After the trial ended and everyone was able to stand up and slowly exit the courtroom, the two families filed out as well, one behind the other. Once again, neither acknowledged the other's presence. Neither, it seemed, was willing to credit the other with existence.

Sentencing was set to take place on January 13.

Immediately after the verdict, Kriss told the *News* that the jury was "the most courageous jury I've ever seen," but he stated he still might appeal their verdict. He cited three decisions made by Judge Corriero that he felt adversely affected his client. The first was the admittance into evidence of certain statements Daphne made during her plea bargain, specifically one in which she declared that Christopher was the person who stabbed and killed Michael. Kriss believed that since Daphne was not available to be cross-examined, her statements should not have been permitted into evidence. Secondly, under oath, one of Christopher's friends testified that Christopher started carrying a knife for protection six weeks before the murder. Kriss believed that this information could have wrongly persuaded the jury to believe that simply because Christopher owned the knife, he was the knife wielder. And thirdly, Kriss was upset by the fact that the judge did not allow two statements Daphne made to cops into evidence: that she was afraid her fingerprints were on the knife and that she burned Michael's business cards after he died.

Jurors interviewed afterward about their decision stated that they had been unable to pin the murder squarely on Christopher, nor could they pin it on Daphne. As a result, they had had to let Christopher off on the more serious charge of murder—that, in spite of the prosecution's contention that it was an obvious case of intentional murder, with over thirty stabbings, including six piercings of the heart. One juror remarked that the deliberations had been emotional and intense and that many jurors had felt that Daphne did the stabbing, so there was a reasonable doubt as to Christopher's culpability. The jurors said that they had considered all the evidence carefully and felt they would be able to live with their decision.

Several jurors expressed outrage that Daphne's plea bargain did not require her to testify at Christopher's trial. "One of the biggest problems was that Daphne Abdela was not available and there was nothing to guide us through it," said one juror to a *Times* reporter. "We just felt that we couldn't be sure what happened and were not 100 percent positive that [Christopher] committed a murder." Another juror said that the majority of people on the jury believed that the murderer was Daphne Abdela. They based their opinion on a combination of the testimony they heard about how she had acted that day, along with the physical evidence presented at the trial. A third juror stated that they had even discussed a total acquittal for Christopher. Several jurors stated that all the jurors were extremely sympathetic toward the McMorrow family and felt that allowing Daphne to enter a plea and not having to testify at a trial was both "wrong and offensive." One juror went on to say that the jury had had the chance to try

Christopher, and ultimately acquit him of murder, but they were given no such chance with Daphne. Another juror complained that because Daphne did not testify and therefore could not be cross-examined, they had had to convict Christopher of the lesser charge of manslaughter. Without her testimony, the juror contended, the defense was able to blame her for the murder and leave the jury with a reasonable doubt as to Christopher's culpability.

One juror said that the travesty in the courtroom wasn't the verdict, but "was a system that kept so much evidence out of the courts, so that in the end, the jury was left with a very limited choice." Another juror concurred, saying that "the only thing they could do was work with the evidence and there were so many holes in it."

One juror summed it up this way: someone walked away without being convicted of murder.

Many jurors were upset at what they considered the light sentences both teens would be serving for the killing. In tears, a juror lamented that nobody was really going to pay for the murder, but they had done all they could and had followed the judge's instructions.

Some jurors stated that many things pointed to Christopher's involvement in the murder, but not necessarily to his being the murderer. They heard testimony that Christopher had a cut finger and many bruises, but jurors felt that these could possibly have come from something other than the killing of a man. Also, they felt they could not state with absolutely certainty that Christopher was the knife wielder, because the handle of the knife had never been tested for DNA.

Interviewed after the trial, Michael's brother, Charlie, said that the jury hadn't had the guts to do what was right and make the correct decision. He pointed out that the killing took a half hour and that Michael had some thirty-five stab wounds. He wondered how a jury could come to the conclusion that that was manslaughter. "I think they took the easy way out so they could go home and go to sleep."

Matthew, Michael's nephew, said that what was done was "murder and not manslaughter." He wondered how anyone could confuse the two. He read an angry statement to the waiting press: "There is no doubt in our minds that Christopher Vasquez murdered Michael in cold blood. All the evidence points to him, and even Mr. Vasquez admitted to several psychologists that he murdered Michael. How anyone could confuse thirty-five stab wounds with manslaughter is beyond comprehension." He wondered how Christopher would be able to live with himself "when he knows that he got away with murder." He felt that the prosecution was not to blame for the outcome. Rather, he believed, it was unfortunate that the jury did not see things clearly. He told reporters that what happened in the courtroom was not justice, but instead a disgrace to the criminal justice system. He lambasted the judge for not allowing the psychiatrists' reports to be introduced as evidence.

Christopher's friends and family viewed the result differently. They felt that the jurors did the right thing, although they expressed sympathy for the Mc-Morrow family. Christopher's uncle Michael Tantillo reiterated his belief that Christopher did not commit the murder. He acknowledged that it was a terrible tragedy and thanked the jurors for not convicting his nephew of the crime, but he reiterated that Christopher was innocent and wished he could be with the family right now.

Many people—law enforcement officials, attorneys, interested onlookers, as well as members of the McMorrow family—were also angered that the reports from two teams of psychiatrists who interviewed Christopher after the murder were sealed and could only have been opened if Kriss had gone for a psychiatric defense. Two law enforcement officials, who spoke on the condition of anonymity, reported that in the statements Christopher made to the psychiatrists, he admitted to having killed Michael. His version of the events, they stated, agreed with Daphne's—that Christopher went into a rage and used a knife to slash and ultimately kill the man, after she kissed Michael, and that she eventually joined in the mayhem, but only by kicking out his feet from under him. Kriss, commenting on the sealed records, defended the decision to keep them sealed, saying that at certain times, certain people say things when under a great deal of stress—things that may not be true—and he emphasized that that had been the case with Christopher. Evidence at the scene and police reports, Kriss stated, did not corroborate Christopher's statements to the psychiatrists. "The science in this case didn't support the statements." Kriss contended that this quiet and meek boy would not have done such a terrible thing, whereas the belligerent Daphne would have. Kriss reiterated that a quick, violent attack was not in his client's character, whereas just hours before Daphne met Michael in the park, she was picking fights with more than one adult. Kriss also pointed out that Daphne had blood on her Roller-blades and Christopher did not—evidence, in his mind, that Daphne was the murderer. Kriss also said that he had desperately wanted to cross-examine Daphne in an attempt to prove that her account of the events was false.

The prosecution was flabbergasted that the jurors had not come to the conclusion that all of Christopher's injuries did not convince them that Christopher was the knife wielder. These wounds, he felt, were consistent with a person on the attack, whereas Daphne barely had a scratch on her. Besides, the prosecution stated, Christopher had been packing a knife, and his blood had been found on it, along with Michael's. What more proof did they need?

Detective Mooney was outraged at the verdict, too. He stated that "she is not without sin, but she is not the stabber."

Lawyers admitted that the jurors probably didn't know which youth did it, especially without a codefendant for them to size up on the stand. One attorney commenting on the case, James La Rossa, said that the prosecutors had a difficult time, since the only witness, Daphne, wouldn't cooperate. The jury seemingly came to the conclusion that the teens were equally to blame. "I think the jury stopped thinking about the crime, and started thinking about which one of them was more responsible for it."

Another attorney, who wished to remain anonymous, wrote a statement saying that Judge Corriero had "grotesquely and blatantly misapplied the law in his jury charge." The lawyer declared that it was without any reason that manslaughter one and two should be considered under the circumstances, considering that Michael had been stabbed so many times, eviscerated, and his head almost severed. How could this possibly be manslaughter? the attorney wondered. It is the equivalent, he said, of a conviction of drunk driving (vehicular manslaughter is second-degree manslaughter). He viewed the jury's decision as one in which Christopher was given a free pass, in much

the same way that the DA had given Daphne a free
pass in the plea.

Another attorney stated that Daphne could have
been found guilty of acting in concert with Christopher
in committing second-degree murder—and not have
been given the opportunity to plead guilty to the lesser
manslaughter charge. He wondered what protection society could feel from juvenile murderers. He also questioned whether or not the judge had been intimidated
by the media, the defense lawyers, and the Vasquez
family itself, who claimed that since Daphne had gotten
off with manslaughter—and she was, presumably, as culpable as Christopher—that he, too, should only get
manslaughter.

One lawyer angrily declared, "Go to a law library
and read the statute on manslaughter and murder
and you will see that only murder fits this case."

The public's reactions to the verdict varied. After an
editorial appeared in the *News* on December 6, titled
"Got Away with Murder," in which the columnist suggested that the jury "ought to be locked up following
the Central Park manslaughter verdict," a letter to the
editor of the *News* put the blame squarely on the
shoulders of the district attorney's office. Robert
Casazza wrote that it wasn't the jury's fault that
Christopher practically got away with murder. It was
the Manhattan District Attorney's Office for the way
they handled the case. From his point of view, when
"Robert Morgenthau and his brain trusts granted a
plea to Daphne Abdela without securing her as a prosecution witness," they deprived the jury of the only
witness to crime, thus dooming the prosecution's
case. Naturally, Casazza suggested, the prosecution's
case against Christopher was going to fail. Lamenting
the result, he concluded that the "latest bumbling" by

the DA's office "will result in the release of two more vicious killers who will be free to roam the streets of New York in a very short time."

Another person commenting on the case labeled Corriero a "shameful judge" and accused the DA's office of "selling out." This person stated that Daphne admitted to having tripped Michael, and that it didn't take a genius to know that if you trip someone while another person is wielding a knife against the person, you want the person dead—that you are trying to kill him, that you have the *intent* to kill. He saw the judge's message as loud and clear: if you are a juvenile, kill in pairs and you will walk.

The DA's office let a cold-blooded murderess walk, said another person commenting on the case, and now the judge had sold out.

The *Daily News* lamented that the two would be back walking among us in practically no time at all.

The plea bargain brokered by Sarah Hines created controversy both during the months leading up to the trial and after the verdict was announced. Lawyers commenting on the case stated that with the plea, the case against Christopher was almost impossible to win, since Daphne could not be called as a witness. After a deal had been made with the main perpetrator in a case, said defense lawyer Marvyn Kornberg, it was hard to get a conviction against another person. Other lawyers agreed, saying that the plea deal left prosecutors with a "flimsy" case against Christopher, especially because the only witness was Daphne, and she was not testifying.

The prosecutors, on the other hand, defended their plea deal, saying that they had been afraid Daphne would not be a very good witness, citing her freewheeling use of curses, her quick temper, and her history of alcohol abuse. They said that Daphne would have made a poor witness because she changed her story so many times and would have been unsympathetic on the stand. They felt that in the worst-case scenario, she would have been such a weak witness against Christopher that jurors might have blamed only her for the killing and let him off scot-free. In effect, then, she would have gotten little jail time, and he would have walked. The prosecutors also stated that they had little forensic evidence linking Daphne to the actual killing. Finally some prosecutors said that if they had allowed Daphne to go to trial, "the wrong jury could set her free."

Both prosecutors and defense attorneys complained that the cops should have gotten a more detailed confession from Daphne about her actions on the night of the murder and that the prosecutors should have gotten a more detailed confession in court from Daphne.

The prosecutors in the case were particularly angry that Kriss changed his defense at the last minute, from a psychiatric defense, citing "extreme emotional distress," under which statements made to psychiatrists could be submitted as evidence, to one blaming Daphne for the murder.

Andrea Peyser, noted writer for the *Post,* had been following the story of the murder since the day it took place. She wrote many columns over the years expressing her opinion about the two perpetrators.

On Saturday, December 5, 1998, the day after the manslaughter verdict was handed down for Christopher, her column's headline was BETTER BE AFRAID OF THOSE KILLER ANGELS ON THE LOOSE. She reported that

Detective Mooney had told her that in his mind, the two teens were very scary people. He commented that looking at the kids, he "stared at a sight more ominous than almost any he'd encountered in 15 years on the job." What exactly was the sight? It was the "cold, remorseless faces of children. Killers without reason. Hormone-crazed mutilators of corpses."

Mooney went on to tell her that usually children who kill do so as part of a robbery or other event. But for this murder, he said, there was no obvious explanation. Hiding behind angelic faces, they were not what they seemed. In his words, they were young, "unrepentant and unpredictable"—with "features of angels."

Peyser warned her readers to be afraid because the two teens got away with murder because a jury couldn't decide whether or not Christopher intended to kill Michael McMorrow. Daphne, she labeled "hard-drinking, tough-talking, thrill-seeking."

Mooney told Peyser that during his hours of interviewing Daphne, he had garnered a version of what took place on the night of the crime. Christopher, he noted, was not well-liked—a "Herb," or a "nerd," as kids in his generation called people like Christopher. He met this young lady, who was nice to him, really nice, and they started drinking and hanging out. The afternoon of the murder, as they were drinking, he asked her to be his girlfriend, and she responded: "Oh, yeah." Christopher heard this as a resounding "yes!" To Daphne, it was pure sarcasm—"Yeah, right." Later, both drunk, they decided to take a cab to her apartment. Along the way, she put her hands down his pants. With his hormones raging and his hope soaring, Christopher asked Daphne if they could have sex later, and she responded, "Oh, yeah." Again,

Christopher was elated, while Daphne was just bored.
Then, according to Mooney, in time, the two of them
and Michael went to the gazebo. All three were drinking beers, and Daphne asked Christopher if he
wanted to go swimming. He agreed. They took off
their clothes and went in. When they came out and
got dressed, Christopher saw her naked. His testos-
terone went into overdrive. However, because the
night air was cool and Daphne started shivering,
Michael put his arm around her, trying to keep her
warm. Then, "as Daphne put it" to Mooney, in a split
second, "the next thing I know, we're kissing."
Christopher became outraged at the older man, now
his rival, who had made a pass at his girl, and yelled
at Michael, not Daphne, "Get up, bitch!" Michael, a
gentle man and even more so when he was drunk,
asked his usual, "Are you mad?"

Daphne tried to calm down Christopher and then
headed off to pee in the bushes, wearing her in-line
skates. When she returned, according to Mooney,
Christopher was already stabbing and slashing
Michael. Daphne decided to help, so she hit Michael
from behind, but Michael knocked her over onto her
back. At that point, she kicked Michael in his right
thigh with her Rollerblades, and then his ankles.
Michael fell backward.

Continuing on with his version, Mooney stated that
Christopher, now on top of Michael, kept stabbing
the man as he lay on the ground, all the while, grunt-
ing and breathing hard. After approximately ten minutes, Michael stopped breathing, and Daphne
demanded that Christopher gut him—"Gut him, he's
a fatty." She then gave him instructions as to how to
do that.

Obviously annoyed that he wasn't doing it quickly

enough, Christopher offered her the knife and said, "Here, you think you can do a better job?" But Daphne didn't take the knife. Soon after, the two pushed the man into the lake, where his disemboweled body was later found.

When asked why anyone should believe this version, since it came from Daphne, Mooney replied that the forensics supported the story: the bruises on Michael were exactly where she said she kicked him, and the pattern of blood was consistent with her story. Furthermore, Mooney stated, Daphne had also told him many other things that he later checked out and found to be reliable. For example, she told him about a Pakistani guy who called himself "Max," a person whom she proudly declared to have slept with in the Elk Hotel on Forty-second Street. As ludicrous as that sounded—a fifteen-year-old from a multimillion-dollar home having a tryst at a fleabag hotel—it checked out, as did other stories.

Mooney said that Daphne had broken down in tears during their many hours together, but he didn't think they were tears of remorse. She was crying for herself. Her version of the whole incident was that she was the unlucky one—her friend went crazy and she was simply in the wrong place at the wrong time.

Mooney said that he believed Daphne knew right from wrong, but he had no answer to the question of what you do when kids kill with no reason, other than to be fearful, because they're going to get out of jail soon and will one day be walking around among us.

Mooney said that after the murder, whenever he was with his own young son and daughter, he often thought of the baby-faced butchers. He said that what went down made him spend even more time with his kids and pay even more attention to them and "love them even more than I thought I could."

He then stated that if Daphne had been given "proper guidance," perhaps the murder wouldn't have taken place. But then, in a contradictory statement, he mused, "But she knew right from wrong. And still, it came to that."

Mooney pondered, "What do you do with kids who kill without any reason at all? What do you do when a jury gives them a sentence that has them back on the street before voting age?"

Answering his own questions, he said, "First you be afraid. Then you hug your kids closer. It's not much, but it's the best we can do."

On the same day that Peyser's column appeared, the *Post*'s front-page headline read: BABYFACE OUTRAGE. In slightly smaller type, the words were: "Central Park victim's kin blast jury for letting teen suspect off the hook."

Another article in the *Post* that day, highly critical of the outcome, stated that crucial information, which could have helped jurors make a more informed decision, was ruled inadmissible—that Christopher told four psychiatrists that he committed the murder; that he was a psychiatric patient who was on two medications for agoraphobia: Zoloft, a mood elevator, and Lorazepam, a sedative; that Christopher's motive for killing was sexual jealousy; that Daphne had sexually taunted Christopher the entire day before he snapped and killed Michael after the older man kissed her. Also they never heard that Daphne had slapped her father in the weeks before the murder or that her drinking problem was so serious that she had been hospitalized for treatment. Other issues, the article claimed, that contributed to Christopher getting away with murder were mistakes made by the cops: Daphne's alcohol level was never tested by police that night, nor were her hands bagged. If, for example, the jurors learned she was drunk or drugged during the killing, they might not have given any weight to her testimony that Christopher was the murderer.

A few days after the verdict, Kriss made his decision about whether or not to appeal the manslaughter decision. He told reporters that he most likely would not appeal, since a retrial would mean "rolling the dice with another jury." Instead, he stated, he might go to a higher court with the manslaughter charge, hoping for a more lenient sentence.

CHAPTER 31

On December 16, 1998, on behalf of the McMorrow family, Joan McMorrow filed a wrongful-death suit for $150 million against Daphne and Christopher. The McMorrow family was enraged that neither teen had been convicted of murder. Joan stated, "Our family's loss is not lessened because Michael was senselessly murdered by a juvenile. Our pain and suffering is not lessened because Michael was brutally butchered by a juvenile. Therefore, why should their sentence be less? What was the point of having them tried as adults only to have them sentenced as juveniles? Why was the jury not made aware that he'd be sentenced as a juvenile?" She went on to say, "Every year we will have to face Michael's killers and plead with two separate parole boards to keep them in jail. What kind of justice is this for our family?"

The criminal justice system failed them, said the McMorrow's attorney Robert Sullivan, so they were forced to pursue civil matters. The suit sought $50 million in compensatory damages and $100 million in punitive damages. Sullivan remarked that since

Michael had not died immediately, the complaint sought damages for the pain and suffering Michael had endured, along with the fact of his death. "This was a wholly innocent person who went through a horrible death." The suit also sought to prevent either teen from benefiting from a book or movie deal. Sullivan said he was doing this in case the "Son of Sam" law was ever repealed, thus making it legal for criminals to profit from their crimes.

Commenting on the wrongful-death suit, Christopher's lawyer, Kriss, said that his client had no intention of writing a book or having a movie done about the murder. Daphne's lawyer did not respond to the suit.

Soon after the lawsuit was filed, Daphne was deposed by attorneys representing the McMorrows, in upstate Johnstown, New York, where she was imprisoned at the Tryon Girls Center. Her lawyer at that time, Paul F. Callan, said that Daphne had expressed great remorse for what happened, and she wanted to stay on the road to rehabilitation. She said that if the McMorrow family would visit her in prison, she would tell them in person how sorry she was. She also admitted, for the first time under oath, that she believed she saw Christopher use stones to stuff Michael's gutted abdomen so the dead man would sink quickly to the lake bottom.

Sullivan doubted she was sincere in expressing remorse for what happened. He revealed that he had spoken to Daphne's family about a settlement, but they had refused. A settlement would mean that Daphne would not have to worry about a later suit, but it could possibly also mean that her inheritance would be affected.

In the end, the McMorrows received a $60,000 settlement from the Abdelas. However, after they paid their lawyer, after they paid for Michael's funeral, and after they bought a bench in Central Park in Michael's memory, the money was nearly all gone.

Although a life can never have a specific dollar amount attached to it, it nevertheless seemed to the McMorrows that their loved one's life was, once again, disrepected and trivialized.

CHAPTER 32

On December 23, the *Post* printed an article written by one of the jurors, Michael D. Kelly. It was the first time a juror had spoken out without hiding his or her identity. Kelly began by saying how appalled he had been by how the deliberations were going—toward full acquittal—that on the last day, he told his fellow jurors that he "could no longer take part in this mockery of justice." Eventually, the jurors were able to calm him down, and they persuaded him to work with them. Six hours later, they had a manslaughter conviction.

Kelly went on to explain that the day after the jurors reached their verdict to convict Christopher of first-degree manslaughter, he was at home, shaking, and slammed a newspaper to the floor, "uttering epithets that unnerved my wife." He called the police work in the investigation "mediocre." He was enraged at the insufficient evidence and bothered by the dubious judicial rulings. But what really got him incensed was reading in the newspaper the morning following the verdict that Christopher had confessed to four psychiatrists that, after being told to do so by

Daphne, he stabbed Michael over thirty times before throwing his dead body into the lake.

Kelly learned that Christopher's confessions were only one of many pieces of evidence deemed inadmissible. The fact that Christopher took drugs for depression, for example, wasn't allowed into the evidence. The facts that Christopher was pathologically shy and suffered so severely from agoraphobia that he had to be homeschooled for two years wasn't allowed into testimony. The fact that Christopher felt that simply because Daphne paid him attention, that meant she had feelings for him, wasn't allowed into testimony.

Juror Kelly railed about the "odoriferous plea allocution" of Daphne, and how, "incredibly," the judge told them that they didn't have to believe the plea if evidence was submitted contrary to it, or if they thought that Daphne was a liar. He complained that the jurors did not have the information that she assaulted her parents, had a serious problem with alcohol since she was twelve, and that she had trysts with a man twice her age in "fleabag Times Square hotels."

Kelly also was enraged that up until the last day of the trial, the judge had instructed them to consider only second-degree murder one, with intent; and second-degree murder two, with depraved indifference to human life. However, on the day of closing arguments, the judge, seemingly from out of nowhere, told the jurors that they would now be considering two additional charges—manslaughter. "My first assumption was that the prosecutor must have agreed to the lesser charges because he concluded his case wasn't strong enough for a murder conviction."

He lamented that after the case, lo and behold, he learned that no such thing had taken place. The prosecutor hadn't agreed to any reduced charges, but, instead, had those charges imposed on him after the judge was persuaded to do so by the defense attorney.

With the second-degree manslaughter conviction, the jurors came up with a verdict "that left a bad taste in everyone's mouth," stated Kelly.

His main outrage, however, was that although one of New York's citizens was brutally murdered, no one was being held responsible for that death.

On January 22, 1999, Kriss asked the court to overturn his client's manslaughter conviction. He said that he believed a jury would have acquitted Christopher if they had known that Assistant District Attorney Sarah Hines, when she made the plea agreement with Daphne, had serious doubts as to Daphne's credibility. This, Kriss said, was stated in the sealed transcript of an informal meeting that had taken place in Corriero's chambers in February 1998.

Corriero stated that Hines's sealed account detailed opinions, not facts, and they did not have to be turned over.

Kriss's motion was denied.

On the day of sentencing, January 25, 1999, Judge Corriero called the court to order.

It was a solemn day. Everyone knew there would be no winners. Perhaps the only consolation that could come out of this day was that maybe each family would somehow come to understand the sorrow of the other.

In his effort to make sure the judge would give Christopher the harshest sentence possible, Bogdanos began the proceedings by describing his version of the murder—how an out-of-control Christopher went berserk with rage at Michael after Daphne and Christopher swam nude in the lake. He stated that Christopher cursed as he wrestled the guts out of Michael, before saying to Daphne, "I always knew I wanted to do something like this." After he concluded his speech, the judge said that there would be two victim impact statements from the sisters of Michael, and a short statement from Charlie, Michael's brother. Joan read hers first, in a quiet, but strong and dignified, voice:

"The images of Michael's sheer terror and pain before he died have filled our thoughts for many sleepless nights. The thought of Michael being tortured and mutilated in his final moments will haunt us for the rest of our lives."

Anne urged the judge to give Vasquez the maximum sentence allowed in the verdict of manslaughter—ten years. "Don't let the judicial system fail us further," she said.

When Anne took her seat, Charlie took a few moments to express his thoughts. He urged the judge to give Christopher the maximum term. He stated angrily that the jury had let a murderer go free, and he vowed to appear at all parole board hearings for both youths to try to keep them from winning an early prison release.

The judge then spoke in a solemn voice. Looking directly at Christopher, he said, "Christopher Vasquez will have the opportunity to explain why this happened, to put to rest the controversy that erupted with the verdict. . . . You have the power to speak the truth . . . to put an end to the mystery that exists in certain people's minds about what happened that evening when you started Rollerblading with your friend Daphne Abdela on a warm spring evening in Central Park. How do we get from there to the death of Michael McMorrow? How do we go from that night to the nightmare? . . . You have the opportunity to resolve all that for us. You'll gain little by your silence. You'll lose the opportunity to speak the truth, explain your behavior, and accept responsibility."

It was an unusual request. Judges don't often ask, or beg, a defendant to speak his or her version of the truth. A shocked and anticipatory audience awaited. Would Christopher speak for the first time? Would he offer his version of the truth?

After conferring with his lawyer, Christopher decided to ignore the judge's pleas and instead read from a prepared statement. He stood up and spoke softly and with no emotion in his voice.

"I understand the terrible pain Mr. McMorrow's mother and his family members must feel every day. I feel so terrible for them and I am sorry for them. I wish that Mr. McMorrow's death never happened. . . . Every day, I also think about that night, and why I went with Daphne to Central Park. If I went home as I always did, and did not stay out late, I would not be here today. . . . I am not a bad person."

After Christopher concluded his remarks, a furious judge shot back, saying that the evidence showed "you had the knife . . . you used the knife . . . you inflicted the wounds that killed Michael McMorrow. I'm giving you every opportunity to explain, to tell us why it happened. Tell me. Explain it to me."

But Corriero received no answer, so he stated: The "inference is that you are guilty of inflicting the fatal wounds. I gave you every opportunity to explain to me where it came from, why did it happen, what pushed you to do this. I don't have that. The jury didn't have it. No one has it. . . . I must therefore give you the maximum sentence allowed, since you won't speak. The only sentence I'm left with is one that takes your youth away from you."

A frustrated Corriero made the pronouncement that Christopher Vasquez would receive the maximum penalty for manslaughter—three years and four months to ten years in prison. He also recommended that Christopher serve his full sentence and not be paroled before he did so.

Under the state's "good time" law, a person must be released from prison after serving two-thirds of his or her maximum time.

Afterward, Charlie McMorrow stated that the family would fight parole. Joan expressed her point of view, saying that in Christopher's prepared statement, "all he did was apologize for missing his curfew that night and for upsetting his parents." Joan wondered out loud whose punishment was the more severe—that of the killers, or that of the victim and his family.

Court observers noted that Corriero had not made the request that Daphne serve her full sentence before being allowed out on parole. Kriss was inflamed at Corriero's statements. He told reporters outside the court that he had advised his client not to implicate himself, as Corriero was asking him to do, citing the constitutional right against self-incrimination. He went on to say, "His was a court of law and not the confessional. [Corriero's] request was totally inappropriate."

CHAPTER 33

To honor Michael, the McMorrow family donated $5,000 to adopt a bench in Central Park. The bench is located in Strawberry Fields and faces north and slightly west, with an upside-down view of the "Imagine Mosaic."

A cherished destination for the entire McMorrow family, especially Margaret, the bench became official on May 29, 2000, a day before Michael would have turned forty-eight.

It is there that family members experience the deepest connection to Michael. If not ever again in this life, they can still enjoy the park together—as they did when they were younger, happier, more hopeful, and more innocent.

The silver plaque on the bench reads:

"In Memory of Michael 'Irish' McMorrow,
'Oh for the touch of a vanished hand,
And the sound of a voice that is still.'"

These words are from the poem "Break, Break, Break," by Alfred, Lord Tennyson (1809–1892):

Break, break, break,
On thy cold gray stones, O Sea!
And I would that my tongue could utter
    The thoughts that arise in me.

O, well for the fisherman's boy,
    That he shouts with his sister at play!
O, well for the sailor lad,
    That he sings in his boat on the bay!

And the stately ships go on
    To their haven under the hill;
But O for the touch of a vanish'd hand,
    And the sound of a voice that is still!

Break, break, break,
    At the foot of thy crags, O Sea!
But the tender grace of a day that is dead
    Will never come back to me.

Margaret McMorrow takes the bus to the park and
then walks a lot before going to the bench. Sometimes, after she leaves the bench, she walks down to
the gazebo where her son was murdered. She said,
"It's an awfully busy place. Buses are always coming
and going. I get depressed, but then someone talks to
me and I feel a bit better. The people who killed
Michael got away with it, they are out enjoying life.
Even after all these years, I'm still trying to make
sense of the murder. Each day I ask myself, why? What
would make anyone do something like that?
    "I believe in God," she said. "It helps."

CHAPTER 34

Soon after her plea deal, Daphne was transferred from Spofford to the Tryon Girls Center, in upstate New York. There, in a single room of spartan simplicity—cinder block walls, a metal reinforced window to the outside, and a solid metal door with a small Plexiglas window—she arose each day at 5:30 A.M. and said her prayers. Until midafternoon, she attended classes and reported to the kitchen, where she washed dishes. During the day, she also attended group counseling sessions in anger management and substance abuse, both required components of her sentence. In her leisure time, she played basketball, chess, and worked at arts and crafts.

While in prison, Daphne earned her high-school diploma, passing the GED test with a score of 324 out of a possible 350. She also took college courses in social and behavioral sciences, with an eye toward getting a college degree, and she studied about a variety of faiths. Some people reported that she converted to Islam. At various times, during her incarceration, she wrote group letters to the teachers from her church, expressing remorse and the desire to change her life.

During the months before the murder, and while she was in prison, it was reported that she desperately wanted to know who her birth parents were. The Abdelas, too, were eager to find out, not only to ease their daughter's mind, but also because they knew their daughter was alcoholic and wondered if her birth parents' genes had anything to do with that.

Under 1997 law, Daphne was eligible for parole after serving two-thirds of her sentence. Had the murder been committed after August 1998, when "Jenna's Law" was passed, she would have had to serve six-sevenths of her sentence. The new law was part of a get-tougher policy, targeting first-time violent felony offenders by requiring longer incarcerations.

On August 23, 2000, Daphne, then eighteen years old, came up for her first parole hearing. It was a short meeting before the parole board, and at the end of it, she was denied release and told she would have to wait the maximum amount of time required by law—two years—before she could appear before the board again.

Interviewed in prison in late 2001, around four years after she was first incarcerated, Daphne stated that going to jail had probably saved her life, since she had been heading downhill. "I'm sure that God has a plan and that in some weird way, this (the murder) was part of it." She stated that she did not believe in God before the incident, but that she had found a god in prison. During the interview, she wondered out loud if the McMorrow family would be willing to forgive her. She said that if she saw them, she would tell them that, if she could, she would turn back the hands of time and without any doubt change the events that took place. Asked if she had any contact with her codefendant, she stated emphatically that she did not, and she had no wish ever to be in contact with him again. She said that some good things had come out of her incarceration. She had learned to accept people, regardless of their race, religion, or economic status. She had become a different person from the "pouting, unrepentant teen" who snarled to reporters after her arrest, "Get outta my face." She said that she had learned "patience, tolerance, and spirituality," and that she sometimes needed to reach out for help and to fess up when she was wrong.

Daphne's second parole hearing was held on July 31, 2002, at the Mt. McGregor Correctional Facility, in upstate New York's Saratoga County. Before the meeting, Brafman stated that Daphne was a perfect candidate to be released. On the other hand, one high-ranking official who had worked on the original investigation saw it differently. He called her a "vicious little freak," and wondered how long she would stay out—if she were let out then—"before she is sent back for another horrendous crime"?

During the one-hour hearing, Daphne, now twenty, admitted to the two parole officers interviewing her that before the murder of Michael she had had a lot of disagreements with her parents, especially about the rules that they imposed on her. She stated that she was acting out to let them know that they didn't understand what she was going through. She also said that her major mistake occurred when she started drinking and hanging out and that that was what impelled her to go to the park that night. She stated that she wished she could go back and speak to the girl who was Daphne then and tell her that things would not always be as they were and that "you know, what's most important is your family and school, and those weren't my priorities when I was home."

During the hearing, Daphne reportedly downplayed her role in the murder, saying that she had been there, but simply as the person who tried to stop a deadly fight between Christopher and Michael. She admitted that she and Christopher were in the park drinking with Michael, but she claimed that Chris got enraged after Michael kissed her and tried to take off her clothes. She told the officers that Michael then grabbed Chris, and Daphne tried to help out her friend by kicking Michael's legs out from under him. She said that after Michael was on the ground, she saw that he was bleeding and having difficulty breathing, but she hadn't realized at first that he had been stabbed and that his throat had been slashed. She said she checked his pulse, and when she found that he didn't have one, she immediately gave him mouth-to-mouth resuscitation two times, but to no avail. She went on to say that she then screamed at Chris and asked him if he knew "what the 'f—' he just did. I told him he just killed someone." Chris responded, "I know." She said she begged Chris to get help, but all he wanted to do was get rid of the evidence, including the body, which he did—alone—according to Daphne.

When asked by the parole board about her admitted statement that she told Christopher to gut him— "He's a fatty, he'll sink"—she responded that she did, in fact, say that, but only when Chris said to her that the "fat motherf'er isn't sinking." She reported that she then said, "If you gut him, he'll sink." It was then that Christopher reportedly told her that he was "putting rocks in him." When asked if she had told Chris to stuff the body with rocks, she said she had not, that it was Chris's idea.

The board members asked her how she was feeling

back then, in the months before the murder and on the day of the murder. She said she was "angry, unfocused, narrow-minded. It was all about me." When asked how she felt about the killing, she admitted that it was something that she wasn't able to forget, even though it took place five years before. "I look back now and how I was, and I was just young and stupid and really not worried about much of anything. It's with me every single day, and it's not something I'll ever forget." She added that the major mistake she made was when she started drinking and hanging out, which led up to her being in the park that night.

During the hearing, Daphne expressed sorrow at Michael's death. She told the board that she had contemplated writing a letter to the McMorrows, but she had reconsidered, feeling that they wouldn't want to hear anything from her. She said that she had put herself in their place and decided that if she were them, a McMorrow, she probably would not want to receive a letter from her. When asked what she would like to do with her life when she was released from prison, she stated that she would like to work with kids.

After the hearing ended, the two parole officers met to discuss what they had heard and to scrutinize Daphne's record. It didn't take them long to come to their decision. In a 2–0 vote, the board denied her parole. They recognized the many positive things that had taken place while she was incarcerated: her behavior had improved; she had received her high-school diploma and completed college courses; she had tutored inmates in mathematics; and she was working toward a career in counseling juveniles convicted of serious offenses. However, they also noted that her prison record included "disciplinary problems" since her last board appearance, and they cited the "particularly brutal" nature of the crime, her "total disregard for human life," and her minimizing of her role in it.

The decision included the requirement that she wait the maximum amount of time required by law—two years—before becoming eligible for parole again, at which time she had to be granted parole—on January 19, 2004. However, it was also possible that she could be granted an early release for good behavior. If she was not granted early release, she might be transferred from a youth facility to a woman's prison when she turned twenty-one, on May 18, 2003.

After the decision denying parole was announced, Brafman expressed his and the Abdelas' bitter disappointment, saying that they felt the board made a terrible mistake. He stated that Daphne did not minimize her role in the murder. He said she was extremely remorseful and now capable of being a responsible person in society.

The decision to deny Daphne parole brought some relief to the McMorrows, who had not been informed ahead of time about the hearing. They had learned about it only the day before, when the *Post*, in following up on the McMorrow murder, discovered the hearing date. Because the McMorrows hadn't had enough time to plan a trip to the facility, they faxed their comments to the parole board before the hearing.

On July 31, 2002, Andrea Peyser gave details in the *Post* about some of the letters that Daphne had sent her during their two-year correspondence, which had begun when Daphne was sixteen. Peyser wrote that when she first received a letter with perfect, boxy handwriting from prison, her immediate thought was to throw the letter away, but she reconsidered when she saw that it was from Daphne. Having labeled Daphne a "demon seed with a platinum card" and a "rich, sexually active, alcoholic teen-without-conscience," she was surprised that Daphne was reaching out to her.

At the start of the correspondence, Peyser thought that perhaps Daphne was trying to show her that she had a conscience. "I believe in God," Daphne wrote. But it soon became clear that Daphne was simply responding to a column Peyser had written in which she worried that prison wouldn't do anything to improve the teen. Daphne chastised Peyser, saying that the columnist should think about what she says about others and "their bad decision-making and mishaps"—but never mentioned that she, herself, should be the one doing exactly that.

In one letter that Daphne wrote to Peyser, on November 8, 1998, Daphne stated that Peyser seemed to be experiencing problems and that she, Daphne, was surprised that Peyser was asking for sympathy after "all the cruel, untrue lies you wrote on me and others." The "problems" Daphne referred to were expressed by Peyser in a column recounting her nightmare dealing with the Department of Motor Vehicles over parking tickets. Daphne warned Peyser in her letter, saying that whatever a person does, comes back "thrice." And she continued, "Do you believe that each and every one of us reaps what we sow? I believe so, and so it is important to watch what we do!"

Peyser couldn't believe the analogous reasoning Daphne was putting forth—Daphne being put in jail for manslaughter and Peyser's problems with the Department of Motor Vehicles.

As the correspondence continued, Daphne alternately baited and tried to impress Peyser. She regaled Peyser with her imagined superior intuition, guessing that Peyser's height was between five feet three inches and five feet five inches—Peyser was, in fact, five feet three inches, and by guessing at Peyser's weight, 135 to 145 pounds, to which Peyser quipped: "Maybe at nine months pregnant." Daphne suggested that Peyser wanted a cat, and Peyser suggested that she certainly would—but only if it was deep-fried. Daphne suggested that Peyser had strong sentiments regarding her father, and Peyser mentioned that her father had died twenty years ago. It was Peyser's belief that in all these details, Daphne was simply speaking about herself.

In discussing her feelings about the crime, Daphne wrote in a letter of July 22, 1999, "I'm sure there hasn't been a day where the impact of foolishness, bad judgement [*sic*], and recklessness hits the McMorrow family. [On all three of our parts], I wish that no one has to endure the suffering and discomfort that all of us in this saga have. The world can be harsh, but it's what you put in it, that you get out. I feel for the McMorrow family, without a doubt. However, there is more than one victim here."

To Peyser, this was simply unbelievable. "More than one victim?" Daphne must be kidding, heartless, or insane to equate herself and Michael as equal victims. The closest Daphne had come to admitting any wrongdoing, stated Peyser, was to say that she had made bad decisions. In the end, Peyser summed up Daphne as "defiant, defensive, begging for respect. And scary." She labeled her a "stone-faced killer."

About a month later, on September 9, 2002, Daphne received word at prison that her adoptive

mother, Catherine, had died. It was a shock, since her
mother had not been sick in the days and months pre-
ceding her death. The following obituary appeared in
the *New York Times:*

> ABDELA-Catherine. On September 9, 2002. Died
> suddenly from cardiac arrest at 60. She leaves
> behind her bereaved husband Angelo, her devas-
> tated daughter Daphne, and her distraught
> mother as well as her family and friends world-
> wide. A service will be held on Thursday, Septem-
> ber 12 at 3 PM at West End Collegiate Church,
> 368 West End Avenue and 77 St. Donations may
> be sent to North American Conference on
> Ethiopian Jewry, PO Box 757, Milwaukee, WI.
> 53201-9338.

Daphne was granted her request to return to New
York City for the funeral.

It was a solemn and particularly poignant service,
with all the parishioners at West End Collegiate
Church painfully aware that Catherine's only daughter was in attendance, straight from prison. Armed officers were stationed respectfully outside.

After the service, parishioners commented that
Daphne was poised but seemed distant. She gave and
received no hugs.

During the early months of 2002, the Vasquez family
hired Jonathan Garelick, an attorney from legal aid, to
submit an appeal to overturn Christopher's manslaughter conviction. Garelick put forth two arguments
to support his appeal. One was that the evidence taken
from the Vasquez apartment should have been sup-

pressed because it was not obtained legally—police were allowed into the apartment by an uncle who lived on the same floor as the Vasquezes and had keys to the Vasquez's apartment, as well as to Christopher's grandparents'. In response, the appeals board said that the police had asked permission to be let in and the uncle did so willingly. "This warranted a reasonable inference by the police that these close relatives had arranged for mutual access to each others' apartments, and the police inquiry prior to entering was sufficient under the circumstances," the appeals panel wrote, as reported in *Newsday*. The second argument was that Daphne's guilty plea statements should not have been submitted as evidence in Christopher's trial. It was Garelick's argument that since Daphne could not be cross-examined—a condition of her plea bargain—his client was not given the right to confront his accuser.

On October 17, 2002, in a unanimous 4–0 decision, the appellate division voted to affirm Christopher's conviction and sentence.

Garelick was out of the country, but his office said they would appeal the decision.

In January 2003, both Daphne and Christopher were moved from juvenile facilities to adult prisons. Daphne was transferred to Albion Correctional Facility, which, like Tryon, was located in upstate New York. Christopher was transferred to Wyoming Correctional Facility, also in upstate New York.

While Daphne was at Albion, Linda Foglia, a spokesperson for the Corrections Department, reported that Daphne worked in the metal-welding department. She earned 32 cents an hour. Christopher was a welding student and also studied general mechanics. Daphne had a clean disciplinary record. Christopher received one disciplinary ticket for smoking.

By law, both Daphne and Christopher were required to be released after serving two-thirds of their sentences, or six years and eight months.

On Friday, January 16, 2004, Daphne was released from Albion Correctional Facility. She was twenty-one years old.

On Wednesday morning, January 21, 2004, Christopher, now twenty-two, was released from Wyoming Correctional Facility.

"If it were up to the parole board," stated Tom Grant, of the State Division of Parole, "they would still be in prison." Each time they came up for parole, the board denied them parole and set the maximum waiting time, two years, for their next opportunity for parole.

On the day of Daphne's release, her father, Angelo, refused to talk to reporters when they came to the Majestic apartment building, where it was assumed that Daphne would once again live. When Daphne did arrive there, she cursed at the crew of reporters stationed outside. It was reported that she told waiting reporters "to get the 'f—' out" as she scooped her right arm up and to the ground, fingers spread, like "some wannabe rapper." Andrea Peyser reported in her *Post* column on January 22: "She went to prison a young punk and came out a slightly older punk." She went on to say that prison had not changed Daphne. Her expression, stated Peyser in her *Post* article, detailed a person who "glared as if right through me." She stated her expression was "as cold and dead as the day she was sent upstate for helping to kill and carve up a man." Peyser reported that Daphne yelled out, "Yo!" to her and "Get the 'f—' out of my building."

The reporter commented on Daphne's "ample figure," which was "swallowed up in a bulky black parka, making her look like the negative image of the Stay-Puft marshmallow man." Peyser reported that Daphne kept yelling at her as she retreated, and labeled this "not a nice way to greet a pen pal." At the end of the article, Peyser stated that she had prayed that prison would soften Daphne's act. "She doesn't seem to have learned a thing," Peyser declared.

Upon his release, Christopher went directly to his father's apartment. When the press tried to photograph him and his father, Gerardo angrily shooed them away. One day after his release, Christopher was seen at 9:00 A.M. walking outside his apartment. He didn't speak to reporters but hurried into a taxi. He had to report to his parole officer within twenty-four hours of his release.

According to the conditions of their release, Daphne and Christopher were required to report to parole officers and stay under the parole board's supervision until May 2007, when their ten-year sentence would end. Neither was permitted to travel outside of the five boroughs of New York City. They were required to find jobs or attend school. They were not allowed to have any contact with each other, except with special advance permission. They were not allowed to drink alcohol or patronize places where alcohol was served. Their curfew began at 9:00 P.M. every night and ended at 7:00 A.M.

When prison officials made the announcement on January 24, 2004, that both Daphne and Christopher were free from prison, the McMorrow family blasted the prison system. With no less anger than on the day Daphne entered her plea bargain or on the day Christopher was convicted of manslaughter, Margaret stated, "They're animals!" She reiterated the question that she still couldn't get out of her mind: how could human beings have done such a thing? Michael's sister Anne said that she was disgusted by their release and their short prison sentences and repeated what had been said about Michael by everyone who knew him: he loved New York and he especially loved Central Park. "I can't believe how unfair they were to him." When Michael's brother heard about the teens' release, he expressed his outrage. "Six years for what they did to my brother?"

Paul F. Callan, Daphne's lawyer, said that he had not been in contact with Daphne since her release and that he would have no comment. Arnold Kriss, Christopher's lawyer, said that the Vasquez family would have no comment and that they were trying to put the entire issue behind them.

The McMorrows were not willing or able to put the whole thing behind them. In an article in the *Post* written by Steve Dunleavy, the reporter detailed how one of Michael's sisters was angered at not having been notified by the parole board of the hearing. Michael's nephew echoed the sentiment saying that the parole board had failed to contact them about two previous hearings as well. Joan reported that since Michael's death, her mother had been suffering from a painful case of shingles. "Obviously, she and our family will never get over it." Charlie, Michael's brother, stated that he was "pissed off" and glad he didn't live in New York anymore. "And I have to relive this all over again. . . . It's not a day I like to think about." Dunleavy ended his column by saying that Daphne was twenty-one years old, pudgy-cheeked, and now knew the taste of prison. "If she really wanted to atone for her sins, and face the worst punishment imaginable, go see the family and try to make your peace with them, if you have the guts."

On January 18, 2004, two days after Daphne's release, Strawberry Fields was covered with snow. Void of people, it was pristine and quiet. As on most mornings—snow or no snow—Michael's park friend Gary passed his buddy's bench to touch it and say hello to his departed friend. That day, he saw a note on it next to a bouquet of frozen carnations. He picked up the note and read it: "Rest easy," it said. "I tried to save you. I'm sorry I failed you. I'm sorry for the pain I caused you & your family." It was signed "D."

Gary immediately knew who had written it, but to be absolutely sure, he took it across the street to the Majestic for confirmation. A doorman confirmed that Daphne had come home two days before.

After hearing about the note that Daphne had left on the bench honoring Michael, two mental-health experts were contacted for their views on it and on the person who left the note. Dr. Marcella Bakur Weiner said that the note indicated that Daphne was still just focusing on herself. "She is a flame that is going to ignite," she stated. Psychologist Estyne Del Rio-Diaz, Ph.D., came up with her own diagnosis for Daphne: multiple personality disorder. She felt that the remorseful Daphne wrote and placed the note in the park. When Daphne's lawyer read this analysis in the paper, he was outraged. He stated that psychiatrists who diagnose patients without interviewing them are "a danger to the medical profession."

Right after the teens were released from prison, the Internet was once again abuzz with postings:

One writer from Stony Point wondered how Americans could have any faith in the criminal-justice system when people who commit heinous murders are paroled after serving the minimum sentence—especially considering the fact that people who commit lesser crimes sometimes serve 30 years of hard time. "There ought to be a law," he declared.

Another writer stated that if the police had done their job that night, Michael would have been arrested. Although it was tragic that he died "at the hands of these two misguided children," they have served their time and they should be permitted to go on with their lives. Daphne is no longer a teen but is now a young woman, declared the writer.

A writer from the Bronx stated that she doubted the sincerity of Daphne's apology, which was printed in the *Post.* She questioned, too, that Daphne was truly sorry for the pain she caused the McMorrows. "If a cold-blooded killer like this can be set loose on an unsuspecting public, something is wrong with the law." The writer was outraged that the parole board never contacted the McMorrows and felt that that alone was a strong reason to make some serious changes in the judicial system. "It seems a safe bet that Abdela will someday again be a guest of the state of New York."

"I applaud Andrea Peyser and the *Post* for bringing to light what a monster this kid is ('She went to prison a young punk and came out a slightly older punk,' Jan. 22)," said one writer. The writer continued by stating that from everything she has read about Daphne, she can't see one bit of remorse. "Prison should be a place of rehabilitation, but it looks like it failed this case."

* * *

On the Sunday after her release, Daphne attended the 11:00 A.M. service at the West End Collegiate Church. Afterward, she seemed happy as she smiled and talked with others in attendance. She also looked more fit—thinner and healthier—and was wearing makeup. She had on a black corduroy coat, a black knit hat, and a pair of gray wool pants. "It was a major transformation from a young adolescent—whom you couldn't tell if she was a girl or boy—to an attractive young lady," said one of the church's Sunday-school teachers. The kids with whom she had spent time in Sunday school embraced her, much to her surprise, and she returned the hugs. When she left the church, *Post* reporters following her asked if she would like to say something to the McMorrow family, but she remained silent. According to the *Post,* she "simply glowered." A man with her screamed, "Leave us alone!" as the two entered a cab. Daphne attended church the following Sunday as well.

On October 13, 2004, nine months after her release from prison, twenty-two-year-old Daphne was arrested on misdemeanor charges in Brooklyn. Police reported that she had been making threatening phone calls to an ex-con she knew from Spofford, who now lived in Brooklyn. According to the report, the two were not close friends. The twenty-year-old woman had been convicted of knifing someone in a malicious attack in a Chelsea park. Daphne was angered because the woman would not allow an ex-con friend of Daphne's to stay at the woman's apartment.

A parole spokesman stated that while the incident was being investigated, Daphne would have her curfew adjusted by two hours, so she would now have to be at home by 7:00, not 9:00 P.M. The curfew was to remain in effect until 7:00 A.M.

On November 10, 2004, Daphne appeared in Brooklyn Criminal Court to face the harassment charge. If convicted, she could be returned to prison. After the pretrial hearing, as reporters waited outside to talk to her, Daphne covered her face with her jacket, but not before she stuck out her tongue to reporters.

CHAPTER 35

To this day, Michael's sister Anne has said, "I cannot even utter their names. The female I laid eyes on in court was ugly throughout, and the street way of speaking and the body language demonstrated that she was less than low-class. Any words from her mouth were meaningless. She is a common criminal and common in every other way. The male murderer was the same mold, but brainless. I do not blame the parents of the female. In fact, I pity them that they reared such a danger to society. I feel she gave them much grief as an adopted daughter, and it is not a product of the environment they created for her, but instead her mentality is of a genetic makeup that made her such a bad seed. Although out of control, she was still their responsibility on that night of unforgivable violence.

"I was told that the parents of the male killer stated to the press after his son's release that his son had paid his dues and to leave him alone. That one sentence tells me a lot about the value he places on a human life.

"I blame the liberal legal system in New York for allowing the lenient sentence they each received for such a heinous crime. Suppressing evidence such as inadmissible confessions and plea bargaining allowed these two devils freedom after such a short time. Believe me, they would still be locked up by Texas law, where the standards are in favor of the victim, not the killer.

"The only reason I ever visit New York City is to see my poor mother, who has endured such a great loss. I have no allegiance to a city where my brother was murdered in cold blood and light penalties were officially given to his slayers."

Joan remarked that she cried for two years following the murder. "I felt separated from life. Nothing mattered." She said that her mother was unable to return to church for a long while. She felt that God had betrayed her. Eventually, however, she did return, but something within her had changed. "She finds it difficult to believe in God the way she used to."

Joan and her family have not found it in their hearts to forgive the two, but Joan did hope that they would go on to do something good in their lives. She didn't think it would have done any good to have given them the death penalty. Joan suggested that since the Abdelas have plenty of money, maybe Daphne could use it to help homeless people or do something else to help others with less than she has.

Joan firmly believed that the two teens had every intention of killing someone that day. She felt that they were losers, who had only each other to hang out with, and that Michael was in the wrong place at the wrong time. She believed they both did it. Maybe neither would have done it alone. "But it's for sure," she said, "that neither ran away in horror at what the other may have been doing, as any normal person would have done. They are both responsible.

"The jail sentence was way too light," Joan remarked. "Plus, neither showed any remorse. They were just sorry they got caught. During the entire trial, Christopher had no expression on his face. Daphne was angry, blaming it on drinking, on the media, on everything but herself."

Joan reported that nobody from the Abdela or Vasquez family ever contacted them to offer sympathy, condolences, or a word of encouragement. Police, on the other hand, were very supportive and sympathetic.

"The dead can't defend themselves, and at one point, it was printed in the paper that Michael must have attacked the kids," said Joan. "That is so hurtful, and untrue. The DA told us not to grant interviews, but we all feel terrible that we weren't able to defend Michael against false accusations. For weeks, though, in the media, they were making Michael out to be the bad guy, as if these two innocent angels couldn't do anything like that. I'm not saying he wasn't drinking—he was. But what the media said he was doing was wrong.

"My mother is often depressed now," Joan continued. "Sometimes she's angry. It depends. After a while, you don't share those thoughts, even with your family because there's no point. Everybody goes through their own grieving. The beginning was the worst. Time does heal the wounds. Of course, you never get over it completely, but you don't cry every day, but you always think about it."

Charlie admitted that immediately after Michael's death, the family tried to keep the lurid details from their mother. They were careful not to allow any newspapers in the house, and they carefully monitored the

TV so their mother wouldn't hear any specific details. However one day, toward the end of Christopher's trial, she did see a newspaper account of the trial, and broke down at the horror.

Charlie said that when he first heard about the murder, all he could think of was, with a little change, Michael could still be here today. "If only . . . he hadn't gone to the park that night; someone had said, let's go to this spot, not that one . . . one of the teens had kept to his or her curfew . . . Michael had taken the bus home. Small changes," said Charlie, "can change the course of history."

Charlie remembered that Michael had it all. He had looks; he was athletic; he was popular; he had the ability to do anything he set his mind to. "He could have gone to the top, but he threw so much of it away," said Charlie. "Nothing seemed to bother Michael very much. He rolled with the punches. Michael was free and easy. Without studying, he'd do great. He had all the girlfriends he wanted, with his good looks. He had a blessed life. Except for one thing," added Charlie. "He never accepted the fact that he had a problem."

Michael's childhood friend Billy said that on Saturday, when he found out Michael had been killed, he read snippets in the newspapers, which sounded like they were coming from a lawyer, that Michael had been the bad guy in this whole incident. He learned later, through unnamed sources, that the lawyers had, in fact, hired an ad agency to spin the story against Michael. In response, said Billy, he and some friends started their own pro-Mike campaign. "I went to Central Park at night, practically every night for two years, getting involved with everybody close to him and everyone involved in the trial. From every person I spoke to, Mike came out clean."

"Mike probably shouldn't have been in there" said another of Michael's friends, "but he was. But I doubt he ever made any pass at Daphne. He just wasn't that type, even if he was drunk. Everybody who knew Michael knew that."

The night of the murder, most friends and park regulars believe, the teens were going to kill somebody before the day was done. "When the cops told the crowd to get lost," said park friend Gary, "the kids followed Mike, and he was on his way home. He stopped off there at the gazebo, where there was a drunken crazy scene. His birthday was within a few days. It was a beautiful night in the park. Christopher was obviously doing acid, the kid was on Zoloft, he had a knife, he'd been jumped in the subway weeks before. He's interpreting things all wrong. He had it out for Mike and went to kill him. What more do you need to know?"

CHAPTER 36

A perfect storm is one that occurs when the convergence of certain events turns what would have been an ordinary situation into an extraordinary one—one that is so exaggerated and out of control that it is almost a mockery of its origins. Had one element been absent from the mix, the situation might well have gone totally under the radar—a nonevent—not the least bit noteworthy. But because just the right ingredients were present in the mix, the situation ballooned into a devastating disaster.

A perfect storm occurred in the early hours of May 23, 1997, after park visitors, who had ambled along the lit paths, hoping for relief from the enervating heat that had descended over the city like a gigantic parachute, had long since returned to the cozy comfort of their homes.

But what, exactly, were *"just* the right" ingredients that came together to cause a relatively ordinary situation to balloon into an extraordinary one? What, exactly, was the dire mix for murder?

Every day, people get drunk.

Every day, people get high on drugs.

Every day, people flirt.

Every day, an awkward outcast dreams of snagging someone clearly out of reach.

Every day, people wake up feeling hostile toward the world in general.

Every day, someone is threatened by the presence of another.

Maybe the situation ends in a fistfight. Maybe in a broken heart. But rarely in murder.

All three of the people at the gazebo could fit any of those descriptions at one time or another in their lives—or many other relatively unremarkable delineations. So what was it that set these people and this situation apart?

Scientists studying the butterfly effect note that a minute variation in the initial condition of a dynamic situation, such as the weather, can produce enormous variations in the long-term behavior of the system. The flap of a butterfly's wings in Chile, for example, *could* set off a tsunami in Indonesia, some claim. Applying this theory to human beings, a small and possibly insignificant incident *could* begin a chain of events that result in far-reaching, devastating, and unanticipated consequences.

But what was the incendiary device?

Was it a whiff of wisteria wafting on a southern breeze, caused years before by a butterfly's wings flapping in Chile, that began a chain of sensory memories that caused one of them to ache so excruciatingly, or yearn so violently, that he or she needed to strike out—immediately and unquestioningly?

Was it a misinterpreted or unintended signal— a glance or sigh or laugh or gesture? Was it a casual remark or a sarcastic retort?

Was it a thought—heinous, humiliating, or grandiose—

that mysteriously wormed its way deep into one of their minds and wouldn't go away?

Or was it nothing, the absence of something, like the color black, like an empty well, like deadened desire?

We may never know what *really* brought these three people to where they were that night.

We may never know why two 15-year-olds were drinking with a forty-four-year-old in Central Park.

We may never know which person did the actual killing, what role each played in it, and why the attack was so vicious.

We may never know what combination of past incidents and present pain—or euphoria—fueled the attack.

As with the aftermath of any of nature's violent acts—a flash flood, a tornado, a hurricane, a tsunami—where people have been left devastated, and forced to contemplate how and why such a cruel thing could have happened, it was the same with this human violent act. Those left in its wake wondered: How could it have happened? Why did it happen? What is the true cause of fury, in nature and in human beings?

Satisfactory answers were hard, if not impossible, to come by, and the survivors were left to weave a cloak of whatever colors and patterns they were able to create to wrap themselves in, to cover and shelter them from the pain.

And inevitably—as sure as there is sky above, earth below, and a horizon out yonder on which to pin one's dreams—the sun rises once again in the east, as always, a now cruel and ironic reminder that life goes on—as if nothing out of the ordinary had taken place.

* * *

Margaret T. McMorrow died on February 5, 2006. Her daughter Joan found her lying on the floor in the apartment when she returned from work. Joan had moved in with her mother to keep her company after Michael died.

Joan recalled that only a few days before, her mother had told her she was looking forward to seeing Michael again. "I miss him so."

ACKNOWLEDGMENTS

I'd like to thank a number of wonderful people for their assistance on this book: Lois Markham, Marjorie Frank, and Jennifer Dixon for their careful reading of the manuscript, delicately phrased suggestions, and enthusiastic encouragement; Dennis O'Sullivan and Jim McShane for filling me in on police procedures, Irish-Catholic culture, and guy stuff in general; Barbara Adelman and her son Tim for their helpful research; Cristian Peña of Carousel Research, Mary K. Baumann, and Will Hopkins for assisting with the photographs; Susan Xenarios for her insights; Hal Sherman for sharing his crime scene expertise; the Central Park "parkers" for taking me under their wing and showing me their side of life; and the many police officers and detectives who, off the record, offered up crucial details.

My deepest appreciation and respect to the McMorrow family—Joan, Anne, Charlie, Matt, and the late Mrs. McMorrow—who, despite their anguish and sadness, shared anecdotes and stories about Michael.

Thanks also to my agent, Giles Anderson, who believed in the project from the get-go; Stephanie Finnegan, copyeditor par excellence at Kensington; and Gary Goldstein, insightful Kensington editor.

And for the support and encouragement of my parents, Sym and Ed, and my sister, Andrea, a big thank you.

I owe a special debt of gratitude to past parker Big Frank. Many years before I ever spoke a word to him, "a big man with white hair and a beard" gave my ten-year-old daughter some change to get on the bus when she had forgotten her money. At the time, his home was a park bench. I doubt he even remembers this incident, but it changed one girl's view of the world, and for that, I thank you, Frank.